Experiments in Life

Experiments in Life

One Man's Transformation from Privilege to Pathetic, Penitent to Professor

Steven Sage

Library of Congress Control Number:		2017904988
ISBN:	Hardcover	978-1-5434-1283-3
	Softcover	978-1-5434-1284-0
	eBook	978-1-5434-1285-7

Print information available on the last page.

Rev. date: 04/07/2017

To order additional copies of this book, contact:
Xlibris
1-888-795-4274
www.Xlibris.com
Orders@Xlibris.com
747710

Contents

"Human beings, who are almost unique in having the
ability to learn from the experience of others, are also
remarkable for their apparent disinclination to do so."
-Douglas Adams

"If you have made mistakes, even serious ones,
there is always another chance for you.
What we call failure is not the falling down, but the staying down."
-Mary Pickford

"The confession of evil works is the first beginning of good works."
-St. Augustine

"Do what you feel in your heart to be right,
for you'll be criticized anyway."
-Eleanor Roosevelt

"I would like to be known as a person who is concerned about
freedom and equality and justice and prosperity for all people."
-Rosa Parks

"I'm choosing positivity over negativity, peacefulness
over violence, and the future over the past."
-Me

Introduction

My name is Steven. I never dropped acid before I was 22-years-old and only did so after several years of fairly serious research. I don't say that to be sensationalistic, but it's important to note, and I'll explain later. I'm very honest, but I've been before, and will continue to be, deceptive where I feel it necessary. I'm in a factual/fictional mode here, recalling details to the best of my ability (not without error, I'm sure) and couching them in a quasi-fictitious setting to protect others. I'm thus using fictional names for those who may not wish to be identified. If you're one and you wanted to be identified, you have my apologies. I'll do the same with some locations. I view this book as an Augustinian-style confession, though I certainly make no claims to sainthood.

I hope for this to be a good read, but also somewhat of an inspiration to those who've made major mistakes and think they can't recover and still make the most of life. I've made many major mistakes in life, and am now on a road to redemption, so to speak. I grew up with major privileges, though I was oblivious at the time and threw it all away. In early adulthood, I 'flirted' with homelessness on occasion and had a serious alcohol problem. I was arrested several times in my youth (though with no convictions). I didn't care whether I lived or died. Many who knew me in my late teens/early adulthood surely thought I'd wind up in prison or dead.

However, I turned my life around and obtained several degrees, culminating in a doctorate, and became a licensed Clinical Psychologist and Full Professor at a university. Having done this myself, I'm convinced virtually anyone can make the most of their own potential, no matter how far off track they veered. As to whether my story amounts to any type of inspiration, obviously you'll decide. I'll give as open and genuine an account as possible. To some, I'm interesting at times. To others, I'm an over-the-top pain in the derriere. You'll judge me, and I accept that. My saga is not for the easily offended, nor for children. It contains profanity (though not gratuitous) and descriptions of unsavory behavior, so please exercise your good sense before reading any further, or recommending it to others.

In my early past, I was predominantly a loud and obnoxious pain in the ass. I'm now aware of my less desirable characteristics and working toward improvement, as I've been doing for more than a couple of decades. As does everyone, I have a tale. It's not better, worse, nor especially different, from anyone else's life story. But it's mine, so I'll tell it. I have some talents, as do we all, and one is writing, or so I like to believe. Feel free to disagree, as some have by now. Sometimes, I'll even dangle a participle. Let the writers among you without literary sin, cast the first stone.

As noted, the following is the truth with a little 't.' I feel it's necessary to condense my story into a semi-fictional framework. This isn't only to provide privacy to others, but also to make it short enough for people to actually want to read. If you don't like parts, skip them, or write your own book. In fact, please write your own book whether you like mine or not. Why not? I wrote this in my 'spare' time. It's taken several hundred hours to complete, and I'm self-publishing it at my own expense. I hope to make back enough to pay for the publishing. If I make more than that, I'll donate at least half the proceeds to worthy charities of my choice.

What knowledge and wisdom I've obtained, have come from nearly 50 years of life and my attempts to consciously evaluate and refine myself to the best of my ability. Especially across the last quarter century, I've diligently worked to become a better person. I've improved my general practice of trying to be a good and compassionate person, and that is an enduring goal.

This work explores various realms of Life as I've come to know them. My contention is all of us humans are 'crazy,' by definition. In other words, we all have hang-ups, eccentricities, neuroticisms, personal issues, and so on. 'Crazy' in this sense does not imply psychosis, nor loss of rational abilities, just that 'normal' isn't something anyone is able to be, at least not all the time. I think most people are not evil, a particularly malevolent form of insanity I'd contend. But we're all a bit odd in our own ways. You don't have to believe me, but consider the notion.

We usually cope with our issues by displaying a facade of 'normality' to others. From childhood to death, we all go 'out of our minds' at least a couple of times, which is a real connection between us all, in a way. You're where you have to be at the moment, as am I, and that's okay. And still, we can all change for better or worse. So, why not strive for better? Whether or not we perceive life or ourselves as being 'good' or 'bad,' is typically a function of our aggregate experience of this world. Philosophers, theologians, scientists, historians, and the like, have influenced my development. I'd say everyone could use edification beyond the typical K-12 grades. But, this doesn't necessarily require post-secondary instruction, as some are quite good at seeking and learning information on their own. However, I've certainly benefitted from my higher education. Having and understanding as much quality information as one can get, is generally a good thing. But, having an education doesn't make anyone better than anyone else who doesn't. I know a lot of great people who have only high school diplomas or GEDs, and some who never completed high school. And, I know some doctors I don't consider to be particularly good people, though certainly many are great, too.

On rare occasions, I've found it was hard to tell the difference between helpers and the helped in mental healthcare settings, given the issues of those particular few helpers. For example, I knew of a psychiatrist who stalked a married female employee in a clinic where I once worked. He'd worked with her in another community 25 miles away. She was frightened by him and switched jobs. He then stalked her. He sent a love letter with a giant finger-painted heart on it, either in dried up blood or chocolate syrup (she showed the staff, and we couldn't tell which). He once waited in the parking lot for her, until she saw his car out the window and called the cops. That's not to slight psychiatrists at all, obviously, but there's a sample of a person in 'charge' of others needing help, who likely needed as much or more help as anyone else. Everyone's heard of some pillar of the local or national community who fell from grace in some heinous manner. Some people just can't keep their inner demons from taking control of their behavior.

At some time or another, everyone, either consciously or otherwise, has been and/or felt crazy, sinful, bizarre, impulsive, selfish, lustful, lazy, gluttonous, angry, mischievous, jealous, self-righteous, and/or ignorant, and/or experienced undesirable facets within their core being. Yet we all try to put ourselves together in a somewhat sincere, but also somewhat superficial manner, so as to hide most of these issues from others. The 10 Commandments, the 5 pillars of Islam, the 10-fold path of Buddhism, and more secular methods such as mindfulness practices, meditation, or yoga, etc., are approaches that help people grapple with understanding and shaping their own personality and behavior. Such spiritual frameworks help us recognize weaknesses are inherent to human nature. Yet they also call on us to better ourselves, and give us guidance for improvement.

This book describes, recognizes, and celebrates in a way, the 'dark' side of human nature, and our ability to positively transform ourselves. 'Dark' in this sense has nothing to do with skin tone. I'll reveal some of my dark side here, but you're asking for it by reading past this point. I do NOT solicit stories of others' dark sides, so please don't look me up to send me yours. I'm a Therapist, so I do open myself to hearing some people's struggles. But when I do, it's in a professional setting with the goal of helping them learn to help themselves. And, I do indeed acknowledge and celebrate the 'Light' and positive side of the human condition, and will cover it in due course. But, it's not with that side of ourselves that we have so much trouble. Goodness is its own virtue and needs no justification. But we can use all the encouragement we can get.

The Yin and Yang is a classic 'union of opposites' symbol, highlighting we can't have good without evil, night without day, happiness without sadness, etc. Usually we get to 'choose sides' ourselves, though sometimes it doesn't seem that way. I prefer the terms 'negative' and 'positive,' to dark and light, as I feel they have clearer connotations. People get hung up on coding and decoding languages, and semantic differences can be important. But, for this piece of 'literature,' I'll not get too bogged down with operational definitions.

I am a philosopher of sorts, a Psychologist and thus a scientist, but I'll couch my work here more in artistic expression than in logical proofs. For various classic views of the human condition, anybody may look up the doctrines of Plato, Aristotle, Hobbes, Locke, Machiavelli, Nietzsche, Augustine (he of *The Confessions*), Aquinas, Wittgenstein, etc., as well as the world's major holy books. I've read a good deal from each of these, and a great many others. I don't take any one view as the 'end-all-be-all,' but rather I try to learn and integrate knowledge from lots of viewpoints. The universe and people are too complex to be easily defined or completely understood. But for me, it's obligatory to attempt such an understanding.

The negative often seems more interesting than the positive, if only for its taboo qualities. That's why slasher movies, horror novels, exploitative talk shows, the news, and other purveyors of 'dreadful' content, sell so well. Human culture seems to thrive on exposing negative behavior, knocking heroes off pedestals, and shaming people. Society soaks it up like a sponge and handsomely pays those dedicated to the dissemination of such things. As Perry Farrell said, "Show me everybody, naked and disfigured. Nothing's shocking." Nothing's shocking indeed, and yet, we seem perpetually taken aback by disconcerting manifestations of human nature. And in many cases we should be, but only to the degree that we work to stop maliciousness, and not just to revel in some self-righteous sense of superiority.

Many artists express themselves on the edge of, or completely within, the negative side of our collective humanity, in works constructed for amusement, shock value, exploration, coping, redemption, etc. Such artistic expressions can be quite interesting and gratifying, even edifying, depending on their modality and personal taste. But with all our negativity, the opposite must also exist. So, I'll also delve into positivity and the possibilities for encouraging the "better angels of our nature," as Lincoln put it. Nothing I'll say here is new, totally unique, or wholly original. "There is nothing new under the sun," as Ecclesiastes 1:9 tells us in the Good Book. I'll throw out caveats as I go, and surely you'll accept/reject/ modify, any of my views, as you wish.

Many place much of our human nature (e.g., desires, oddities, fantasies) into pejorative categories such as 'moral failings,' 'sin,' 'heresy,' 'hedonism,' or 'evil.' However, thoughts alone do not constitute one's essence, and there's nothing negative about which we each cannot think. If I say "don't think of a pink elephant," you almost certainly will anyway. But bringing negative thoughts into our shared reality via actual behavior which adversely affects others, is unacceptable to me. And yet it happens, a lot. Most would like to assume a person who commits such an evil act IS evil, rather than as a person who made a very regretful and clearly unacceptable choice, but who still has the capacity for positive change. It's easier to believe the former, than to grapple with the complexities of the latter. Moses and St. Paul were both literally murderers, yet were also later chosen by GOD to be changed for the better, and ultimately changed the world. We are exquisitely complicated.

Clearly, there are some very obvious examples of people who essentially exist as a manifestation of pure evil (e.g., Hitler, ISIS, and the KKK). However, they likely believed they were 'good' people nonetheless, doing what they felt 'called' to do. Such examples are thankfully relatively rare, and what we have most of the time is garden-variety human beings doing things they know are wrong, and not being able to resist the impulse. Sometimes, it's circumstances which pull for negative behavior. The Zimbardo Prison Study and Milgram Authority Experiment, showed how 'normal' and 'good' people can be induced to do terrible things, within experimental settings. Those studies and others, have real-world counterparts; examples which bear out their conclusions that ordinarily 'good' people can be pulled to do terrible things, under the influence of particular conditions.

Most can typically relate to the statement that "We all make mistakes." If that's true, and I think it is, why do we have such a hard time forgiving others, instead of adhering to the principle that "Everyone deserves a second chance," and being quick to forgive transgressions? Forgiving doesn't imply forgetting, but does reflect the concept that people can, and often do, change for the better. Alas, unfortunately, some do not.

Dogmatic rejection of the negative side of our human nature, as a necessary aspect of the soul, is questionable. Carl Jung said we all have a 'shadow' self, largely outside of conscious awareness, which consists "...not just of little weaknesses and foibles, but of a positively demonic dynamism." He noted we're all "constantly living on the edge of a volcano" of sorts, saying further, "we carry our past with us, to wit, the primitive and inferior...and it is only with an enormous effort that we can detach ourselves from this burden." Nonetheless, Jung felt this 'shadow' side was a source of great creativity.

Conquering the shadow within, at least to the point it doesn't control our souls and behavior, is a major component in the quest for spiritual enlightenment. It's the proverbial inner battle of Good vs. Evil.

But, nobody can control all their thoughts at all times. Very few people sit around saying to themselves, "I'm going to think a really disgusting or strange thing." Yet, nobody can honestly deny they sometimes have hideous or shameful thoughts. Those of us who are honest will tell you we think weird things at times and that our dreams (thinking while sleeping) can sometimes be outright bizarre and disturbing. Thoughts by themselves have no consequences in our world, aside from any emotional states they may produce. But, when thought gives way to behavior, they become a part of our world, for better or worse. And it's actual behavior, not just thoughts, we must worry about, in general.

To make any person out to be less valuable or 'normal' because they're struggling, and having trouble keeping their superficial mask together, is degrading and wrong, in my view. And it flies in the face of the "there but for the Grace of GOD, go I" type of wisdom. For those who engage in behavior cruel to others, they should surely be stopped and held accountable. Most societies in approximating Justice to the extent possible, attempt to prevent the *willful* doing of wrong to others (with exceptions for *accidental* wrongs). We endeavor to have offending individuals make amends, and rehabilitate themselves. Once coming into a position of needing, wanting, or being forced to get help, everyone should have an opportunity to change, and be given as much support as possible to assist them in that effort. Taking responsibility is crucial.

Notwithstanding legal punishments or other serious consequences from bad choices in life, I like Carl Rogers' empathy concept: meet a person as a person on his/her level with the purpose of helping them become better people. At least that's how I interpret it. There are of course exceptions to every rule, so give me that much leeway in my statements. All complete generalizations are false, including this one. With that said, I'll proceed.

Chapter 1

Phase I, Getting Started

I've been told many times my life would make a great book. With no intention of boring the reader, I'll give a fairly complete but hopefully somewhat brief synopsis of it, and what I've learned. If you skipped the introduction, which is fine of course, I'm taking a fact-meets-fiction approach, changing names of people and some locations, to do right by others, while keeping my account as accurate as possible, to the best of my ability to recall details.

I was born in Charlotte, NC, in 1969. I was born to a good woman and good man. At the time, my Mom was a Registered Nurse who'd switched to the role of Housewife, and my Dad a Businessman just underway, but who'd ultimately attain an executive position. On the way to such a position, one seems to encounter a lot of time-consuming tasks. Consequently my Dad was gone a lot, at the office or a business trip. Mom stayed home to raise me, which was a Herculean task as I had an unruly temperament, stubborn attitudes, and a finicky constitution.

In 1973, Mom gave birth to my brother Luke, who I was to alternately love and torture from then until my late adolescence. Soon after his birth, my parents' marriage dissolved. I remember being told my Dad would be leaving and not coming back to the house, and that I could see him on weekends at his new home. My only other memory of this was crawling behind a chair after I heard it. My next substantial memories began when I was about 6 and living in an apartment complex off Providence Rd.

From that time, I recall Mom working a lot after their divorce, having gone back to being a Nurse. I had my own room in our townhouse-style apartment. My Dad always helped out financially, and as a child I always lived in privilege that I didn't understand or appreciate at the time. I'll return to that theme throughout. I remember watching Ultraman in the afternoons and playing with my Spiderman wrist web-launcher, and a church bus that came through the complex on Sundays and picked up some kids. I recollect once getting picked up by the front of my shirt, which was collected in one hand of what seemed at the time to be the largest, most threatening teenager in the world. I'd been teasing his little brother and he came to give me a scare that would make me think twice about it next time. It worked, at least temporarily.

It was the last time as a young child I would live in our 'own' house. It seems silly now, but suffering is highly relative and everyone has some burden they think is their own unique cross to bear. I'd always be lucky enough to have a room for just me, or me and Luke, but until my Mom's second divorce when I was almost 16 and we moved to another townhouse, I always felt like a 'guest' in the houses of my stepfather and Dad. I didn't particularly see myself as a true member of either household. It wouldn't be until my adulthood that I'd find an appreciation for the life I was privileged to live as a child. The last thing I remember in that original apartment was my Mom marrying my stepfather at the church where we'd soon become members. Then we moved into his house. I was about 8 years old I guess, and Luke about 4.

My stepfather, Jerry, lived in an upper middle-class neighborhood in southeast Charlotte, though I didn't know anything about social classes at the time. The house itself was really nice: 2 stories, 4 bedrooms, a den, a playroom, a large kitchen/breakfast room, a large front yard and huge wooded back yard, with a bike trail running through the area. It was at the bottom of a hill at the cusp of a cul-de-sac, one of 7 houses on that dead end. He had 2 boys, one a year older than me, one a year younger. It was their house really, though they lived with their mother during the week. They were there almost every weekend for the next 8 or so years. Even though they stayed in a room together while my brother and I had our own rooms, Jerry always let me know where I stood with him, which is to say, he didn't like me. I now know Mom was my only advocate and any indulgences I got from him, came solely from her insistence it be that way.

At first Jerry seemed cool, but I was only 7-ish when Mom and he got together and I was probably easy to impress, given my Dad wasn't around much. Before Jerry and Mom's marriage, my Dad moved about an hour and a half away. Though I saw him once or twice a month, it seemed he was half a world away. Jerry played it cool until after the marriage, and then his bizarre personality started to seep out of the cracks in his mask. He could get totally tore up about one stupid issue or another, and fly into a rage. Many of his tirades were directed at me, the kid who seemed to be doing nothing more than taking up space in his suburban castle. He never hit me, but he would physically intimidate me by grabbing me or cornering me. Every now and then he spanked me, which I resented more than anything.

He did kick my skateboard at me one afternoon after a 'hard' day at work, because it was in his royal way. I instinctively jumped as the yellow nose of the fiberglass board pierced the thin wood paneling, leaving a 3-inch hole in the wall where I'd just been standing. That served to confirm he hated me, which in turn fueled my hatred for him. I never saw him and Mom argue, so I assumed she was happy. But he had a sound-proof office built in the back of the house, after we'd lived there several years. Mom later said arguments regularly occurred inside that isolation chamber. When we finally left, it was a weekday near the end of 9th grade, while he was at work. Mom told me the night before we were going. I was thrilled. Two of her close friends came, we packed everything that was ours, and moved to a townhouse she'd rented with Dad's help. She organized this secretly for fear of how Jerry would react if she told him ahead of time.

Jake and Terry were my first stepbrothers. Jake was younger and Terry older. In retrospect, both were good kids in a situation not of their own choosing. Like Luke and me at my Dad's house (about which, more later), they shared a room at their own dad's house. I came to hate Terry and love Jake. Terry was Jerry's favorite. He could do about anything and it was okay with Jerry. Jerry paid far less attention to Jake and me, and didn't seem to like Jake that much, though he definitely didn't like me. As Luke was much younger, Jake and I spent much of our time together when he was around. On weekends, during the summer, on long station-wagon trips to Jerry's parents' farm in Virginia, and family 'vacations,' Jake and I were inseparable. His presence made being around Terry and Jerry more bearable for me.

Dad later married a woman, Laura, who was good to me and Luke. She had 2 boys, both older than me; Fred by a year, and Lee by two. When Luke and I went to stay at their house, usually one or two weekends a month, we shared a room. It was also a really nice house, off a country club golf course. So I had it good materially, no matter where I was, but neither place felt like 'my' home. Fred and Lee both liked to mess with me, but not in a harsh way. For example, Fred would goad me into trading knuckle shots to the arm, where I always wound up black and blue. I seemed unable to faze him or give him any lasting marks. I really liked them both, and Fred is still like a brother to me, though we lost Lee many years ago (also about which, more later). So in my early world, I had 5 brothers, and 2 sets of parents that were fairly preoccupied with their own lives. And that's where I began to become the loud, obnoxious kid I'd be into my 20s. Competing for attention perhaps, or just staking claim to my own ground, I became the proverbial squeaky wheel that couldn't be ignored.

I did love Luke, but was never close to him until my early 20s. As we grew up, all us 'brothers' tortured Luke, like boys back then were prone to do when easy targets existed. He was never a 'deserving' victim. And, I don't mean 'tortured' as in teased, though we did that copiously; I mean physically hurt, intimidated, humiliated, etc., on a near constant basis. I feel especially responsible for Luke's maltreatment, as I should have protected him. About a decade or so into adulthood, I apologized to him for all the mean things I did to him. Mostly so I'd feel better, I asked him to punch me in the face while I stood with my hands behind my back, but he refused. Apparently his good character was more powerful than his resentments. Nothing I could say or do would, in reality, make up for my negative treatment of him. He did however, become very independent and tough as nails. He's an avid rock climber and rugged outdoorsman. I have tremendous respect for him and try to forgive myself for what I did, by thinking that maybe all those years of abuse produced an extraordinary man. I can't really take credit for what a great person he became…that would be too self-serving.

What was the case for me and Jake was the opposite for Terry and me. Maybe it was the tension inherent in the odd step-union that'd been formed, or perhaps it was competition between the 2 eldest male children of 2 families. Jerry was certainly an aggravating factor since he didn't like me and encouraged Terry to dominate me when we were at odds. A huge problem for Jerry was that in wits and fighting, I dominated Terry. He was taller than me though not much heavier, and any time we tangled I got the best of him, sending him running to Jerry to make me stop. That always pissed Jerry off and he'd scold Terry for not being tougher and kicking my ass. I'd go berserk on Terry and he'd get scared and run away. That was my first inkling that having others think you were 'crazy,' was self-protective. Of course now, I don't have any animosity for Terry, and hope he's done well in life.

Jerry was into sports and coached little league baseball. Terry was his 'star' first baseman, pitcher, and all that. Terry was actually a good athlete while I'd little interest in organized sports. Since Jerry coached, I was expected to play baseball and did for years. It wasn't until my last season that I was any good and actually enjoyed the game. Before then, I was a 'bench warmer' and outfielder, and my hitting was never outstanding. That last season, I was given a game ball once for making 5 fly-ball catches. I was on a team with a different coach, Mr. Sampson, who was kind. He cared more about the kids than winning. He'd tried to get me to catch fly balls with 2 hands, but after that game he started calling me the "1-armed bandit" and told me to catch any way I wanted. I liked him for that. It takes a big person to change their opinion in light of new evidence. After that season, I was allowed my own decision in the matter and I quit altogether.

I never liked many of my coaches (especially Jerry, whom I endured as head coach for 3 seasons), as most seemed to be over-compensating assholes who enjoyed screaming at kids, and who always selected their own kids for the best positions in the field and batting order. When Jerry was coach, I played with Jake for 2 seasons and of course, I didn't mind him. But the seasons I played with Terry really sucked. He was a starter every game as either pitcher or first base, naturally. As usual I played bench or left field; more the former than the latter. No coach ever worked with me individually, so my skills were weak. But I did have a hell of an arm, and could throw the ball from deep left field to home plate without it hitting the ground.

I guess Mom persuaded Jerry I should have a chance to play infield, and I figure it was after much coercion. All of a sudden just before a game, he called me out of the outfield to play third base. I had absolutely no experience playing infield, except as a T-ball catcher when I was said to have climbed the chain-link backstop. During the pre-game warm-up he put me on third. I'm guessing he intended to embarrass me and/or Mom, who kept score for our team. The only instruction I got was if the ball was hit to me, I should throw it to first, to Terry. Jerry had a kid named Taylor pitching and at the time he was warming up with the catcher. Meanwhile, Jerry hit grounders to the infield and fly balls to the outfield. I stood my ground ready to try, totally naive of the probability that I was being played for a fool instead of a third baseman. Jerry drove a hard grounder right at me. It rolled up my glove, hit me in the chest and bounced on the dirt before me. I grabbed the ball and threw it as hard as I could toward first base. I'd never thrown in the infield and threw it with the force it would take to propel it from left field to home plate. That ball would have gone right into Terry's waiting glove at first with the force of a freight train, if it hadn't been for Taylor standing on the mound. Instead, it hit Taylor in the side of the head and he went down hard. I felt absolutely awful as people rushed over to his aid. After several minutes he got up and was assisted off the field. He turned out okay and I think he actually played later in that same game. At some point I apologized to him. Needless to say, I was sent directly back to the outfield and was never invited to play infield again. Jerry won, though I doubt he wanted anybody to get hurt over it. Incidentally, a few years later I bought my first nickel bag of weed from Taylor in the 8th grade. Other than those 2 significant events, he and I never spoke.

I did have a few decent coaches or assistant coaches, but they couldn't make up for those for whom controlling children and vicarious winning were a thrill. Jerry and Terry were probably the reasons I came to dislike watching televised sports. Until the last 20 years, as my own son became a sports fanatic, I couldn't stand to watch sports. As a child, sports were on TV all weekend long, and Jerry and Terry would spend most of their time watching and talking about players/teams. At first I tried to join in, keeping up with professional teams as best I could, but it eventually became apparent they didn't accept, like, or respect me; so I stopped watching. I couldn't stand hanging out with them, so televised sports became something I totally avoided.

There was a tennis/swim club to which we belonged in Charlotte. Mom was a very social person and played a lot of tennis and cards. She was always on some committee, working some part-time job for 'something to do,' on the phone, or attending or hosting a party. She was also the Youth Activities Director for the club for a while. That place never hit it big with me. The only thing I liked was that they had a couple of old-school arcade video games. But the older kids dominated the machines, so typically all I'd do was watch from behind the crowds who gathered around them. I played tennis a couple of years, because I was told to, but I was mediocre at best. I never liked swimming. When I was small, Jerry used to splash me and hold me under water, and encouraged Terry to join in, though I'd usually get the best of him. I hated the ever-present competition, but I wouldn't be beaten. So, I usually avoided the pool and sat around waiting for the time when we could go back to the house, trying to avoid getting pushed around by older kids. I was skinny with acne, and a smart ass, so I was an easy target. But, I fought back fearlessly when pushed, and held my own most of the time. I was reasonably intelligent, but kids don't seem to value that quality and being 'smart' can be perceived by other children as a bad characteristic and used as criteria for bullying or exclusion. So, many kids learn to hide intelligence. I didn't, as that was my only real 'weapon,' other than a willingness to fight.

I don't remember much about kindergarten or first grade. I do remember a few kindergarten experiences at Billingsville Elementary. It was next to a government housing project, to where I was bussed. My teacher, Mrs. Hatcher, was a 'hippie' with long red hair. She was very nice and I enjoyed my time in her class. I didn't realize socio-cultural differences existed between races in Charlotte, or anywhere else. Later, when our baseball team went to play a game at the school's field, next to the 'projects,' which were predominantly African-American, the other team didn't show up. I heard adults and kids say it was because they wouldn't come to such a neighborhood (though that wasn't how it was put). The teams in our league were all White children and coaches. I couldn't understand what was 'wrong' about the place, and thought it was great given I went to school there. That was my first experience with overt racism, without knowing it. Racism is insidious, and it eventually infected me. My family didn't teach it to me, but neither did they teach me it was wrong.

My real schooling began at Sharon Elementary in first grade. It was a new school located in an affluent area. I was told in second grade that I was a good reader, by Mrs. Gentle, a kind lady who lived up to her name (her real name was just as tender). I was also told in second grade by my math teacher, Mrs. Gulag that my work was "chicken scratch" and was how math should "not be done." She did this in an aggressive, loud manner in front of the whole class. Thus I 'learned,' I couldn't do math. Until I entered community college, I simultaneously loathed and feared math. I used my intellect to successfully avoid it from about 6th grade through high school. On the other hand, I quickly took to reading, and ultimately writing, because I 'learned' I could do them well.

I never really liked school, especially the arbitrary control exerted by teachers, staff, etc., and I eventually came to hate it. I remember once in third grade I got a pint carton of milk in the cafeteria that had gone bad. I was telling other kids about it, and was taken out by the Principal and told I was causing "mass hysteria" and shouldn't say bad things about the food there. There were the occasional cool teachers or peers, but for the most part, school wasn't for me. I did fairly well up until the fourth grade where Mrs. Sehouse taught my class which was divided into halves: fourth graders on one side and fifth graders on the other. She demanded what I thought was a ridiculous amount of work and discipline. I was a fairly hyper kid and I still tap my fingers on table tops like drum sticks while my knee bounces up and down. With my habits I was often called down in her class and I began to fall short of her academic expectations. I held on and made a comeback in fifth grade when I had Mrs. Billet. She was a kind and caring woman, and that was the last time I made straight A's during my public school education.

Chapter 2

Phase II, Breaking a Bit Bad

When 6th grade came, I met Tom. We shared a passion for all things related to World War II, which was fueled by one of our teacher's passion for the same. We had 2 teachers, Mr. Byrd and Mrs. Stevens. The school apparently thought it was a good idea for kids on their way to junior high to get experience changing classes. We did math/social studies with Mr. Byrd and then changed to Mrs. Stevens' class for language arts. Her class was on the other side of a thin partition, so changing classes involved walking all of about 30 feet from one desk to another.

Mr. Byrd made class fun, at least for me and Tom. He'd show long World War II documentaries, and then run them backwards in their entirety. He let me run the movie projector; my first 'tech' gig. He once played parts of The Who's *Tommy*, and we watched a lot of 'educational' TV. So, he killed a lot of time. He had us build and launch model rockets and make active volcano sculptures. He also had lots of World War II collector's catalogs and let Tom and me go through them during breaks. Mrs. Stevens was a lovely, classy older lady, who encouraged me to write. She once let me write an extra credit poem when the band kids and a bunch of others left for some reason. I didn't 'know' what I was doing, but I wrote something that rhymed. She said it was very good, and encouraged me to write another. I've never stopped writing since. I felt she really appreciated me as a person. This just goes to show how we begin to define ourselves quite early based upon the criticism or support we receive from influential people in our lives.

While I was unruly in certain contexts, I was pretty straight-laced until I began to hang out with Tom, who lived in the next neighborhood over. I'd ride my bike to his house and hang out after school. We kids were allowed to do pretty much anything, as adult supervision seemed minimal to absent in that era. He had an older brother, Jeff, in high school who was always getting into trouble. Jeff hung out with the other older kids in the neighborhood who were also 'troublemakers.' Tom told me about their exploits with enthusiasm. They did drugs, listened to rock music, had 'slutty' girlfriends, broke all kinds of laws, etc.

One of Jeff's crowd lived across the street from them and one night this kid's dad shot him in the back, right in the front yard. Supposedly he and his father were both drunk and arguing. He went to the hospital and recovered fine. Oddly, I'd wind up working as a carpenter on his framing crew when I grew up, but at the time I only knew of him as a local 'legend.' This was quite the story for the neighborhood as stuff 'like that' never happened around there. I remember an adult on our cul-de-sac taking his son's moped to go see the blood in the yard for himself. Tom later showed me the blood stains on the grass where the kid had fallen.

Tom had all sorts of rock albums he got from Jeff and we'd spend time listening to them in his room. Tom's mom didn't seem to care what he did, although she seemed to be a nice person. I never met his dad that I recall. Tom and I started hanging out on the bike trail. We'd take model airplanes, boats and cars, and set them on fire. Tom was the first kid I knew with his own lighter. On Halloween of 6th grade, I went trick-or-treating with him. I was rambunctious to say the least, but I was a pretty good kid and allowed to do all manner of things that in retrospect should've required supervision. A young kid on his/her own has no way to evaluate the rights and wrongs of options presented. On your own, you tend to wander wherever your mind decides to take you. Like most things in life, wandering is in and of itself neither good nor bad. But a child without appropriate guidance will take the easiest and most satisfying routes, be they good or bad. And, 'bad' was more satisfying to me.

Anyway, Tom and I were on our own for the country's more or less officially sanctioned night of masquerade and pranks. We dressed as

World War II US infantry men of course, though so inadequately that we were hardly identifiable as such. We went all around, got pillowcases full of candy, set off firecrackers, and basically raised pre-adolescent hell. Later we were hanging out in a creek as though it were a battle trench when Tom produced 2 cigars. I didn't want one, but he lit his up. A couple of puffs later, I fired mine up, too. I felt pretty 'cool,' to be honest. There I was with no supervision, hanging out with my friend doing anything I decided to do. Mom never detected that or anything else I did. It was not so much her fault as parents want to believe their children and I was deceptive, and damn good at it. I enjoyed the 'freedom' from real life. Still, it'd be some time before I'd really break bad.

Also in 6th grade, I met Mark Hill, who'd just moved to Charlotte from Texas. I really liked Mark and he lived in my neighborhood at the other end of the bike trail. He shared my interests in World War II, bicycles, playing in the woods, fire and fireworks, and especially music. He was super nice and to this day though I know a few as smart, I don't think I've met anyone more intelligent. We gradually became best friends. When Tom moved away to lands unknown, I started hanging out with Mark almost exclusively. He had 2 brothers, one a year older than me, Calvin, and one a year younger, Byron. Both were as nice and interesting as Mark. I became best friends with all 3 and treasured our experiences together. I don't want to get them in trouble here, because Mr. and Mrs. Hill were like parents to me. But as we've all survived and since their boys have prospered in their own ways, I'm sure they'll forgive the past and me for telling it. I don't see most of my childhood/young adulthood friends now as that's life. But just to let them and the reader know, I love them all and we'll always be friends.

When Tom moved away, that removed a huge negative influence from my life in terms of predicting my future behavior; though I enjoyed hanging out with him. But I didn't fit in with any of the junior high crowds and I developed a lust for the wilder side. I had no idea at the time how wild it'd become. I was in the Academically Gifted program up through 6th grade, but my interest in academics fell off to the point that I dropped out of the program. I knew those classes in junior high were harder and required more work, and I was lazy and wanted no part of that.

For 7th grade in Junior High, I was prepped by Mom for 'social success' with new jeans, new shoes, button down shirts to be tucked in, belts, etc. I wasn't socially adept and felt awkward in 'dressed up' clothes. Tom was big on looking 'slack' and very down on the 'preppie' look, but he was gone and I did what I was told. It was Alexander Graham (A.G.) over on Runnymede Ln., a mile or so from South Park Mall. I doubt I made any real impression on anyone during my first semester there. Mom was friends with a cute 9th grade cheerleader by virtue of her position as Youth Activities Director at the club. Her name was Deidre and she was popular. Apparently Mom asked her to talk to me at school, because before I got to A.G. she never spoke to me. She came up one day while I was at lunch, and made small talk about classes. I responded in kind, but she soon went away as though she'd fulfilled her duty. She did that a couple more times and stopped. One day I overheard her talking to other girls, saying how they hated a guy with a 'uni-brow,' which I was developing myself. I know it wasn't directed at me, but I'd gone into full-blown 'crush' mode on girls about fifth grade, and didn't want to repulse the ladies. From then on, I tweezed the center of my brow, to avoid being 'horrendous' on that point.

The only 2 significant female experiences I had during 7th grade that weren't of the fantasy variety, were both somewhat negative. First in my math class a gorgeous blonde, Cindy, sat on the front of my row. One day I asked her if I could borrow a pencil or something, and she literally told me to "Go fuck a tree." It wasn't the reply I expected. She never spoke to me again until my Jr. Year in high school when she happened to be at the shop where my car was being fixed. I had no ride home and was planning to walk. She was picking up her green Mustang convertible (our school mascot was a mustang, and our colors were green and white) and she spoke to me. I couldn't believe she remembered who I was and was actually being nice. She offered to drive me home and obviously, I accepted. We shot the breeze a bit as we drove with the top down, her hair flying in the wind and looking like a fashion model. I never saw her again.

The second experience was with an odd girl named Monica who took a fancy to me for some reason. She was trim, female and thus 'hot' as far as I was concerned. At Mom's suggestion, I went to the first school dance, dressed as I'd been for my first few months of junior high. I didn't really want to go, but I did. It was the last school dance, or any after-school function, I'd ever attend. I just didn't get into that scene. Rick James' *Super Freak* was playing, and I was doing whatever I thought would pass for dancing with Monica when she unbuttoned my shirt. I was okay with that and we kissed a little. The dance ended and I went home while the 'cool' kids went to Grandfather's Pizza, where it turned out I'd later work. Monica began to call me constantly. She refused to hang up when we finished talking which I thought was weird. I'd no way of dating her anyway, so I broke it off. I didn't like her phone antics, and decided I wasn't *that* attracted to her.

To kill the suspense, I didn't have sex until I was almost 17 (at the beach; I was very drunk and don't remember her name) after several 'almosts' with various girls. I met those 'almost' girls at camp, church youth group functions, the beach, etc. We'd get interrupted while making out, headed to what I was hoping we were getting to. Otherwise for the most part, I was a social pariah until 11th grade when I fashioned a reasonably likable personality out of my obnoxious self. I found a couple of girls at A.G. and several afterwards, to be 'goddess-like' in their attractiveness, and began having occasional obsessive infatuations. I developed an early habit of putting girls I liked on a pedestal, regardless of whether they'd have anything to do with me. There were at least a half dozen that made it into that category for me, all whom I went to school with or who I met on the club scene in Charlotte when I was getting around as a late teen/young adult. I usually didn't speak with girls until high school, when I developed a tremendous amount of courage for such things.

So, back to 7th grade. As I was a social failure, my interest in 'dress clothes' quickly waned. Since then I've often described myself as fashion 'unconscious.' I took up the dress of a true 'slack' connoisseur. Burnouts, potheads, losers, and wastoids, were common labels used to describe people who dressed in such a manner. I was thusly labeled though I hadn't done any drugs at the time. The 'uniform' consisted of faded blue jeans, untucked black t-shirts with rock band logos, tennis shoes and of course, long hair. The Hill brothers and I'd discovered Black Sabbath, Ozzy, AC-DC, and many other heavy metal/hard rock bands. I remember buying Van Halen's first album on cassette. I thought I had a piece of gold, and perhaps I did.

One of the most appealing things about heavy metal/hard rock was that to a middle-class American White boy, it was rebellious and anti-Establishment. Of course, that was the target demographic, though I was ignorant of that. I was upper-middle class, socio-economically, as Dad was a successful white collar worker, as was Jerry. I could've easily been groomed for a professional career of some sort, but I didn't want that. I didn't see value in the 'Establishment' way of life. I'd been listening to music my whole life, but only the 'easy-listening' AM stations my parents listened to in their cars. The 'freedom' issue rang clear as I established myself as a fan of music most people hated. It was loud, over-stimulating, and often aggressive in content. I'll go ahead and address aggressive factors of my life, as it has important relevance to my overall development.

Chapter 3

Phase II Continued, Developing, Then Disowning Aggression

I mentioned I used to kick Terry's ass, and picked on Luke relentlessly. I also had my ass kicked at times, early on. There were 2 high school boys in my neighborhood who lived next door to each other and 2 houses up from me. When I got off the bus in fourth and fifth grade, they'd be waiting. I had to go past them to get home, and they were only there to accost me. I tried talking to them, fighting back, and running around them, and sometimes I got past them. But usually, they'd grab me and throw me to the ground. They'd wrench my arm behind my back until I said some stupid thing or another. After 5 or 10 minutes they'd tire of it and let me up, and I'd shout obscenities as I ran away. I was feisty and this got me into all kinds of sticky situations.

They changed to a different school schedule one year, and just disappeared, which was fine with me. Throughout my elementary school years they and a few other older kids would sporadically set up fights between me and my next door neighbor, Drew, for their amusement. Drew was a year younger than me, and 'crazy.' As an example of his oddness, whenever kids were in the street, he'd jump up and down naked in front of a window. He had an older brother who'd hang with the others I mentioned. On weekends and summers we'd encounter the older kids together, and usually they'd have other friends with them. Drew was easy to rile up and would do just about anything. We were both in elementary school at the time. Ordinarily I had no problems with him, though I didn't like him much. They'd start egging him on by saying I'd been talking shit about him. He'd get angry and they'd say he should fight me. He'd obligingly direct his anger toward me. Then they'd say to me, "You're not gonna let him talk to you like that, are you?" Having them falsely accuse me of talking shit about him, him yelling shit at me, and being fairly aggressive myself, a fight was inevitable. He was a bit smaller, but just as tenacious as me, and we'd hit and tear at each other. We'd both come away bruised and tired. The older boys thought this was hilarious.

The only time I came away from a fight far worse off than when I went in (aside from the 2 older boys who would jump me, but those weren't really fights more than beatings), was my first school fight, in second grade. A Black kid with a shaved head who was wearing a red and white striped shirt on this occasion, and I were on the playground. I was on top of a concrete pipe section about 3 feet off the ground, which was covered in pellet-like gravel. He came up from behind me and shoved me off the pipe. I was wearing shorts, so when I landed on my hands and knees, they got cut on the rocks. He jumped on my back and started pounding away on my head. A teacher ran over and pulled him off, and sent me to the office to see the nurse and report the incident. He never bothered me again, but I was shocked he'd jumped me for no reason. That was the last time anyone really got the better of me, though I've 'tied' a few times.

My fighting and aggression were not of an extreme nature in my eyes. It was a 'tough' male-dominated world in which I lived. I figured I was doing what I had to do. I always thought I had good reason to be aggressive (except in the case of Luke). I never brought a weapon to a fight and I only used one once as a very young adult (a hammer, which I'll relate soon), and I did so in self-defense. When I was about 10, Jerry and Mom took me to see a Therapist, regarding my aggression toward Terry and Luke. I didn't say a word and never went back. Luke and I were forced later to be a part of family counseling just before Mom left Jerry, but again I was totally uncommunicative. I suppose it's a tad ironic that I became a Therapist myself.

I eventually became a pacifist, though I'm hardly a 'passive' person. I've not been in any way violent toward another person for over 2 decades. This was by my own choice and I'm very firm in my peaceful beliefs. I've been able to 'test' my resolve with several would-be aggressors, and succeeded in talking them down. I'd certainly defend myself if attacked by someone trying to do me serious harm, but only to the point of stopping them. I'd also defend family members, friends, and innocent parties, if any were to come under attack; again just to stop an attack, not to self-righteously 'punish' the aggressor with retaliatory violence. I call this 'modified pacifism.'

I've found most disputes arise due to lack of communication or misunderstanding. So most can be talked through, if you're willing to accept when you're wrong and apologize, or if you'll attempt to understand the other's position. My conversion toward peace had a little bit to do with strategic LSD usage, which I'll address soon, but mostly it was a decision to assess myself and eliminate my potential for violence. I'll address my remaining history of aggression now, jumping from period to period in my life, then return to a more standard chronology.

I fought a boy named Don, in 6th grade. He was a pretentious kid who'd said some smart ass thing to me in class. I've probably deserved most smart ass comments directed at me. Anyway, I took offense and Tom set it up where I'd meet Don after school near the bike trail. He was about my size and I was ready to shut him up. Don showed up 'late' with another boy, wearing shorts with his shirt tucked in, and a really nice watch, as I recall for some reason. He and his friend were trying to talk me out of the fight, but I was pissed and Tom was shouting me on. Don ran and tried to put a tree between us, but I caught him and beat him up.

In 7th grade there was an incident with this kid at A.G. Mark Hill was in the school band and we'd discovered the music building was open before school and nobody was ever there. I tore the room up on an almost daily basis, slinging chairs and music stands, banging drums, etc., without being caught. One day coming from the music building and headed to class, I was running and came upon this shorter Black kid head on. I dodged him to the side, and raised my arm over his head to get by without colliding into him. He and his friends apparently thought I'd singled him out and was making fun of him, so he started cussing me with his friends egging him on. This caught my attention and I headed back. He came at me and we went to fighting. Being smaller than me, I dominated him, until I was pulled away by a teacher. We were both sent to the office and sat before the Vice-Principal. He started crying and said I was making fun of him and that he didn't want his friends to think he wouldn't stand up for himself. I told him I was just trying to avoid running into him. I apologized and he apologized, and that was it. I saw him several times afterward and we were always on friendly terms though we didn't hang out. It was at that moment in the office that I rejected the racism I'd been conditioned to have by the society around me. I had an epiphany of sorts, realizing we were both in the office, both in trouble, both misunderstanding each other, both sincerely apologetic, and there was no essential difference between us. I'll address that issue more, later.

There were several times where I thought I might have to fight by virtue of my association with Dick who was a 'crazy' guy I used to hang out with at A.G., during 8ᵗʰ and 9ᵗʰ grade. Dick was highly entertaining if you weren't his target and he had an attitude a mile wide. He wasn't particularly big, but he was obnoxious and highly aggressive. He played soccer and would sneak metal cleated shoes into games, put them on and gouge a competitor whenever he could get away with it. For a short period, he'd walk up to unsuspecting people in the hall, grab them by the shoulders, and lay into their forehead with a completely committed head butt. I saw him randomly drop 2 people to the floor in this manner during class changes. He'd immediately disappear, running into the sea of people.

Dick would talk shit to anybody, but his favorite targets were those he called 'jocks,' 'preps,' and 'deadheads.' Some seemed to fit all these criteria and interestingly enough, these cliques blended to form the most popular crowd. At one lunch Dick had about 7 or 8 of the biggest and most popular males surrounding 3 or 4 of us, and there were at least 50 others around us watching. I don't remember what he'd said, but they were ready to kill him and I assumed they'd do the same to those of us who happened to be with him. He was a true bullshit artist and he talked them down, convincing them they'd mistaken his words, and they left. Once we were down the hill behind the school, and about a dozen Black kids came after Dick for something he'd said to one of them earlier. He took up a 'crane' stance and started saying things that sounded Japanese (if you don't know Japanese), and cutting his arms back and forth like he had a black belt in martial arts. One of them said "He's crazy, just leave him be," and they left. I never had to fight anyone he pissed off, but I was prepared to do so on several occasions, in the interest of my own self-preservation. Aggression just seemed ever-present in my world.

Also at A.G., I got into a fight on the bus on 2 different occasions with 2 different people. The first was a kid in my neighborhood about a year older than me. He was in my opinion at the time, a dumb ass that always had something to say when he shouldn't. I verbally assaulted him a couple of times in response to something he'd said, in front of other people. He had 2 friends who were brothers. One I thought was pretty cool and the other hated me, and the feeling was mutual. The latter convinced this guy he should fight me. The situation built up, so I expected a move against me was coming. On the bus one morning, he started talking his shit and I started talking mine. He took the first swing and grazed my cheek. We went to the floor in a tangle of arms and were soon broken up by the driver. I got back up and was still yelling at him when someone pointed at my face. There was blood on my fingers when I wiped my cheek and someone else picked up what he'd used to do it. It was a wine cork with a nail pushed through it. He'd tried to drive that nail into my head, but missed. That really pissed me off, but we were whisked away to the Assistant Principle, Mr. Cardison, when we arrived at school. The cork/nail was left on the bus and I'm guessing it was hidden by one of the brothers because it wasn't found and they denied he'd ever had it. Cardison was a tall, skinny man with a long thin face who was called 'Birdman' and other names by many kids, including me. I regretted that later, as he was actually nice and fair-minded. By this time he'd dealt with me so much that he didn't believe my story about the weapon, so that ended it. I got in some trouble, but I can't recall what kind.

From 7th grade on, I was punished often by Principals, Assistant Principals, Teachers, and 2 Coaches 'posing' as Teachers. My penances included staying after school, coming back once during the summer to clean the school, writing repetitive sentences about what I shouldn't do, cleaning blackboards/erasers/classes, isolation at lunch, In-School-Suspension (which to me was better than being in class), and one paddling in the country high school I went to for a semester-and-a-half when living at Dad's house. I'd been punished at home as well for all manner of transgressions, by grounding, privilege removal, spanking, extra chores, withholding allowance, etc. But punishment never stopped me, so I guess punishment never makes up for what was lost in the first place, whatever that may've been. Something drives bad behavior.

The second bus fight involved a Black kid named Jim who came from a new government housing project near the affluent South Park area. I don't know how it started, because I remember him as being an okay guy for the most part. He was obnoxious and so was I, and he'd been getting on my nerves for days with his attitude toward some other people on the bus. One day he talked some shit to me or someone I knew and I stood up on my seat and jumped headfirst over another seat into him. We went at it for a bit and then just kind of disengaged when his stop came up. He got off and that was the end of it. From then on, we were on good terms. It's odd, but when guys fight, no matter how it turns out, they often become friends. At least that was the case with me a lot.

In high school, I didn't fight nearly as much physically as I did verbally. I threatened one guy for making fun of the first girl I actually fell in love with, Donna, for calling her a 'slut' amongst other derogatory things. She liked cocaine and her boyfriend was out of high school and a dealer. She never said she'd leave him, but I thought she'd want to, since I cared about her and he didn't. I was wrong. Anyway, the guy I threatened was saying what he felt, because she'd had sex with him and dumped him the week before. He had a car and I didn't anymore as I'd totaled mine (about which, more later), so she got with him briefly. I thought she deserved better treatment, basically because I was still in love with her, and I demanded he stop. He did, and we got along afterwards. Another fellow I threatened over a girl was more deserving, in my opinion at the time. She was a beautiful blonde who seemed to be crazy about me, named Sharon. As noted, I'd totaled my car, so I couldn't really see her outside of school. But I totally fell for her and because she wanted to, I was going to the prom with her (I figured I'd get someone to drive us), which would've been the only school function I'd attended since 7th grade. However, just before the prom I found out she'd gone to rehab for cocaine addiction, so we didn't go to the prom after all. I knew she liked drugs, but I didn't know how much until I also found out she'd been 'dating' a dealer on the side.

I was depressed to the point of carving her name into my arm. I'd taken up self-injury after hanging out with an older fellow, Kirk who was friends with W.B., my best friend from late high school on. Kirk would get us drunk on Wild Turkey and high on great weed, and we'd listen to Thin Lizzy and other great bands. He was in a long-distance relationship and would get into arguments on the phone with his fiancée, and disappear into his bedroom. When he came out, he'd be shirtless and bleeding profusely from deep gashes he'd cut into himself with a razor blade. He was an extremely macho guy and we looked up to him. I figured if that eased his emotional pain, it might work to quell my own distress. Eventually, Donna and I were off-and-on after high school, and I passed out when I was supposed to meet her, and she dumped me again. In my drunken depression, I cut a gash into my left upper arm with a razor blade. When my first wife questioned my loyalty to her, noting that the long vertical scar indicated my dedication to Donna, I 'proved' my love for her by cutting a horizontal slash across it, making a scar that resembled a cross. All these years later, both scars have faded to the point of obscurity. Kirk eventually died from what was likely complications related to his severe alcoholism. And, I gave up self-injury after making the cross-scar in my arm.

Anyway, I hated that coke dealer for taking Sharon from me, and for facilitating her addiction to the point of her having to go to rehab in high school. I later saw him at a concert talking in a group. I walked up and literally spat in his face. He looked at me like I was 'crazy.' I cussed and yelled at him for a couple of minutes in an attempt to provoke him. When he refused to respond with violence, which would've 'justified' my attacking him, I left him alone.

The only actual fight I got into in high school started out in my verbal defense of another girl, Lana, who in retrospect, didn't need it. She was a friend of mine until I finally figured out how 'crazy' she really was, years later when she was with my friend Henry, and later married W.B. At any rate, this fellow who to me always seemed bothersome, was talking shit to Lana one day. I thought he was out of line and told him so. He stopped and apologized to her and me. He sounded sincere and I thought that was the end of it. During a class change later, a friend of mine said as soon as I'd left, he'd started calling me all kinds of names. That sounded like something he'd do, and was all I needed to get wound up. Instead of going to class, I went looking for him, since like me, he often skipped classes. I found him walking through the parking lot. He waved and said "Hey!" as though nothing had happened. I ran up to him and we wound up on the pavement, with me on top of him pounding his head with closed fists. I was pulled off by one of my teachers who was a very big guy. He saw the incident from his class window and came out to stop me. When we went to the Assistant Principal's office, the guy said he'd never called me anything. I didn't believe him, but afterwards we got along well.

That teacher's class was Horticulture, which I took because I thought it'd be easy…it wasn't, but I didn't care. One day, and this was well beyond my racism enlightenment, a bunch of White kids were saying there was going to be a 'race riot' in the parking lot that afternoon. I stood up and loudly told them they were all idiots. I wasn't afraid of anyone or anything, so standing up to a crowd wasn't something I considered as threatening to me personally. The 'riot' never happened, but they were hoping it would, as they were all racists. So at that point, I'd become an 'enemy' to those who hated others based on their race, where they thought I was some kind of 'traitor' to my own race. I didn't care about that either. Later in trying to make my own amends, and trying to promote racial understanding and equal rights for everyone, I've been accused of being "anti-White." I don't even understand how I can be 'anti-what-I-am.' I've never been anti-White, just anti-racism. In fact, I'm not anti-people of any kind, as everyone can change for the better, as I did. I'm just pro-everyone-respecting-and-helping-one-another.

After graduation, I started dating a girl, Janice, with whom I'd been friends in high school. We got naked together once, presumably to have sex, but had no condoms and decided it was better to wait than risk pregnancy. But, I cheated on her before we had a chance to become that intimate again and I was honest about it, so we broke up. I've never cheated on women I was dating, and the girl with whom I cheated was a good friend of mine's long-time girlfriend. She said they'd broken up, and she was really attractive, so I disregarded my friendship. When you're drunk (as I almost always was on the weekends and at the beach with my friends, which is where it happened) and an attractive girl wants to be with you, it's hard to resist. It turned out she got with me to make him jealous, and she had no further interest in me. I felt horrible about betraying him, once I sobered up. Anyway, my present point was my aggression. One day after we'd broken up, Janice came to my apartment very upset, saying her ex-boyfriend (who was still friends with her parents and came by their house fairly often, like he lived there) had grabbed her and injured her wrist in anger. I immediately went over to her house where he was still hanging around, went straight up to him and punched him in the face. He fell back, turned and ran away so fast I couldn't catch him. I was satisfied leaving it at that and never apologized.

A couple of years later I was at a party with a lot of friends. This one guy there who wasn't part of 'our' crowd was drunk, loud, and obnoxious, and talking shit to a lot of people. Really, he was a lot like me and maybe that's why I didn't like him. Me and a buddy of mine named Obie, were poking fun of him a bit. But another friend of ours, Vinnie, a long-haul truck driver, told the guy to shut his mouth or he'd do it for him. He apologized and quit until Vinnie left, and then started right back up again talking shit. I don't know what possessed me, but I felt he needed to get hit. I'm sure others have felt the same about me, but I stepped up and punched him as he was spewing his garbage. He hit back and tackled me. I put him in a headlock and he grabbed my hair and pulled it hard. We stalemated quickly and as I'd started it on a whim, I suggested we quit. We did and I laughed about it, and he left shortly after. Obie told me it was a 'pussy' thing to do, to 'sucker punch' the guy, but that he thought it was funny. I agreed it wasn't cool to strike someone without warning, and I never threw a 'first punch' again.

The last fight I had was on a job site a couple of years later, when I was working as a carpenter trimming the exteriors of new houses. By that time, I'd learned 3 trades including floor installation, sheetrock hanging/metal stud framing, and carpentry. I'd changed jobs many times due to conflicts with my superiors, and I was working at this point as a 'long-hair' with a 'redneck' crew. I don't say 'redneck' to be derogatory, just descriptive, as that's how at least 3 of them described themselves. I was no longer racist, and in fact was anti-racist. I'd also been in several bands by that time. One was a rap/soul band where I was the only White member, playing guitar for a female singer and 3 guys who rapped (about which more, later). At the time of this last fight, I was in a band with my best friend W.B., and 2 other guys who happened to be Black. There was one fellow on the crew who was a hardcore 'redneck' and proud of it. They all gave me shit for my long hair and my opinions and such, but that guy seemed to hate most everybody. We called him Goose, because as soon as he ate lunch, he would go take a shit and do it almost anywhere. He'd also intermittently bring back his feces wrapped in paper, and leave it as a 'present' for others. He was very stocky, and mean as a snake. I felt I couldn't hate him for hating others or I'd be just as bigoted as he was, so I respected that he'd at least stand his ground for his beliefs, however 'crazy' they seemed to me. I always disagreed with him and said so, but he never got ill with me about it. He just seemed to like arguing, and I surely did.

Another guy about my age had been with the crew much longer than me, but still took a lot of verbal abuse from the older guys. They called him Jethrene after the Beverly Hillbillies character, where the guy who played Jethro dressed in drag as his own sister. This Jethrene got drunk on liquor a lot and would fight whomever. He was a bit bigger than me. I think Jethrene resented that I could hold my own so well with the other guys, that I could take their shit and give it right back, and often gave it back harder than it was given to me. Being the 2 lowliest members of the team, we often had to work as a pair doing 'grunt' work. One morning Jethrene was feeling rough from a drunken night, and took to making fun of me in cruel fashion. I was used to that and didn't think anything unusual was going on. He mostly made fun of my band and called me an 'n-word lover' (from my own learning experiences, I haven't used that word for an exceedingly long time, and I won't print it here) and stupid shit like that. I assumed it was part of the regular day's abuse and gave back far harder than I received, as verbal cruelty was a specialty of mine. We finished the house on which we were working and went to the next job. Dino was the boss, and he, Goose, Jethrene, and Mel (a.k.a. Messy Mel from Hell, King of all Trailer Parks, his self-proclaimed title, who was an old friend of Dino and a crack addict), always rode together. I drove separately since I lived a long way from Dino and I didn't want to ride all the way from various regional job sites to Dino's house and then have to drive back to my place. On the way to that next job site, Jethrene must have told them about our morning's conflict.

I must preface telling about the rest of this conflict with an observation I'd previously made of Jethrene. One day he was engaging in some shit talking with Goose about 2 Latino workers who were a couple houses down, calling them "Taco Bell" and much worse. Unaware of the verbal jests made at their expense, one came to our site to ask if he could borrow a tool. Dino didn't seem to care one way or the other about their ethnicity and helped them out, while Goose gave him a very obvious evil eye and wouldn't speak to him. Jethrene on the other hand, was very friendly toward him, saying "Hi!" and asking how he was doing. When he left, Jethrene resumed making fun of them. I didn't say anything, but I took in the situation. So after we got set up at the next job site on the day of our fight, I was on a ladder at one end of a long fascia board over the garage, and Jethrene was on his ladder at the other end of the same board. We got it tacked up when Goose made some ignorant comment about my playing in a band with Blacks. He laughed uproariously at his own 'joke' and said, "Or is that too close to the family, Sage?" People have always seemed to prefer calling me by my last name. I said it wasn't 'too close' to anything and that I expected nothing less from him. Jethrene took immediate offense and asked why Goose could give me hell and I just let it go, when I'd given him a bunch of shit earlier that morning for doing essentially the same thing. I said, "Because at least Goose isn't a hypocrite." That was it for Jethrene. He practically ran down his ladder and grabbed the bottom of mine. He told me to come down and "let" him kick my ass.

I was surprised to say the least, and didn't know what was any different from earlier in the day. I told him to quit acting like a 'dumb ass' and to get back on his ladder and keep working. He called me a 'pussy.' That word is commonly used as one of the most derogatory in White male culture, in my experience. I told him I didn't want to fight him, but that I was no 'pussy' and I climbed down to talk face-to-face with him to prove it. Before my foot hit the last rung, he tackled me, knocking me to the ground. I really didn't want to fight him and grabbed him in a headlock and pinned him where he couldn't hit me. An old painter was standing in the doorway of the garage where we'd rolled, entangled on the floor. He said we were both a couple of "stupid shits" acting like children. I told him I agreed and pushed away from Jethrene. We stood up and walked out of the garage. I was facing him with my hands to my side, my tool belt empty as all my tools had fallen out. I said again I didn't want to fight and asked why he'd attacked me. He said, "You called me a hypocrite!" I said, "I called it as I saw it." When I made the "hypocrite" comment, I was thinking back to how he'd talked shit about the Latino workers, but then smiled in the guy's face when he came over. And how Goose was always everything he seemed to be, and wasn't two-faced about it. Jethrene said, "Well I'm calling it as I see it, and I'm calling you a pussy!" At the moment he called me a pussy, he landed a right hand 'sucker punch' across my face (as I had my arms to my side and thought we'd stopped fighting).

Something happened inside me and I went into a semi-unconscious rage. I didn't even know where my hammer fell, but all of the sudden it was in my hand. It was a 24-ounce straight claw, and I drove the steel claws into the side of his left knee. As he grabbed his knee I started to swing it at his head, when for some reason I froze instead and dropped the hammer. I then threw both of my arms around his waist and picked him up, spun him around and tripped over a rock. His face fell hard into the ladder I'd just been working on. This knocked loose one of his teeth. He didn't want to fight anymore. I sat down with Jethrene and explained I'd never intended to piss him off, and apologized for hitting him with the hammer and knocking him into the ladder. Dino then took him to the store to call his brother to come get him, so he could get a dentist to look at his tooth. I later asked Dino what he thought had been the problem. Dino said that on the way to the store, he'd asked Jethrene why he jumped me. Jethrene said it was because I called him a hypocrite. Dino asked if he knew what the word meant. Jethrene said he didn't, but he knew it was something bad.

While working for Dino, I was confronted by another situation I thought I'd have to fight my way out of, and was pretty sure I'd lose. We were working at this house with an embankment in need of a retaining wall. There were 3 gigantic guys with buzz cuts installing railroad ties to make the wall. If you don't know, railroad ties weigh in the neighborhood of 150 pounds, and these guys lifted them onto their shoulders with no assistance. They had a Doberman pinscher with them with a bad attitude, but had him tied up. We finished our work and Dino told me to get the extension cord up. I had to go past them to get to the power pole. The dog started barking viciously as I passed, and when I got to the pole, the biggest guy let the dog go. The dog ran straight at me and stopped about 10 feet away, looking at me like a piece of meat, growling and barking in attack mode. I was in a standoff with a dog. The guy who let the dog loose was laughing as were the others, when he said, "Watch out boy, he'll bite your ass!" I maintained the appearance of calm on the outside, thinking fast, knowing if I hurt the dog defending myself I'd then have all 3 of them to deal with. I also knew nobody on my crew gave enough of a shit to get involved. I put my hand on the hammer I spoke of earlier, as I was still wearing my tool belt. I looked at the biggest guy and said, "If that dog attacks me, I'll crush his skull." I don't know if I passed their test or if I just scared the guy by telling him in a convincing manner I'd kill his dog, but he called off the dog. He said they were just kidding. I said that was cool, but I was just trying to do my job. We left the site and I was glad to have gotten out unscathed. I've always had the appearance of utter confidence, but it was a façade in that situation. I thought I was going to get the worst of it, one way or another.

Usually though, I had the confidence that came from having cultivated the label of 'crazy.' A case in point was how I found favor with a Lumbee Indian sheet rock Crew Chief, who called himself the 'Fascinator' (it was actually written across his belt). He was shorter than me, but he was huge, and it was all muscle. Like me, he also had long hair and wasn't concerned with how he appeared to others. He and some of his crew sold cocaine on the side and on the job. His whole crew was 'hard core' and didn't talk to people not on their crew. I was working for the same company they were, but was an independent employee while they came as a crew from eastern North Carolina. I worked near them often and being a fairly open and generally friendly person, initiated conversations with a few of them. Fascinator did a lot more talking than working, but could do any job there was to do, and as their leader he didn't have to work if he didn't want to. He'd talked to me a couple of times and it seemed he was trying to intimidate me for reasons I didn't understand. At one point he pulled out a hook-blade knife and started telling me how he could skillfully and quickly kill me with it. All of a sudden he lunged at me with the knife and stuck it to my chest, dead center. When he started the move the blade was pointed right at me. While I never saw him do it, he'd flipped the knife around so the handle was what he pressed into my chest. I'd not moved at all and I think this impressed him, because afterwards he always talked with me. Another time he had me stand against the wall and said he was going to throw his hatchet (used to shave sheetrock or cut small holes) into the wall and miss me by several inches. I told him I thought he could do it, and yet believed he wouldn't try, so I stood ready. He acted like he would, raising it and making the motion as if he was going to let it fly, but then he didn't and laughed. He said, "I can't believe you didn't even flinch!" If you were friends with him, he'd crack you up. If you weren't friends with him, I imagine he'd just scare you. But that job was one of many.

The only situations with potential for male-driven violence since the incident with Jethrene, were ones I avoided by talking it out face-to-face with the person who had a problem with me. I'd converted to my version of pacifism within a couple of years of that construction site fight, after divorcing my first wife (about which, more later). But it's one thing to say you're non-violent, and another thing entirely to test such a theory in threatening circumstances. One such incident happened when I was in a local rock club, hanging out with my buddy Henry, not doing anything special. This gorgeous blonde woman would walk by every now and then, and I watched her as she passed. I thought nothing of it, until her very drunk and very large boyfriend came up to me and said he wanted to go outside and fight me for trying to pick up his girl. He was backed up by his buddy who was just as big. But I was committed to remaining non-violent, if at all possible, or getting just physical enough to stop a fight, should one actually start. I told him I'd never even spoke to her, and certainly didn't try to 'pick her up.' I even said I was sorry if she or he got the wrong impression. He insisted we should fight and so did his friend. Henry was quite non-violent himself, and was amused with the whole situation. I became amused as well when the guy wouldn't accept my explanation and apology. He never threw a punch and he and his friend walked outside disgusted, so I followed them. I told them I wouldn't accept that they wouldn't accept my apology. The guy was wearing a necklace with a peace symbol. Henry asked if he was all about fighting, why would he wear a peace symbol? The guy then ripped the necklace from his throat and threw it down and said "Come on, let's go!" I said if either of them hit me first, I'd defend myself, but that I wouldn't throw the first punch and would only stop them from attacking me. Eventually they calmed down. The guy's girlfriend had tired of his drunken stupidity and told him to get over it, accept my apology, and shake my hand. Finally, they did.

Another incident happened when Michelle, my second wife to whom I was married at the time, and I went to wash some clothes at the laundromat and the place was packed. I saw one machine open and went for it immediately. I put some clothes in, when a voice from behind me said in a very harsh manner, "That's MY machine!" It came from a huge guy who was loading another machine. He was about a foot taller than me and almost twice as broad. Though I didn't notice him at first, I knew it was possible he was planning to use the machine

I'd taken, so I began to give it up. However, I didn't like the way he told me it was 'his' machine, so as I pulled my stuff out I said in my own smart ass fashion, "Well, I didn't see your name on it." He took offense and immediately started saying how he wasn't going to take any shit off of anyone. He told his son, who looked to be about 12, to go get his 'piece' from the car. I said I thought he was overreacting. He said he didn't think so and we could take this outside. I grabbed his hand with both of mine and shook it while looking him in the eyes. I said I didn't want it to come to that, but I'd go outside if that was the only way he saw to resolve the issue. I apologized for any offense he took for what I said. He seemed stunned that I didn't run away or cower from him. He reluctantly accepted my apology, got the machine in question, and we both went on about our business as I looked for another open washer. His son never did go to get the 'piece' and seemed embarrassed by his dad's behavior. It became apparent later the guy was being obnoxious to other patrons, as some came up to me covertly and said they were glad I'd stood up to him. He kept avoiding me while we were there, going around a large table to the door or garbage can instead of passing in front of me, which was the shortest route. Just before we left, his son who was standing beside me, pulled some quarters out of his pocket and in doing so, dropped a small bag of pot on the ground. His dad saw that I saw it. He came over, picked it up and then looked at me and said smiling, "We're cool!" I smiled back and said, "We're cool." When we left, Michelle gave me hell for almost getting shot over a washing machine, but I tried to get her to see it as a 'growth experience' for me.

The last incident was perhaps the best test of my non-violent position. I was at a pizza joint in Boone, NC (having moved there for graduate school), where I occasionally played music for fun. That particular night I wasn't playing, but just hanging out and talking with the owner. The place attracted lots of unusual people who were usually a peaceful bunch. Having been there a while, 2 wiry 'skin heads' came in. Oddly, they were identical twins who wore identical clothing, and had identical shaved heads, tattoos, and patches on their jackets (including a swastika), and apparently an identical need to cause trouble. They came with a tall skinny guy who had dark, wavy, shoulder length hair. I noticed the 'twin heads' looking at me with evil glances every now and then. I'd catch their eyes and wave with a smile, and they'd turn away. I later pieced together what exactly happened, with the help of other people involved. The 'twin heads' were coming down from an acid trip and had been drinking most of the night in a bar down the street. They came in looking for a fight. The taller guy with hair apparently decided the target would be a guy who was well-dressed and unsuspectingly enjoying a meal with his girlfriend and her brother. The tall fellow went up behind the young man sitting down, and gave him a hard kick to the back of his head. After a very brief moment of dazed shock, he got up and the 'twin heads' were there with shirts off ready to fight, and fight they did. There were 4 males in the fight, the twin heads, the target and his girlfriend's brother. The tall accoster had slipped away into the night as soon as he'd finished his 'sucker kick.'

So all of a sudden there was a chaotic fight, taking down tables and chairs. Being an adventurous person who used to work for rock bands, I'd done my fair share of 'bouncing' out-of-control patrons. I never tried to hurt anyone I helped remove, and in a couple of cases I prevented bouncers from doing serious harm to people being thrown out, by talking down one or the other party. I went over to help break it up and move the conflicting parties outside, as they were tearing up my friends' restaurant. In the moment, I had no idea who was fighting who or over what. I was so intently looking into the ball of fighting, trying to figure out who to get ahold of, that I didn't notice one of the 'twin heads' had slid out of the pack. He came at me from behind with a full on right hook to the jaw. He hit me hard and went immediately back into the main brawl. I just shook it off, which is the crucial point. At that point in my life, I'd said for several years if someone hit me but wasn't continuing an attack on me, I doubted I'd hit back. Not only didn't I hit him back, but other than the intense pain in my jaw, I was utterly unaffected. My heart rate didn't rise and I wasn't upset or angry at all. I knew he didn't know me from anybody and had no idea I wasn't trying to attack him or his brother. Judging from his former glares, he'd likely wanted to hit me anyway, but it didn't matter to me. The owner and a couple other patrons stepped in and there were at least 4 of us trying to break it up. We pulled them apart as someone called the cops, and we got them all to stop for a minute. Before long though, the original victim started talking all kinds of shit to the 'twin heads' and they started up the whole melee again. As they went back at it, I said to the combatants, "Come on! This isn't Jerry Springer!" The 'twin head' standing near me screamed, "This IS Jerry Springer!" and fell over a chair and into a table as he scrambled to get back in the fight. We eventually got them outside and the cops came and took over security duties. I went out and looked at the guy who'd hit me and asked why he did it. He looked at me and asked if he'd really hit me. I said I was just standing there when he laid one across my jaw. He actually hugged me, and said "I'm sorry, brother." I said it was okay, noting I didn't have a label saying 'neutral' on my chest. He looked really sad and said, "My jacket's still in there." I went in and got his jacket and shirt for him and they eventually went on their way, as no charges were pressed. I now had extremely tangible proof for myself that I could remain calm and peaceful, even if unjustly and painfully attacked.

Now I'll get to the acid and the issues with my first ex-wife which led to my modified pacifism. I tried a few different drugs in my teens and early adulthood, namely alcohol, marijuana, LSD, psilocybin, codeine, Xanax, Thorazine, and Klonopin, where none of the latter were prescribed to me except codeine. I was also a copious user of caffeine and nicotine. I was never in control of my alcohol use, and eventually stopped drinking all together, which I'll address more fully, soon. Weed was a daily habit, but never caused me any trouble directly. I started drinking at 12-years-old and smoking pot at 13. I had no problem trying those, but I was quite wary of others, fearing addictions to things I couldn't afford, so there are many drugs I've never used, though they were all around me at various times. As noted, I've considered myself a writer since the 6th grade or so. I've written tons of poetry, some short stories, and more lyrics than I can possibly remember. I've also written some pretty weird stuff, though I've never published anything non-academic except this book you're reading. Having read cool but weird stuff by people such as Edgar Allen Poe, I've also heard people put down such work on the basis of how the authors lived. They'd say things like, "He was just an opium addict, so of course he wrote strange stuff," or, "He wouldn't have had to do drugs, if he had any talent." In other words, some dismissed such writers' creativity out of hand, attributing their work to drugs as opposed to talent. I never wanted my stranger work (again, not that I actually published any of it) to be taken as 'just' the product of hallucinogenic or opioid intoxication. So, for a long time I never tried hallucinogens or opiates (other than codeine, which I'll get to soon), and just stuck with weed and alcohol, not seeing any irony there. The upshot is I decided not to do certain drugs in my teens.

During my young adulthood, I hung out with lots of drug addicts, many of whom I considered to be very good friends. I saw up close and personally, how cocaine and crack, crystal meth, heroin, and the like, took over some of their lives. I saw how some eventually came through okay and how some lives were destroyed. Having seen those tragic situations, and concerned my 'addictive personality' would take over, I never tried any of those particular drugs. As my 'junkie' friends and other addicts would testify, as quite a few have to me, choosing not to do those specific drugs were some of the smartest decisions I could've made. I'll detail some of my experiences in the drug world later, but my ultimate decision to use LSD, was directly intended to help me improve my self-control and abate my violent tendencies.

My first wife, Anne, was the sister of the singer of the band I worked with as a roadie. I'll call the band Creature Sack, and those associated with them will know why (2 of the 4 members have died, both having struggled with drug issues, which is a real shame because both were such wonderful and amazingly talented people). They really were one of the most gifted and original rock bands I've ever heard, and were all very close friends of mine. There was also a circle of dozens of other friends that oscillated around the band, and we had our own sub-culture of sorts. This was an amazing assortment of all kinds of people, and they deserve a book of their own. In fact, a guy I've never met recently contacted me, having been so moved by their music decades ago (up north) that he's planning to write such a book. He wanted stories about my interactions with the band. Anyway, Anne was a very good person and her family were all very nice people. Luther, her brother, was Creature Sack's singer. I was pretty good friends with Luther before I met her. When we met, I was 19 and she was 18. She and I never got along very peaceably, but we did seem to be in love. When we first got together I was again without transportation, due to my own drunken stupidity, having totaled another car, and this time (unlike the first) it was DUI-related (I wasn't convicted; a situation I'll detail later). She lived about an hour away and came up to see me on weekends whenever she was off from work. We thought we'd move in together to see how things worked. However, her parents adamantly didn't want their daughter 'living in sin.' So she said she'd marry me, and her parents put together a very elaborate wedding. I was barely involved in the process, except to show up as the groom.

We fought about everything. She was young and her parents were rich, so she was somewhat spoiled, though she was far from arrogant. I was young, argumentative, poor, and an absolute drunk. I couldn't stop drinking, or wouldn't. Our fights got worse, and even though I didn't drink liquor anymore (I'd quit drinking liquor after totaling that second car, and almost running over my roommate, W.B., in the process, but I certainly didn't quit drinking heavily, and did so on a daily basis). I still 'blacked out' regularly on beer, malt-liquor, wine, or fortified wine. Being a compulsive arguer, I was verbally abusive toward Anne when drunk, but she could hold her own in that realm. I also intimidated her now and then by getting right up in her face and yelling at the top of my lungs. But I never assaulted her physically, and never thought I'd do that to any woman. Once though, after about a year of being married, she said I'd grabbed her. I'd totally blacked out and didn't remember it at all, but she was no liar and I'd no reason to believe I wasn't capable of such awful behavior. Nonetheless, I still had a hard time believing I would physically threaten her, beyond being an in-your-face verbal bully, which was bad enough. Shortly thereafter, she said I tried to choke her and I couldn't remember doing any such a thing. Again I'd blacked out, and again I believed she was telling me the truth, and it scared the hell out of me. I asked her to please go through with her regular threats to leave me. I never wanted to hurt her in any way, and certainly not physically, but I didn't think I could quit drinking and was now becoming afraid of my own drunken temper. She left and we divorced. That major wakeup call was the impetus for my inward evolution toward non-violence. After she left, I made it a goal in life to never hurt anyone. For the most part I haven't, but I slipped a couple of times until I became alcohol-free. After I quit drinking, I was absolutely sure I wouldn't again, and never have. The transformation wasn't easy and required a lot of conscious and subconscious effort, as being aggressive seemed to have been 'hard-wired' from childhood.

I'd been reading various subjects related to unconventional views of reality and altered consciousness since I was 16. While in high school, I had an experience of being paralyzed while lying on the couch at home. I was watching TV and all of the sudden it seemed I couldn't move. The program on TV continued and the room appeared the same, but I couldn't do anything physically. I freaked out and concentrated every ounce of my energy into moving my body. I dislodged from my position on the couch and rolled into the floor, and instantly recovered. Nothing like that ever happened before, so I became intensely interested in what occurred. To the best of my researching abilities at the time, it seemed to me what had occurred was a prelude to astral travel –essentially the inner astral self (a reflection of soul, as it were) leaving the physical body. I've read enough scientific sources since to know now it may've been what's described as a hypnagogic response. Essentially, as the body prepares to sleep it becomes paralyzed, but the mind isn't yet in sleep mode and can produce hallucinogenic experiences, as though fusing waking and dreaming states. The first set of explanations regarding astral travel that I found in my teens were fascinating, and led me to read more about altered consciousness. I've always liked to read and learn, and I've got an open mind, but not so open that my brains fall out, so to speak. I always retain a healthy skepticism, but consider all manner of plausible alternative explanations.

A few years later an almost identical thing happened, coincidentally on the same couch, but in a different home after I'd moved out. Mom gave me the couch and other furniture when she remarried and moved. This time a couple of different people appeared to come in through the front door, while I was in a seemingly paralyzed state. Obviously they weren't really there, but they certainly seemed real. Again I brought myself out of it by willing myself to shake loose the paralysis, and came back to waking consciousness, at which point they disappeared. After a close friend's death, it happened again and I actually felt I'd completely left my body briefly, but nothing like it has happened since. That last one is worth telling, but I'll wait until I get to my friend's (Krull) story. Anyway, I do read and have read a lot about all manner of spirituality and consciousness, and that included subjects related to the use of hallucinogens. By the time I divorced Anne, I was a virtual expert on the subject of lysergic acid diethylamide (known as LSD-25 chemically, and as LSD or acid popularly), mescaline, psilocybin (magic mushrooms), the ergot fungus, and peyote.

I'd read about Dr. Tim Leary's and Dr. Richard Alpert's Harvard studies on altering negative personality traits with the controlled (or as close to controlled as possible) use of psilocybin and LSD. However, their research program was completely shut down, and both were tossed out of Harvard in disgrace, and these substances were made illegal in the prelude to our 'War on Drugs.' In the 60s, people totally unprepared for the effects of hallucinogens had been taking them as 'party' drugs, and having 'bad trips,' often winding up in the hospital from being unable to cope with their bizarre experiences, and occasionally getting injured or killed from highly risky behavior while under the influence. Both Leary and Alpert became counter-culture gurus (Alpert changed his name to Ram Dass, after moving into spiritual practices), and they continued to publish in the realm of consciousness and personality change. Their idea was that people should be thoroughly educated about these drugs (and use of spiritual practices, in Dass' case), and use them to alter their 'programming' to effect positive personality changes.

Of late, some of the research into beneficial uses of psychoactive substances (other than standard mental health medications) has begun again, especially in Europe, and particularly with ketamine (which can have hallucinogenic effects) and depression. The jury is out on whether there is any real or lasting benefit, but it's interesting to note a return to research on how these drugs might be used to positively change mood and personality. Also interesting, is the U.S. government's recent refusal to re-schedule marijuana, and refusal to endorse any potential medical benefits of THC, despite the move by quite a few states to legalize its use for medical and/or recreational use. As I'm now a more positive and productive citizen, who's also treated many people with addictions, and having experienced addiction myself, I'm not one to advocate drug use in general. I do know some people will always choose to use drugs, and I think those who do so should be highly educated about what they're doing, and very careful so as not to put themselves or others in danger. And, of course, children should never use psychoactive drugs, as they're not really able to engage in 'informed consent.' With the potential for negative consequences, people should be very careful with what they put in their bodies, and especially so with hallucinogenic drugs. As I say frequently, those who never use drugs will never have problems with them. Again, I know a lot of addicts and former addicts, and not one ever started using drugs with the belief that they'd develop problems, but they did. Not everyone develops addictions, but to reiterate, it's important to be as careful as possible, and nothing is more careful than not using. The most dangerous drug there is, is alcohol (in terms of causing the highest rates of deaths, injuries, property damage, personal struggles, and serious family conflicts, amongst many other negative outcomes). But our society has deemed that to be a legal drug under certain circumstances, intended for recreational use. Thus, we have an odd approach to deciding which drugs are legal for personal use, and which we must go to 'war' over. I'm not trying to be flippant; I'm just pointing out this is far more complicated than many people suppose.

I know it may sound like a cop out to some, but one can do a lot of personality work when the rational ego has been deconstructed, if knowledgeable, willing, and mindful. As Leary said, "Just Say Know," meaning the unknowledgeable and naïve should not take drugs with the power to essentially 'explode' traditional consciousness and the otherwise stable sense of self. That is a recipe for a 'bad trip,' which is apparently a terrifying and potentially dangerous thing. I've never had a 'bad trip,' likely because I was so fully aware of what I was getting into. But I've read about many of them and spoken with many who've had that experience. Of course, acid is far from the only way to create positive change. Any major and positive personal change takes a radical shift in overall perspective, and determined effort. While difficult, this can be achieved without drugs, and not just using spiritual practices as suggested by Dass, though for some, that works quite well. Essentially, that's the goal of psychotherapy: achieving positive self-change of significant and lasting quality, through work of an effortful and persistent nature. In therapy, change is guided and supported by a trained professional, though it's the person in therapy who makes it happen. Some make major strides in a self-help mode, also without using drugs.

But, back to my original point. I knew of the potential for working toward positive and deep personality change quickly, by taking acid consciously and carefully. So I decided to use LSD specifically to become non-violent, after my first wife left me (with good reason and essentially at my request). After my first experimentation, I used acid a few more times. I'd heard some courts consider a person 'legally insane,' if they've used acid more than X (some arbitrary figure) times in their life. I can't now recall where I'd heard that, but I'm far from 'insane.' In fact, despite having cultivated a self-protective label of 'crazy' in my teens, I'd say I'm as sane and rationale as a person can be; or so I like to believe. So, my main goal was to attempt to 'reprogram' myself as a more peaceful person. I've not had alcohol in over 2 decades, and I've also not used marijuana for over a decade and a half, and neither have I used other types of drugs, including hallucinogens, since about that same time. I was successful in the non-violence endeavor except, as noted, when I was intoxicated on alcohol. While drunk, I was twice violent in minor (no injuries caused) and self-defensive, but inexcusable, ways. This happened with 2 different women with whom I was in committed relationships. Again, I found my actions to be repulsive. Clearly, no matter what work I'd done on myself in cultivating a peaceful disposition, severe alcohol intoxication undid that work under conflictual circumstances.

Disputes with lovers are not as easy to walk away from, because the conflicts are waiting when you get back. The first of these 2 incidents was with a girl I'd been dating and was more or less living with at the time. She was pissed at me for something, and attacked me. I used my foot to kick her off of me, and she immediately desisted. I was very drunk, but it didn't matter…I hated that brief lapse in my non-violence. It never happened with her again. We still argued, but she never struck me again, and had she done so, hopefully I'd not have reacted physically. The other incident happened with my second wife, Michelle. When we first got together I was still drinking, but was 'down' to 'just' 3 quarts of malt liquor a day. I didn't black out much anymore, but did so every now and again. Once, I blacked out at a friend's house where we were playing in a band together, and we gave each other total hell all the way home, all in the presence of our 10-year-old daughter (my step-daughter at the time, whom I later adopted), but I didn't remember it the next day. I heard about the start of the fight from my band-mates and Michelle (who was also drunk, but didn't black out), but apparently that situation didn't become violent. As you'll see later, I'd given up driving intoxicated, and she'd driven us home.

The critical incident happened at our place a few days later when we were arguing. I was drunk and lying face down on the bed and she hit me hard from behind. I'm sure I deserved it, but instead of taking my medicine, I got up and shoved her. She'd been in abusive relationships before and though that was the first time I was rough with her physically, she wasn't going to take that from anyone. She said she and her daughter were leaving the next day. There was something about that child, where I'd never planned to be a parent and I'd never had a dependent child under my care before. She'd never had any stability in her life, and apparently I had a strong paternal instinct. I knew I needed to give her my all as a parent. Thus, that was the moment I knew I had to quit drinking. Michelle didn't really believe I would quit, but she stayed anyway. And, I haven't had a drink since then, August of 1994. I've also never been violent toward anyone since. Alcohol is a blinding drug and I was blinded for a total of 13 years, but now I see. I'm not moralizing, because I don't have anything against others who use alcohol, especially if they stay under control. But alcohol controlled me far more than I did it, and now I'm free of that burden. The major point here was that in quitting alcohol, I fully became the non-violent person I'd worked so hard to become. Having grown up highly aggressive, physically and otherwise, I was able to shed the physical aggressiveness of which I'd become quite ashamed. Before this section on my aggression, and subsequent change to a committed position of non-violence, I was talking about being a rebellious delinquent in my junior high school years, so I'll return to those aspects of my socialization.

Chapter 4

Phase II Continued, Breaking Worse

During the rest of junior high, I became a menace to the 'Establishment,' whose job it was to teach us. People decided I was 'crazy,' as I'd do almost anything I was dared to do, and rarely needed a dare to act out in an extreme manner. I found the label 'crazy' had lots of benefits, as well as some disadvantages. When people think you're 'crazy,' few want to fight you, and no one expects much from you, either. Again, I know there are many people with very real incapacities who are not in control of their own functioning to a large degree, but I'm not talking about that. Everyone has a different set of circumstances with which to cope. We all 'lose it' in some way or another, at one time or another, but most of us eventually recover and get back to doing what we believe we should be doing. Anyway, I used this 'crazy' label to manipulate others and situations to my advantage. I harassed almost all of my teachers at A.G., and I'd boisterously annoy the Vice Principal and even the Principal. I liked Mr. Cardison, the Vice Principal, but I bothered him constantly. He'd brush it off and give me a lecture about proper behavior, but I'd just laugh and he never imposed any consequences.

One day the principal, Mr. Crane, was standing out by the busses as he did in the afternoon. I had a window seat facing his direction and gave him the 'middle finger' as our bus pulled away. I didn't want to get caught, so I pressed my hand against my head which was against the window, so it looked as if I wasn't looking at him. But he was looking at me and immediately stopped the bus. He got on and told me to get off the bus. I did and he sent the bus on its way. He took me back to his office and accused me of flipping him off. I played dumb and said I was just scratching my head and didn't even see him. He gave me a big lecture which included a description of the downfall which awaited me if I continued my offensive behavior. Prior to this, when I'd see him in the halls I would yell, "Mr. Crane, Whooooooooooo!" and give him the metal music sign of extending the pinky and index finger while retracting the other fingers and thumb into the palm. During this after-school conference, he said he'd had enough of those types of greetings and my 'devil horn' hand signals which he said he knew meant "party, party, party." I said that in my sub-culture it was a sign of respect and friendliness, and I didn't know what he meant about partying. He didn't punish me other than to make me walk home and he told me to think about how I was living my life.

I did all kinds of 'crazy' shit in junior high. I once pitched a large glass aquarium off the raised courtyard onto the concrete below, just to watch it smash. Remember my 'crazy' buddy, Dick? He and I once replaced posters for the upcoming student government elections with "Ozzy for President" signs. After classes were in session, Dick and I snuck out the windows onto the roofs of the walkways that surrounded the courtyard, and put them all over, covering or removing legitimate posters. During lunch, a football player named Johnny came up behind us and tapped Dick on the shoulder. Dick turned to face him and Johnny asked him if he'd put up those Ozzy signs and taken down the real ones, because he was going to kick the ass of whoever did it. Dick was about to answer when Bryce McGillian came up behind Tommy and said "I did it, what about it?" Johnny turned around to threaten the boy who had just spoken to him, and when he did, he looked squarely in the chest of Bryce. Bryce had just come to our school from we didn't know where. He was huge for an 8th grader, with a full beard. He was as 'slack-looking' as us, and always kept to himself at lunch. Johnny looked at Bryce, backed up a little and said "Oh nothing, that's cool, I was just wondering who did it, that's all." He then left. We thought Bryce was awesome and after that he hung out with our group.

As I said above, I'd started smoking pot in junior high. I bought my first nickel bag of weed for 5 dollars in 8th grade from that kid Tyler, who I'd accidentally knocked out with a baseball years earlier. In the summer before 8th grade I went to the beach with my Dad's extended step-family. My step-grandfather was a fun guy whom I liked a lot, and he started sneaking me drinks one night. I loved the 'buzz' I got, and essentially became an 'instant' alcoholic. I'm not bitter about it, because he didn't know that would happen, and my alcoholism helped shape me into the person I am now, and I really like who I am now; and if he hadn't done it, I'd have found it sooner or later. That evening after the adults all went to bed, I got trashed on liquor, taking a little from each bottle so they wouldn't notice any was gone. I had a blast, getting drunk all by myself. The next day when everyone was at the beach, I poured myself an enormous glass of vodka. I had a great 'drunk walk' alone. On the last night there, my step-brothers Fred and Lee, told me the adults 'expected us' to finish off whatever liquor might be left over. Again I got drunk and of course, I was hooked. It was all so inevitable.

So in becoming an alcoholic in junior high, and picking up weed use, I became the 'burn out' I'd already been labeled by others. I was never 'burned out' in any real sense though. My energy and determination have always been forces to reckon with, but for a long while my energy and determination were devoted to finding ways to catch a 'buzz.' In 8th grade I resolved to have as much fun, and to do as little work, as possible. I stopped taking home books and started a 'no-homework' policy. I made rare exceptions to those rules when a teacher I liked was in charge or when I actually liked the subject material. But I got drunk or high whenever and wherever possible. My family never knew, except for Fred, Lee, and probably Luke. At school, my friends and I continued doing whatever entertained us. I decided in 9th grade that going to class was optional and I thought the same about school in general by 10th grade.

I skipped my first whole day on the last day of 8th grade. Mark Hill and I decided to ditch the bus and hang out in the woods until our parents left for work. Mark was never caught, but somehow it was determined I wasn't there. A guidance Counselor, Mrs. Welsch, who'd taken interest in me at my Mom's behest, called home to check on my whereabouts. I was busted. As a punishment, they decided I would spend an entire day of summer vacation cleaning the school with the janitorial staff. I went that day and found that the janitors only planned to strip and wax the gym floor. I worked with them a couple of hours and they were done with my 'services.' They couldn't have cared less what I did, so I went off to explore the empty school. There was no one in the halls and all the doors were open. Teachers' desks and file cabinets were also open. I found all kinds of stuff and figured if I was going to be 'forced' to spend my day there, they'd 'pay' me for it. I took whatever I thought was cool and put a bunch of stuff into my bag. I stole tons of plastic passes needed for being out of class, in the hall, going to the office, etc. They were 8 inches long, but thin. My bag was already stretched to the point of bursting with other things I'd grabbed, so I stuffed the passes into my socks underneath my jeans. In the main office at the end of the day, I told them I'd enjoyed my work and I'd see them in the fall. They didn't notice anything unusual and neither did Mom when she picked me up.

Ninth grade was pathetic, academically speaking. My family was distressed about it, but they couldn't motivate me to succeed. I did start learning to type that last year at A.G. (a skill that's served me well over the years), and was in Industrial Arts. My Granddaddy was a master carpenter and a full-time sales representative for a major machinery manufacturer. He went to schools across North Carolina and sold them Industrial Arts equipment. I respected him and so I took up carpentry a bit. I liked typing and wood working. Other than that, I got nothing but boredom and trouble from school. My Granddaddy actually made me a wooden device that held 4 pencils, perfectly spaced so that each would write on a separate but consecutive line of notebook paper. That way I could write my frequent 'punishment sentences' in a quarter of the time they expected it'd take me. I also did my first In-School-Suspension. Before the end of the year, we'd split from Jerry's house. Mom went back to work as a Nurse and Dad helped her get a nice place, as it was an expensive area to live in. They didn't want me to have to leave the neighborhood where my best friends lived. Both my parents were upset that I flunked Science and so I was sent to live with Dad to attend summer school.

Dad has helped me throughout my entire life, financially and legally, and with moral support. No matter what was going on with Mom, he always made sure we had good clothes and a nice place to stay. When I got arrested, he bailed me out several times and got me a good lawyer. He had his opinions, and quite a temper with no patience for 'games,' and he'd always tell me what he thought I should do. But he never rejected me, no matter how bad I became and I could always call with a problem. He'd tell me what I didn't want to hear and I'd later find out he was usually right, as good ole Samuel Clemmons did with his father. Dad always saw me when he could, though he was a workaholic and was almost always busy with something. He's a wonderful person, and I can't fault him or Mom in any way for my life's problems. A divorce is a divorce, of course of course, but I now know he and Mom were incompatible and I'm glad they've finally found good partners with whom to spend their lives. They're both on their third, but long-lasting and successful marriages. Likewise, Mom always loved me unconditionally and supported me, though she was pretty much clueless as to the trouble I got up to in my teens.

I got into other mischief in junior high, especially pyromania and minor vandalism. Me and my friend Mark played with fireworks a lot. During our respective families' summer trips to the South Carolina beaches (it was illegal to sell fireworks in North Carolina) we'd stock up and smuggle them home. We concealed our activities and had camouflaged caches in the woods where we'd store cigarettes, alcohol, fireworks, etc. We'd create 'weapons' to discharge bottle rockets in a directed fashion. His designs were better than mine, because like I said, he's a very smart guy. We'd roam the neighborhood and fire bottle rockets at whatever, and would occasionally get up with other kids for firework 'wars,' firing them at each other.

I lost myself in my adolescent life, without any focus other than a desire to play music for a living and get drunk or high, or cause trouble for my own amusement. Mark never let his school work fall behind and had unsurpassable grades. He's a Psychology Professor at a university now, married to a wonderful woman with kids, and I'm very proud of him, though I only very rarely see him. I eventually wound up on the same professional path, but that would be much later than Mark. He did everything well and stayed on the societally-expected trajectory. He was really a much better person than I was. I was the negative influence, though he avoided actually developing any serious problems or getting into trouble, whereas I wound up with all sorts of problems and trouble. In junior high, Mark and I terrorized the neighborhood in an anonymous fashion, rolling trees with toilet paper, ringing doorbells and running, soaping windows, setting small grass fires, discharging fireworks in the middle of the night, and things like that. One thing we did was to have him spend the night with me at Jerry's house, and we'd stay in the first floor recreation room. Mark didn't like Jerry either and so after Jerry and Mom went to bed, we'd sneak out and fire bottle rockets at their bedroom window. We'd run back inside and pretend to be asleep before Jerry got up to see what'd happened. Sneaking out was easy for us and we did it often.

The Hill brothers and I often did such stuff together by the end of junior high, though Byron wasn't usually involved. Mostly it wasn't bad stuff, just hanging out and listening to music. But one day, Calvin drove his moped and I sat on the back with a bat and smashed a mailbox in the neighborhood next to ours. Someone saw us as it was daytime, and called Mr. and Mrs. Hill. They took us to the man's house. I denied having done it. The man proceeded to tell us how his wife had cancer and how his life had become very hard and that this was the last thing he needed to deal with. My stomach turned in knots as I listened to him. I stuck to my lie, but seldom have I felt worse about anything I've done. Living with the guilt ensured I'd never repeat the act. We were privileged middle-class kids with little constructive to do. We found entertainment in ridiculous activities. We made all types of prank calls at all hours of the day and night. We did all the classics and made up many.

I'd likely have qualified for the diagnosis of Conduct Disorder about that time in my life, doing all kinds of illegal and antisocial things, but I did feel bad when the consequences were brought to my attention, if someone was negatively impacted by my deeds. Having that conscience was likely what kept me from developing Antisocial Personality Disorder, a chronic and terrible thing to be plagued by, where others suffer as a result of a person's impulsivity and lack of empathy, and their willingness to manipulate or hurt people for their own benefit or amusement. But unlike those with APD, I didn't persist in the antisocial aspects of my bad behavior past high school, for the most part.

We did other stupid things as well. We went out one night, along with Dick, throwing eggs at random targets. Dick, as I said, was wild. He's now an accomplished guitarist, who's played with 2 fairly major bands. At one point that night, we were chased by some guy who was next to his car when it got hit with eggs. Calvin was driving and easily lost the guy as we had a major head start. However, another fellow had come out looking for the vandals who'd hit his car with eggs. He later said he found us out because he saw Dick hanging out the front passenger window waving an egg carton, when we'd driven back down his street. He took down the license plate number and got the Hill's address, and came over the following Saturday. I was out of town at Dad's house when the bust came down. The others wound up going over to wash his car for several hours until he was satisfied. Again in hindsight I felt bad, especially as my friends were punished for something I did, too. I'd escaped being humiliated in front of Mr. and Mrs. Hill, by a guy who didn't deserve what he got. Eggs wouldn't likely hurt people if hit, but I found out later if they're not cleaned up quickly, they can ruin paint. But for all the negative stuff we did, there were positive aspects to our lives, nothing more so than music.

Mark, Calvin, and Byron, formed a rock band when I was in 8th grade. I'd received a guitar for my confirmation into the Episcopal Church and badly wanted to be a musician. However, I worked hard to just become mediocre. The Hill brothers were the absolute opposite. They had natural talent and all quickly became virtuosos on their respective instruments. Mark played drums, Calvin guitar, and Byron took up bass and keyboards. They started out playing cover songs, almost exclusively Black Sabbath. They named the band Power Mouse (not really, but I'll call it that). Eventually they played to fairly large crowds and earned respect from many musicians, because they could play any rock song note-for-note. I loved to hang around and hear them practice. In the beginning, they had a second guitar player, Paul, who had shared musical tastes. I was not remotely good enough to play with them. They got a friend named David to sing, but he was very shy on the mic. He'd practice in another room, away from the band. When they got their first gig at a local school festival, I became their roadie.

I loved them and felt I'd never be able to play well enough to be in a band, so it was an honor for me to help carry and set up their equipment. I was a roadie for several other bands over the years until I married my first wife. I loved to do tech work for bands. Eventually, I became the guitar technician for Ian who was the guitarist and a backing vocalist for Creature Sack, prior to them leaving to do the 'starving artist' thing in LA. I'll get more into that crowd later, but I think other than Calvin and another friend of ours, Dusty (who replaced Paul in Power Mouse), Ian was the greatest original rock musician I ever personally knew, and I know a lot of musicians. I also worked a few times for the Visigoths, a very popular local rock group who once got on a nationally televised talent show. In addition to lugging gear, I was also the tech for their guitarist, Vinnie, who worked at the major musical equipment store in Charlotte, and was revered by many. It was a true privilege to work for all those bands. I found there were many benefits to being a roadie, if partying is your 'thing,' and it was very much my 'thing.' You get into shows free, drink free, throw obnoxious drunk people off stage (if they weren't your friends), hang out with beautiful girls backstage, have access to great weed (and other drugs, though I didn't do those), and go to parties after the shows. That job fit my description of a great time, but I never did it professionally, though I might have if I hadn't gotten married.

I remember the summer after the 9th grade when Power Mouse played in a bar in Kannapolis called Cargo's. By then they had an older and serious singer, Roddy, who could sing anything. We were all under age except Roddy and his best friend Carl. Carl had a gorgeous girlfriend named Beth. They were both nice as could be and if they're lucky, may still be together. They practiced in the back room of a basement in a warehouse owned by Roddy's dad, and we partied hard there. But this night, I was thrilled to be in an actual bar. This gigantic dude, Darryl, was really getting into the band. I was working with them and since he liked them, he took a shine to me. At this time I was a few inches short of my full adult height of 6 feet. He was huge, standing a foot taller than me, with a foot-long beard, wearing overalls without a shirt underneath and a hat that had the letters FTW on the front. He had lots of tattoos, one of which was also FTW. I asked him what that stood for and he said, "Fuck the World." I'd think he would've been scary to most people, but he was nice to me. People often perceived by others as intimidating, strange, crazy or whatever, never bothered me. Perhaps that's why I got along with people who were actually psychotic in mental health settings much later down the road. I always treated them kindly and with respect, and got the same in return. Anyway, Darryl carried a pitcher of beer around at all times, tucked in the top of his overalls. Standing up front, where I always stand watching a band, he'd come up and rock out with me. Then he'd put his left arm around my shoulder so that no one could see me from behind, since I was obviously underage, and with his right hand he'd hold the pitcher of beer up to my mouth, and let me guzzle from it. I didn't even expect to be able to drink that night, which made it all the cooler of an evening to me, being already an alcoholic.

That same summer I had to do summer school at my Dad's. I saw Judas Priest that summer on their *Defenders of the Faith* tour. This was a big deal to me and my friends. It was only the second concert I'd been allowed to see. Before then, I'd hoped to see Ozzy's *Speak of the Devil* tour with the Hills, but Mom wouldn't let me go. After they returned alive, I made the case that I should be allowed to go to concerts. I was supposed to see Rush's *Signals* tour in the winter of 8th grade, and got my ticket. However, I was supposed to bring all my grades up to a 'B' to be allowed to go. I did exactly that, except for one subject, where I still had a 'C'. Report cards came out the day of the show. I begged, pleaded, and lost, as Mom wouldn't let me go. It was snowing and I asked her how I was supposed to sell my ticket if I wasn't allowed to at least go scalp it. She told me to get over it. This was one of the few times she stuck to her punishments, but since I'd improved my grades so much, I felt it was unfair. I thought I'd be melodramatic, since it was only a $10 ticket (times certainly have changed), and literally called a randomly number in front of her, to see if "anyone wanted to buy one Rush ticket." A guy answered and I asked if he wanted to buy it. He asked how I got his number and I told him I'd dialed it randomly. He told me to hold on. Amazingly, when he got back on the line, he said he'd buy it. A family friend, Donnie, drove me over to his house. I saved my $10, and made some sort of point in the process, perhaps. Oddly, much later, Donnie would be killed by a home owner who'd said he came knocking on his door insisting he was looking for the "Stairway to Heaven." Donnie was in college at that time, and likely on some type of hallucinogenic drug, which was also odd, because he was a star athlete in high school, and pretty straight-laced before he went to college. Again, the potential for tragic outcomes for the uneducated user of heavy psychedelic drugs was ingrained in me, through this loss of a personal friend.

I saw my first concert the second semester of 8th grade, Iron Maiden's *Piece of Mind* tour. It was incredible to watch and to experience. Tickets were general admission so seating was first-come-first-serve. I went with the Hills and a couple of others and we got decent seats. People were openly smoking pot all over the place and drinking from pint-sized liquor bottles they'd snuck in. It was really a quite impressive show, especially given my state of mind and lifestyle at the time (I felt totally at home passing joints down the row, sharing weed with strangers). They played a flawless show and I was blown away. I've seen 100s of huge

concerts since, and countless bands in bars, clubs, and parties. For the
Judas Priest show, Dad let the Hill brothers and their first singer David,
come stay at the house. Judas Priest was great. Though I knew I wasn't
that talented on guitar, I could see myself doing that kind of thing
for the rest of my life. That was the only highlight of that otherwise
miserable summer in the middle of nowhere.

My first quarter in 10th grade, I failed most classes except for
English, which I still liked. I made a couple of 'D's but to my family
it was the same as failure. So I was shipped off again to live with Dad,
my step mother Laura, and my step brother Fred. Fred's older brother
Lee was in college at UNC-Chapel Hill at that time. I liked Lee a lot,
but he was rarely around and when he was, he often stayed alone up in
his room. Lee actually committed suicide in his senior year of college.
No one saw it coming. He had a high GPA and having the privilege of
being a White male (again, something I didn't understand at the time),
who was also good-looking, nice, athletic, and intelligent, one would've
thought he had the world at his feet. For whatever reasons, Lee decided
to check out of this world.

Lee's suicide happened after I graduated from high school and was
living a drunken life as the only member of my family left in Charlotte.
I was living in such an oblivious, sleazy lifestyle of constant intoxication,
that Lee was buried before anyone could get hold of me. I was terribly
affected by that...in fact, I'd considered suicide several times, and came
quite close to attempting twice. On the surface, I seemed over-the-top
in terms of self-esteem, cocky and boisterous, but inside, I had nothing
of which I was proud. Having been arrested a few times at that point,
I'd felt shame at how much I'd put my family through, as they loved
me and tried to set me straight. Lee's death took the suicide option off
the table for me.

I know Lee never would've wanted to hurt anyone else, and I
figure he somehow thought he must've been a burden on others and
was helping by leaving life, but it absolutely devastated that side of my
family. Seeing what it did to others, I decided no matter how bad life
became, whether I wound up in prison or a mental asylum, I wouldn't
ever take myself out intentionally. I still behaved very recklessly, such
that I could've easily died many times, but was Blessed enough to live
through it all. I'm especially grateful I never hurt or killed anyone else

with my stupidity. Dad and Laura divorced not long after Lee died, but I still consider Fred as a 'real' brother.

Getting back to when I lived at Dad's in 10th grade though, Fred was a blessing and a curse. He was popular and had a tight group of friends. They were a good group of people in retrospect, but nothing I did or liked fit into their idea of what was cool. Fred and I both smoked weed, drank, and skied together, so we had that much in common. That was about it though. Dad gave Fred hell a lot of the time, and Fred gave it back, and neither was too happy with the other. Sometimes Fred would be real nice and include me in what he was doing. Other times, he'd just try to see how much shit I could withstand. As much shit as I'd put Luke through, I certainly deserved it coming my way. I went to Fred's high school out in the county, a rural institution of almost exclusively White, lower and middle-class kids. I was not liked, with my long hair, torn jeans and black t-shirt ensemble.

Almost nobody would talk to me, except to make fun of me. As I would verbally slice and dice them when they did that, it didn't happen much. There were a couple of girls, and a couple of 'burnouts' who talked to me, but that was about it. There was one very unusual, very pretty girl named Charlene who'd talk to me. We sat at the back of the class together and she'd entertain herself by meowing like a cat, drawing pictures, and sliding notes to her friends in the class on the other side of the classroom partition. We were taught by a coach in that class. He preferred to be out of the room and to over-control everyone when he was there. He once came in on several of us talking in the back of the room and decided we needed to be paddled. I had never been paddled, but the others had. They couldn't get away with corporal punishment in the Charlotte school system, but out in the country it was a common practice. He didn't paddle Charlene, but the rest of us got several hard strikes by a rapidly swung, 2-inch thick, wooden paddle with several holes drilled through it to reduce air resistance. I took my licks and ceased to get in trouble in his class. I hated being away from my own friends and in a school where I was totally unwanted. I got into far less trouble. I made 'A's or 'B's in all my classes for the rest of the school year, so I'd get sent back home to Charlotte when the year was out.

Fred and his friends had given me a lot of grief about my hair. My hair is extremely straight with no natural part. Mom cut it when I was a kid, and it always formed a perfect 'bowl' shape. I didn't like it, and was invested in the rock culture as well, so I preferred it longer. Before the semester was over, Fred made the point that I couldn't know if I liked my hair short or not, because I hadn't cut it for years, and I was growing as a person. I took that as a valid point and decided I'd cut my hair to the standard short length, just to see what it was like. His barber gave me the cut as Fred stood watching. It felt weird to have my head lighten up instantly. I went to school the next day and a 'miraculous' thing happened. All the sudden I was an okay person to talk to and more people spoke to me that day than the entire time I'd been there. I got all manner of compliments on my new haircut, though I felt I looked goofy. That type of superficial recognition, with me apparently now being 'worthwhile,' just pissed me off. I was nice in return, but I knew they didn't really care about me unless I met some ridiculous 'appearance code.' I never cut my hair from then on (until my third marriage), except for the bangs which I stopped cutting several years later.

Until my first marriage, I always let the bangs grow to about my chin, then cut it above my eyes, without really having a reason to do so. My first wife wanted me to cut the back, and used the fact that I cut the front as rationale for why I shouldn't care about cutting the back, since she wanted me to. I said she had a good point about the front, and never cut it again. All the women I dated said I should 'trim' the back to get rid of 'split ends,' but I didn't care about that, so I never did. By my third marriage, where my wife gave me the same feedback, I figured maybe I was just being an asshole about it. If it mattered to her, and she mattered to me, and I really didn't care like I said, why not cut it? So she cut about 6 inches off, and said it looked great. About 6 months later, she wanted to do it again, and by that time we were having serious relationship issues, so I declined, and haven't cut it since. My fourth wife (about whom, more later), has never mentioned it, so she accepts me just as I am, which I really appreciate.

I don't do anything except wash and brush it once a day. I've many reasons for retaining my hair in its 'natural' state. I've got a bit of Native American heritage (Cherokee), and so I feel a minor connection via my hair to that culture. I'm also in pretty good company if Jesus in fact, had long hair. But I've also found it to be an excellent gauge of a people's attitude toward others. I experienced 'prejudice' in early employment situations that I could've alleviated simply by cutting it. Instead, I left those jobs, figuring if they didn't want me as I was, they could just as well do without me. In construction, nobody cares what you look like, so long as you can do the job and show up. Construction was a natural choice for me when I got out of high school, though I fell into it. It was a hard life, but I was never excluded from working due to my appearance.

After 10th grade expired, I moved back from Dad's house to Mom's townhouse. It'd been a year since we left Jerry's house. Right after their divorce was final, he got married to another divorcee who lived 2 houses down. Mom told me while I was living at Dad's that Jerry did some bizarre stuff. He'd leave empty boxes on her front porch with notes saying "you left this." He also followed her multiple times. She was on the apartment balcony of a guy she was seeing and Jerry parked his car where he could shine his headlights on them. When the guy went down to confront him, Jerry drove away. Today, that's what we call 'stalking.' When I found out what he'd been doing, I wanted to get revenge on him for messing with Mom. She totally discouraged me from doing that. I never did anything other than sneak into his house to get some stuff I'd left because we were in such a hurry to leave. What I wanted was in his attic, which was my baseball glove and some other stuff of only sentimental value. I figured he'd throw it out if I told him I was coming to get it. I waited until he went to work, climbed up to the back porch roof and crawled through his bedroom window, which was always unlocked. For a while, I wanted to vandalize his house. Mom's friend jokingly said she'd help me. Of course, Mom protested and I never did anything, though it was gratifying to think about. I wanted to destroy the bridge over the creek he'd had my Granddaddy build for him for free. Granddaddy and my Grand Uncle built him a super nice, huge, elevated deck on the back of his house, in addition to that bridge. They did it for free as a favor to Mom and Jerry barely spoke to them the week they were there. I also didn't want to mess up their hard work, so I let it be.

I only saw Jerry once more aside from the day before we left, after I graduated high school. I was pretty much over my anger toward him. He was at a local grocery store and he actually said "Hi" to me. He asked how I was and I said "Fine," and that was it. I saw Terry only once after we left. I know he's a good guy. I just wish things hadn't been so bad between us growing up. I saw Jake a couple of times more; he even drove over to Mom's house a couple of times to say "Hi," when he was able to drive. But after high school, I never saw him again.

I got my driver's license the summer after 10th grade. I was given a car by Dad (again, a privilege not everyone gets). It was a Buick and it could move! It drove like a yacht, drifting to and fro on an asphalt sea. I couldn't do anything mechanical with an automobile. I didn't have any interest in figuring out how to make an internal combustion engine hum with precision. I wish now, of course, I was able to effect normal repairs on my vehicles, but I must defer to qualified professionals. I've always gotten along with the mechanics and shop owners who've taken care of my cars. I have a deep respect for people who work in any type of skilled trade, and also for those working in service and retail positions. They rarely get the respect they deserve. I never worked retail (never fit the appearance code), but I've done tons of other jobs.

I got an allowance of a few dollars a week from pre-adolescence into my teens, and did odd jobs to make money on the side. Usually I'd do yard work or detailing automobiles for my family or their friends or neighbors. However with a car and a mischievous agenda, I needed steady money. Most middle class kids don't know how good they have it financially, including me. I had no rent, no bills, no car payments, no insurance payments, no medical bills, etc. All the money I made went to the 'me fund.' I spent a lot on gas, pot, alcohol, and junk food. I did eventually make enough during my 16th year of life to buy a Marshall amplifier and a white Les Paul Custom guitar. The next 2 years I got a Marshall half-stack and a second Les Paul, this time a burgundy Studio model. Dad fronted me the money for all of it, and I made good on paying him back, except for the Studio Les Paul which I bought shortly before Mom remarried and I'd graduated and moved out on my own. I paid him some of it back, but real-world expenses and my addictions prevented me from putting away any cash for musical equipment. It would be another dozen years before I bought any more major music-related items.

After I got a car, I got a job. I worked for a 'fancy' grocery store over in South Park mall. By that time, my hair had grown back to around my collar. I was vying for the position of bag boy, and would also be cleaning the store, blocking shelves, and retrieving carts from the lot. I'd be making minimum wage, $3.15/hour. I got the job and wore the proper attire which included a button down shirt tucked in. I was always on-time and self-supervised. You'd think this adequate for a bag boy. After 2 months of employment, my hair grew past my collar. At this point, the manager told me I must get a haircut. I thought that a ridiculous requirement. I ignored his directive and continued to do a good job. About a month later, he said to cut my hair above my collar or I'd be fired. I told him I appreciated him giving me the job, but that I quit. This was sometime near the end of the second semester of 11th grade.

After that, I started working at Grandfather's Pizza, the place all the A.G. and Myers Park kids still went after school functions. Calvin already worked there and had put in a good word for me. I was a cook, cashier, janitor, and busboy. The Manager was a silly man named Johnnie Dirkman. He was in his 30s, with short, spiky, brown hair, and a terrible sense of humor. He made jokes like: "My dick is only 3 inches......but the wife likes it that wide!" He had 4 kids of various ages from infancy up to about 10-years-old. He was a drunk and eventually got fired for letting it affect his job. When I worked for him, he stayed out of major trouble and just seemed to like being a control freak. He'd change people's schedules after he'd posted them, then act like that was the way he originally wrote it, and that you were the 'problem.' I enjoyed the company of most of the other employees, and none of them liked Dirkman.

Dirkman seemed to get a rise out of telling me to do some stupid shit and then having an argument about the legitimacy of his request. One night a girl who'd worked there longer than me, had some friends come in. She was on the clock, but was basically paid to hang out with them. I took their order, rang it up, cooked it, served it to them, and cleaned their table after they left. When I was bussing their table, I found they'd left a $2 tip. Nobody ever tipped there, so I was impressed and assumed it was my money. That girl had the audacity to tell me they'd left the money for her. I told her she was crazy, that she did nothing but shoot the shit with them the whole time, while I did everything for all of them, and it was mine. She argued with me and Dirkman told me to give her the money. I told him he was crazy, too, and went back to work.

Another time Dirkman told me that to save money, I should take all of the scraps off the 'make table' and blend them to make Supreme pizzas. I said the scraps had usually been lying around for hours and were stale at least, if not going bad. I also told him we'd be putting toppings on that someone hadn't ordered and may not want. He said nobody would notice, and proceeded to make one that way for a customer. I said he was cheap and that I wouldn't do it. He said I'd either do it or get fired. I never did, but he never checked, so it seems he just wanted to run his mouth that evening.

One night Dirkman secretly changed my schedule. I had the following Saturday night off according to the schedule he'd put up the day before. I then saw my original day off had been replaced by an 8-hour evening shift where I'd be closing at 2am. I confronted him and he said the schedule was exactly as he'd put it up and he hadn't changed anything. I told him he was full of shit because I'd seen it the day before and even made plans to do something on my day off. I pointed out the faint stain of the red rubber eraser he'd used to change it. He blew up and told me I'd either work that night or be fired. I'd had enough of him and said he couldn't fire me because I quit, and went on to tell him all about him being an asshole, and to shove the job up his ass. I was young, impulsive, pissed off, and thought he deserved it. Dirkman then played 'tough guy' in front of other employees and asked if I wanted to take it outside. I said "Definitely!" and stormed out with him following saying he was going to wipe up the parking lot with me. As soon as he got outside he started telling me to calm down. I told him to fight, if he was any kind of a man (machismo runs deep in male culture). I told approaching customers he was an idiot who kept unsanitary conditions in the restaurant, which was true but exaggerated in my tirade. He said I should stop frightening his customers. I told him we could take it around back if he wanted. He said alright and we went around the corner. I turned to face him when he said if I didn't get off the property, he'd call the police. I told him to hit me if he was going to, but he didn't. He repeated his threat to call the cops, so I stormed off. He yelled at me to give him the restaurant keys. I pulled them out of my pocket and threw them at him from about 50 feet away. They landed at his feet and that was the last I saw him.

W.B. worked for Dirkman after I quit. I'd come to know W.B. throughout the summer between 11th and 12th grades. He'd quit high school and was living with his mother. Like Mark, I doubt anyone is smarter than W.B. He was a virtuoso on the bass guitar and we played music together at my Mom's townhouse. W.B. stayed on until after

Dirkman was fired. He said Dirkman had become severely depressed about work and his family life and would ask W.B. and whomever else to stay after closing and drink beer with him for free, just to have someone to commiserate with. He said Dirkman would get so drunk he'd pass out in his office in the back of the kitchen. Eventually he got caught and was fired.

The Hills and I were partying over at Dusty's house (his mom was out of town) one night and waiting for W.B. to bring over some pizza. I'd scored a case of beer and drank almost all of it myself in short order, slamming them to get a quick, strong buzz. I blacked out. At some point Calvin was asleep in the living room lounge chair, and apparently I urinated on his leg, thinking I was in the bathroom. He woke up and went off on me, as would anyone being peed upon. I had no recollection of this and shortly thereafter passed out, but the next morning they all told me what I'd done. I was ashamed as I'd never been before. They tried to clean the chair using bleach, to 'sanitize' it. But, it was a brown chair, now with bleach stains. Dusty was obviously worried what would happen when his mom got home and saw it, as he wasn't supposed to have anyone over. Mark and I went to the store and got some brown dye, and tried to fix the bleached spots. We did it carefully, and she never found out, as far as I know. I apologized profusely to Calvin and Dusty for what I'd done. They forgave me, and we're all still friends to this day. So I was really no better than Dirkman, as my drunken behavior was just as bad, though I was much younger than him, so he should've theoretically been much more mature than me.

After quitting Grandfather's Pizza, I went on several interviews for other minimum wage jobs, and encountered much enthusiasm for my prospects until the question arose, "would you be willing to cut your hair?" Without exception, I told them thanks, but no thanks. If being a clean, properly dressed, responsible, and motivated worker wasn't enough for them, I wouldn't work for them. I had quite the 'attitude problem.' After a few weeks of looking, I finally found a place that accepted me as I was. Again, Calvin worked there ahead of me, having quit Grandfather's himself, and he suggested I try to get hired. The place was the Ring Clean Carwash, wiping down cars coming off the automated wash line. I found they'd hire anybody who wasn't openly psychotic. People who couldn't work elsewhere worked there, including long-hairs, alcoholics and drug addicts, mildly 'crazy' people, etc. The pay was minimum wage, again $3.15/hour, but you could make up to $40 on a nice weekend day with cash tips, which was pretty serious money for me, and others who couldn't work elsewhere.

I started in the summer. There was a week of temperatures just over 100 degrees, and I sweated profusely. It was dirty, boring, and somewhat tiring work. But, they never cared what I looked like. So long as I wore my blue Ring Clean t-shirt, I was fine by them. I actually became the Crew Chief (under only the Manager and Assistant Manager) of the place, which came with a 'huge' 10₵/hour raise. I got keys and opened the place on Saturdays and/or Sundays. So, out of 40 or so mostly adult employees, the one 'most qualified' to 'supervise' was an obnoxious long-haired, 17-year-old. I made many friends on the 'fringes of society.' I became friends with a Black guy named Charles who was a nice person, but also a drunk like me, and of legal age to buy spirits. He didn't have a car so I'd occasionally drive him home after work. We'd go to the ABC store and I'd give him money to buy me a fifth of 100-proof vodka. We'd go to his mother's house, where he lived. He'd take a few swigs from the bottle and I'd leave with the bottle in my trunk, to get trashed somewhere. That was my first experience actually inside Black culture, though I'd been going to school with African-Americans my whole life. I'd never been in a house that was so eclectic. Pictures of extended family were everywhere as were pictures and figurines of Jesus and Mary. The rooms were painted bold colors. I'd engage much more closely with Black culture later, and I'll get to that later, as well.

I mentioned above I got 'laid' for the first time just before my 17th birthday, which happened at Myrtle Beach, South Carolina, in the summer after 11th grade. She was in her early 20s. I was very drunk and smoking hashish. We were done quickly and she seemed satisfied enough, so I gave the room back to my friends who'd stepped out for us. I then left her in the parking lot and went on my drunken, stoned way. She saw me the next day and was pissed I'd left her. I told her we both got what we wanted and she didn't want to hang around me anyway, because I wasn't worth it. But, we got together once more. As I said earlier, I don't remember her name. I don't know if she even told me. So much for chivalry. I'd been wanting to have sex for a long time and finally did. To some, this may seem silly and asinine, but such status was coveted amongst males at the time, or at least those I knew. I didn't have sex again with anyone except myself until I began 12th grade, a few months later. My newly discovered sexual self-confidence prompted me to interact with females much more freely. Unfortunately for me and others around me, I was still quite obnoxious in general.

One day that September, a gorgeous grocery store clerk named Donna caught my eyes and held a firm gaze, and I had a 'love-at-first-sight' moment. It turned out she was a junior at my high school. At first, it was a strictly sexual relationship. And it was incredible, for a while at least. She and I skipped school many days and spent them driving all over town, and frequently in bed. I soon found out about her cocaine addiction and her cocaine-dealing boyfriend to whom she was utterly 'devoted,' and who was in his 20s. I couldn't compete with him, so I was just a secret affair on the side. But, I totally fell in love. She was my first 'true love' and while I'm totally over her now, it took a long time to get that way. She loved that I had a car and she also hated school, so I was a way for her to get off campus to enjoy life while her dad was at work.

After I moved back from Dad's, I'd resumed my pathetic academic performance, but by this time my parents were too frustrated to do much about it. I'd screwed up all of 11th grade, academically speaking. During the beginning of my senior year, I took to earnestly screwing up my life in general. One Friday in October when I got off work from Ring Clean, Charles bought me a fifth of vodka. He took 2 big sips and was content to let me leave. That left me with almost a whole bottle full. I went out that night with Calvin and W.B. We went to the top of a parking deck, about 10 stories high. Neither was interested in drinking straight vodka and chasing it with Hawaiian Punch, but that didn't matter as I had enough interest for us all. I was to go early the next morning to my maternal Grandparents' house with Mom and Luke. I'd just eaten a large meal. My plan was to chug the whole bottle, and before the alcohol went through the food and hit me, I'd drive straight home and go to my room and enjoy my drunk. I seriously miscalculated though. I drank the whole bottle in 10 minutes and started down the parking deck.

Even though Calvin and W.B. both asked to drive, I absolutely insisted that I'd drive, even though they were both totally sober. By the time I got to the bottom of the deck, I was wasted and blacked out. What I know of the rest of the night is from what Calvin and W.B. later told me. Apparently, I decided we'd stop at Burger King a block away and get a cup of water at the drive thru. We waited in line behind a few cars. I guess I felt it was taking too long, so I got out and walked up to the window. There was a large dog in the car ahead who barked ferociously at me, and I barked back. I then came back to the wheel and when the path opened up ahead, I burned rubber past the window, nearly hitting the building. I seemed to have decided we'd go to Wendy's, several miles away, to get my water. They said they tried repeatedly to persuade me to give them the wheel, fearing for their own lives. I was loud and obnoxious naturally, and when alcohol was added, I'd be a total asshole, who was always 'right.'

In driving to Wendy's, I cut in front of another car, while I was only doing about 20 MPH in a 45 MPH zone. A police officer named Tessler, in a cruiser a few cars behind me, came around and stopped me. Totally coincidentally several years later, I was speeding and he pulled me over again. I actually ran that second time, though I was sober. I saw a cruiser coming the other way down the divided 4-lane road and saw its brake lights brighten after it passed the other side. Already going 60 MPH or so, I punched the gas and high-tailed it up into a maze of roads in the neighborhood next to where I'd grown up. I parked in a cul-de-sac and shut off my lights, figuring he'd never find me. He did though. He asked why I ran. I was honest with him, saying I had a lot of tickets and was trying to avoid another. He asked why my name was familiar to him. I saw his name plate and told him I remembered he'd arrested me for DUI when I was 16. He gave me a ticket and advised me not to run from the police in the future. By this point, I'd learned to always 'be nice to your officer.' They put their lives on the line for others every day, and are just doing their jobs, so by now I figured if I got caught doing something illegal, the least I could do was admit it and show them respect.

Anyway, back to the first night in question, the night he arrested me for DUI. I pulled over and had rolled down my window. He asked for my license and registration. At the time, I watched this cartoon called *Thundercats* and thought the female cat was 'hot' for an illustration. She was Chetara and animated to resemble a robustly built blonde pseudo-cat person. Being an odd kid, I had a sticker of her in my wallet, which I'd gotten from a bubble gum machine. Instead of producing my license and registration, I gave him the sticker. He wasn't impressed and told me to get out and touch my nose with the index finger of each hand, while standing with my head tilted back, eyes closed. I did poorly. I was then told to walk the dotted white line that divided the lanes on our side of the road. As I did, I fell on the hood of his police car, at which point he handcuffed me and placed me in the back.

The next thing I knew, I woke up in a jail cell with 5 other drunks. I was still quite drunk. One of them started laughing, saying, "Man, you were giving those cops hell last night!" I'd never been in jail before, and it took a minute to get oriented. I asked what he was talking about and he said I'd been verbally obnoxious when I'd been drug in by the police. I asked if I'd physically attacked the cops, praying I hadn't assaulted officers. He said I was too wasted to hit anything but the floor. For that I was thankful, but I still didn't know why I was there. When I was transferred to a small cell by myself, I learned I'd been arrested for DUI. The officer who escorted me to my cell said I'd passed out when they attempted to finger-print me. They'd sent me to the hospital, where my blood alcohol content (BAC) was measured at .385, which I was told was "near death." I'd pissed my pants in the hospital, but they were pretty dry by the time I woke up. The deputy (a city cop arrested me, but the jail was run by the sheriff's department) found the whole matter amusing. As he was talking about my night's events, I realized Mom and Dad must have already heard what happened and there was nothing to do but to wait for the inevitable confrontation. Neither of them even knew I drank, much less how often or how much.

My new cell held only me and was 4 by 6 feet, with a metal toilet. It had a metal bunk with no mattress and holes one inch in diameter drilled all across its surface. It protruded 2 feet into my 4 foot cell width. The walls were concrete and the door had bars 2 inches in diameter, with an opening through which food could be passed. It had 3 cross bars across the width, spaced evenly from floor to ceiling. I began to act the fool and climbed up on my bars and started singing. A deputy came and told me to get down. I did and climbed back up when he left, but didn't sing. I had no idea if anyone would bail me out. After a bit, a guard came by and handed me a paper cup of purple liquid. I was totally dehydrated and as I drank it, I realized it was unsweetened. Water would have been far more palatable and cheaper, so I assumed it was a punishment. I asked the deputy why they served purple water, instead of just water. He sarcastically said I could have more, since I 'liked' it so much. I was dry and so I took him up on the offer and downed another cup.

I got bailed out later that morning. We were many hours late leaving for my Grandparent's house. Mom never told them what happened, and neither did I. I was ashamed because my Grandparents on both sides were honest, moral people. I didn't want to be a huge disappointment to them and was already a disappointment to my parents and ever-increasingly to my friends. Calvin had driven downtown with W.B., to see if they could get me out of jail. On his way, he was pulled by a cop who said he ran a red light. He denied it and W.B. backed him up, but Mr. Hill still had to get him a lawyer to defend against the charge. He won his case, but it was my fault he had to go through it. W.B. had called my Mom to come bail me out of jail. He didn't know what to say to her, but told her the truth. Mom and her good friend went to the hospital after I'd been taken there and then set about bailing me out.

Mom and Dad were upset, but tried to help me out. I know they loved me very much and I think they believed their divorce contributed to my problem behavior, so there was probably some guilt as well. Dad got me a 'high-dollar' lawyer. I wound up with a punishment that was not technically a conviction, but rather an adjudication, called a 'Prayer for Judgment Continued.' It included limited driving privileges for work and school only, attendance of Alcohol Driver Education and Traffic School classes, 24 hours of community service, and a 2-year suspended jail sentence, which would go away if I satisfied the terms of the agreement. The judge pronounced the judgment and saved the jail part until last, when he said "…shall serve a sentence of no less than 2 years in the Mecklenburg County prison………(at which point he fell silent and my heart dropped, because I thought for a second he was done)." Then he said "…suspended on the following conditions…" Though I didn't know at the time, this was part of my privilege, for sure. I was a young White male, with a father who had enough money for a good lawyer, and they saved me from screwing up my record and my future. Had I been a male of color, or from a poor family, it would've likely gone very badly for me. I knew I'd been wrong to have acted so irresponsibly and I set about fulfilling the adjudication requirements.

This was the first time I seriously considered suicide. There was a parking deck across from Cotswald Mall, near the Wendy's to which I'd been headed when I got arrested. I drove to the top on a Sunday morning, sober and depressed, and ashamed for what I'd done to my family. I looked over the side to make sure nobody was beneath. It was deserted, except for me. I lined up my car and got ready to hit the gas and attempt to burst through the railing and plunge to my death. I figured if I was going to take myself out, it'd be a spectacle. It was incredibly selfish. I revved my engine and got ready to take my foot off the brake and speed towards the edge. Something made me stop. I went home and told no one what I'd contemplated. I totaled that car at the end of that December, totally sober.

It was over Christmas vacation and I was at Dad's for a few days. His birthday falls just after Christmas and I'd gone to the mall and bought a coffee mug that said "World's Greatest Dad", to give him. I was sober, but going way too fast for the road I was on. I considered myself an excellent high-speed driver, but I was on a city road that led into the country. I was unfamiliar with the route I was taking back to his house. It was a 35 MPH speed limit and I was doing at least 60 MPH. Suddenly, I came upon a sign warning of an impending 'S' curve. As I entered the first curve I skidded across the double yellow lines into the oncoming lane. I could've held on and made it through, except another car was coming, head-on. I'd have hit it for certain, so I steered hard to the right as I headed into the second curve. I plowed straight into a drainage ditch and my car flipped end-over-end, twisted and rolled, coming to rest upside down. I'd avoided the oncoming car, which continued on its way apparently unconcerned that I'd crashed. There's no way they didn't see me crash.

Houses lined the street and I'd landed in a large front yard, about 20 yards from the house. Fortunately, nobody had been in the yard. I wasn't wearing a seat belt, but I was unhurt. I crawled out my smashed window and surveyed the damage. All the glass had been smashed out, the passenger's side roof was crushed in, and my stereo was still blasting Dokken's *The Hunter*. The homeowner started coming toward me and I began to feel like an idiot. I cut my hand crawling on glass shards to turn off the music. The stereo was the only thing in working condition as the car was totaled. The people who lived there were very nice and called the police and a tow truck. I was honest and the police were sympathetic, and didn't even give me a citation. I called Dad and told him what happened. What a present for my Dad's birthday! He was just glad I wasn't hurt. I knew it was another terrible disappointment to him, for me to have driven so irresponsibly yet again. For the rest of the school year, I was without a car, which is when Donna dumped me.

The Hill's drove me to school every day. I quit my job at Ring Clean, as I'd no way to get there. I felt terrible and I didn't know why I was so out of control.

The last semester of senior year was disappointing academically, but no one expected anything else. I was a regular in the Assistant Principal's office, being called down during second period every week and sometimes daily. They gave me In-School Suspension a couple of times. I had problems with most of my teachers at some time or another. I skipped any class I felt like. There were 2 Assistant Principals who handled all discipline issues. Mine was Mr. Clemmer. He saw me so often that we'd just wind up shooting the breeze or discussing why I continued to hold the 'anti-Establishment' attitude which brought me so much trouble.

Once I was in History class where I had a fairly nice teacher, Ms. Shelling. I liked History and listened in class, and sometimes would even read the book. I still didn't do homework, except for a couple of creative writing assignments in English, which I wanted to write. We'd taken a History test on which I'd made a perfect score. The rest of the class did abysmally, and Shelling was chastising them for their poor performance. She concluded by saying she'd re-teach the entire section the test covered. I'd no interest in hearing an identical series of lectures. I was tired from staying up late, drinking and smoking the night away, so I quietly laid my head on my desk to catch a nap. She took immediate exception to this. She told me to raise my head and pay attention. At that point, she was polite to me and so I was polite to her. I said that as I'd made a 100 on the test, and while I understood she wanted to teach the class the same material again, I'd prefer to quietly rest. This piqued the interest of the class, many of whom started laughing. She then escalated and told me I'd better get my head up and pay attention. I said I'd 'prefer not to,' 'Bartleby-the-Scrivener-style.' She hit a boiling point and said, "I request you pick up your head and pay attention!" I replied "Request denied!" The class burst out in laughter and she exploded, telling me to go straight to the Assistant Principal's office. I calmly said I was okay with that and went to see Clemmer. I explained what happened and he said I shouldn't upset my teachers. I told him I didn't try to, but that I thought I'd just go home. In fact, we agreed I could leave school any time I had a conflict with a teacher. He said to leave them alone, come to his office and tell him, and I could go. That seemed reasonable to me.

In addition to being an avid pot-smoker, I was also now addicted to cigarettes. Donna smoked and in-part to gain her attention when we got together, I took a drag off one of hers and got a 'buzz.' It was short-lived, but I really liked it. I'd only tried cigarettes once before with Mark, back in junior high, and didn't take to them then for some reason. I hit another cigarette of hers between the next classes, and got a similar 'buzz,' but it went away more quickly. But, I was 'instantly' addicted. They let students smoke in high school back then, and there was a tree where they gathered to hang out and smoke. Once I was coming into a building, and just kept on smoking my cigarette, when I ran into the Principal coming down the stairs. He was shocked I was smoking in the building. I said I'd simply forgotten it wasn't allowed, took it outside and put it out. He didn't do anything but give me a short lecture.

Another incident occurred that year in Geometry. While living at Dad's, I'd intimidated a young, bashful Algebra teacher at the school. I'd utterly failed that semester with ridiculously low grades, but I said if he didn't pass me, I'd have to take Algebra again and wouldn't be allowed to move home to Charlotte. I didn't actually threaten him, but I was very aggressive saying he needed to pass me anyway. He passed me. So, I never got anything out of Algebra, but had a passing grade and couldn't take it again, so I had to move to Geometry. I was in a class with a few other burnouts and we didn't do anything but talk or sleep. One day a month into the semester, the teacher had enough. She didn't want us to keep disrespecting her and disrupting class. She went off, winding up her comments with the statement: "Whoever doesn't want to come to this class to learn, shouldn't come at all!" I took her up on that invitation. I got up and quietly walked out and never went back. It was the last period of the day, so I just left school early every day. That was fine with her until the last weeks of the semester, when she started turning me in as she'd found out she'd get in trouble for not reporting my skipping. Clemmer called me into his office. He asked what the problem was between me and my Geometry teacher. I told him we didn't have a problem, because she didn't want me there, and I didn't want to be there. I told him she'd said for anyone like me not to come, so she'd actually given me 'permission' to skip. He asked how many days I'd missed. I figured it to be in excess of 90. He said if that was the case, he wasn't going to make me go now. I thanked him and left.

I got high and drunk all the time, but I didn't do drugs at school until senior year. I started hanging out with John, a classic 'burnout.' He was new and we got along great. He had several tattoos, prison style, which he did himself. On his left fore-arm was a large word that read "Cocain," missing the 'e.' I asked why he left off the 'e,' and he said he was high when he did it and never finished. He actually smoked pot in class one day when the teacher was out of the room. It was in Horticulture and he sat by the window and toked up, blowing the smoke outside. Someone said they were going to report him. He said, "Go ahead, and I'll kick your ass!" John was skinny, but was the only kid with tattoos. He was very convincing and wasn't turned in. He tried to grow some pot plants in the greenhouse, but the teacher found them and threw them out (so he said). I smoked weed with John several times on campus, while skipping.

One day (before I'd totaled my car) I went home after the first couple of classes and hit the liquor cabinet. I don't know why, I just did. I picked the lock and replaced the missing liquor with water, so it looked like the bottles had the same amount in them, as I always did. Many years later when I told Mom, she realized that's why she never got a buzz when she made drinks. I had a huge glass of about 10 different spirits and got a good 'buzz' going. I went back to school drunk. I went to Psychology where I had a nice, but naïve soccer coach as a teacher. I was acting a little too happy. The teacher didn't notice, but the kids around me did. Right when class ended, one girl told me I had better get the hell out of there before I was discovered. I asked if it was that obvious, and she just shook her head at me. I left immediately and got away.

At one point that fall semester (again before I'd totaled my car), I contracted tonsillitis. I was in terrible pain and taking literally 8 ibuprofen tablets at a time (which you shouldn't do, I found out later). Mom got a tonsillectomy scheduled. Before my surgery, I skipped a couple of classes one day, went home and smoked pot. I was stoned and went back to school. I neglected to leave my quarter bag of weed at home and had it in my pocket. I was walking down the hall when a Counselor stopped me. He asked where I'd been. Mom had called to check on me and he said they couldn't locate me. He took me to his office and started to give me a lecture. He noticed my glassy, red eyes and correctly inferred I was stoned. So, there I was with a bag of pot in my pocket and this guy was on to me. He accused me and I got scared they'd find the weed and have me arrested. So I turned the tables on him. I told him I didn't even smoke pot and I'd gone home because of the pain I was in, and that I'd taken pain medication which explained the appearance of my eyes. I said I was offended he'd accuse me of such a thing and I was going to have my parents speak to the Principle about his behavior. The bluff worked. He apologized and went on to explain that a lot of kids who skipped school also took drugs. He even empathized with my pain, because he'd had a tonsillectomy as well. I walked away and went home.

One day (after I'd totaled my car) I missed my ride with Mark one morning I'd overslept. I was wondering what to do when I thought of a 'burnout' girl that lived nearby. I walked to her place and sure enough, she hadn't left. She said she'd drive me to school. I waited for her to finish getting ready and we left. She pulled out onto the road and then pulled out a bowl. She said it was 'skunk weed' and we smoked all the way to school, but I never got high. I thanked her for the ride and went to class. We missed first period, but I was on time for English. I thought it was odd I didn't catch a 'buzz,' as it had a pungent odor. I walked in just as the late bell rang. As soon as I sat down in my seat, it hit me like a sledgehammer. I was so high I didn't know what to do. I became paranoid that everyone around me would see how obviously high I was and turn me in. I sat with my head down looking at a blank sheet of paper. The teacher started randomly asking questions. I was sure she'd single me out and I'd be unable to do anything but mumble or drool. But, I got through class without anyone speaking to me. As soon as the bell rang I stood up and my high was instantly gone…it was weird.

After I got back from Christmas vacation, Donna dumped me, as noted. Without a car, I couldn't get her away from school anymore. We'd still hang out at school together, but with other friends as well, and never alone. She'd never taken me as her 'one and only,' and now she didn't want me at all. I figured girls didn't want a boyfriend with no transportation. I 'dated' a couple of girls who drove me around, but never got anywhere relationship-wise. I was dependent on friends and Mom to go anywhere. That's when I took up with Sharon, the girl I'd soon lose to the dealer, and who'd gone into rehab just before prom. I was in Clemmer's office one day after getting back from vacation, totally pissed about something, and hating school more than ever before. I called Mom and told her I was quitting. She said if I did, she'd throw me out of the house. For some reason, after all the trouble I'd recently caused, I believed she was serious. I knew without a job, there was no way I could pay rent, even if I found a roommate, so that I'd quickly be staying with friends (which seemed unfair) or homeless. So, I stayed in school. I was faced with not being able to graduate without another semester's credit in Math, having failed Geometry that past fall. I had to take a remedial math class to get a Math credit. And, I had to take an after-school class to get enough credits to graduate. A cool guy named Bob drove me to the other school where he took the same course, and we'd get high before and after our class. My situation was such that it was highly in doubt that I would graduate at all.

But I walked across the stage and got my diploma, wearing my mirrored shades and hair hanging down. It was only the day before that I learned I'd actually graduate. I had to 'threaten' another teacher to pass me in my Typing course. I'd taken Typing the whole year and my teacher absolutely hated me. She was high-strung beyond belief. I never did anything the way I was supposed to, but I was literally the best typist in school, likely because of my guitar playing. She'd scream at me for drumming on my desk, which always made me laugh since the class consisted of making tapping noises on the keys. She said I made her 'nervous' with my drumming. The thing that really set her off was when she had a typing contest with a cash award of $10. Everyone in all her classes participated, and it turned out I won. That pissed her off. What's more, when the school gathered for an assembly, she called my name in front of all the faculty and students to come up and receive my award. I wasn't there. Even though I was on the roll as being present, I'd skipped and was at Hardee's eating. To top it off, I had the gall to go to her a couple of days later and ask for my money. She was livid I'd blown off the assembly, but she gave me my $10. She was going to flunk me that last semester, and had every right to do so, but I needed those credits to graduate. I told her if she didn't give me a passing grade, I wouldn't graduate. I said that meant I'd have to come back the next fall to get a few credits. I told her I would take one easy class to get my credits and would take every one of her classes with the remainder of my day. The thought of spending multiple classes with me was 'threat' enough and she passed me, and so I got my high school diploma.

That last semester, I was doing my 'Prayer for Judgment Continued' requirements. I took my tasks seriously because I didn't want to go to jail or have anything on my record, and I set out to get it done. I was given a choice for community service. I could work on weekends picking up trash on public property. Or, I could wash police cars. I had lots of experience washing cars, but I shivered at the thought of washing cop cars. My last option was to work at the Salvation Army, which I took. Mom dropped me off at 7:00 on a Saturday morning. They had a night shelter for homeless men downtown. I asked if I could just work my 24 hours in a single stretch and be done with it. The guy in charge said it was okay with him. So, I scraped paint off windows all day with a little retractable razor blade. I kept it and put it in my pocket for protection that night. That evening they drove me to the shelter and I helped the guys 'in charge' check-in homeless men. The guys 'in charge' turned out to be in the same community service program as me, but literally had thousands of hours to serve. They'd worked there for months and were now the night supervisors.

There were some wild people that came into the shelter. Almost all of them were dirty and disheveled. They had a maximum capacity of 150 and we quickly reached capacity. Later that night when the men were supposed to be going to sleep, a gigantic man came in drunk with a limp, yelling at everyone in his way. He had a scarred and contorted face, with patches of hair missing. He was obviously looking for trouble. The supervisors turned him away, telling him there was no more room and even if there was, he couldn't come in drunk. I thought he was going to attack them. I was sweeping the staircase, trying to stay out of the way. He didn't get physical, but he was threatening it the whole time. He turned to leave and walked up to me in a storm of violent emotion, and said, "What the hell are you looking at?" I didn't reply and he brushed by me in a huff. He was screaming in the street below the office window. The supervisors were laughing and told me he did this kind of thing all the time. They said he regularly assaulted other homeless men. They said a couple of weeks before, he'd passed out in an abandoned warehouse and was beaten silly by guys who used a 2-by-4 stud on his head. Someone found him and they sent him to the hospital. When he woke up, he went on a 'crazy' screaming trip, and left.

The guys in charge let me go to sleep for a few hours. They were nice to me and were interesting. Other than their convictions, they seemed pretty normal. I got up at 5:30 a.m. and helped make and spoon out a barrel full of grits. One of the occupants was wearing a KISS shirt from their solo album tour. It was in good shape. I only had $2 on me, but I asked him if he'd consider selling me his shirt. He asked what I'd give him for it. I said I'd give him $2 and the shirt I was wearing. He said, "Fuck you!" and went on to eat his meager breakfast. He knew his classic shirt was worth more than $2. At 7:00 a.m. that morning, my 24 hours were complete and my form was signed. I left and started walking home. I didn't want anyone to have to come get me that early on a Sunday morning, so I thought I'd walk the 8 miles to Mom's. I gotten about a half mile when the husband of my Mom's best friend drove up and asked if he could give me a lift. He knew I hadn't asked my Mom for a ride, and came to find me. I had all kinds of good people looking out for me, in spite of myself. Yet another type of privilege I only later learned to appreciate. Not everyone has a solid family or social support system to help them out in times of trouble.

Thus, I made it through high school and got a genuine diploma, but I never felt it was worth much. It came from a system I'd come to despise. I only went to the ceremony at Mom's request. I didn't respect the degree or the school. I knew W.B. had dropped out and he seemed way brighter than the majority of kids receiving diplomas that day, including myself. But still I knew society looked down on a 'drop-out' and employment would be harder to come by without some certification that one had a basic education. W.B. had taken the General Education Development (GED) test without studying, and made the highest grade the scorer had ever seen at Central Piedmont Community College (henceforth referred to as CPCC). Tons of people I know went there, and eventually I did, too.

On Luke's birthday in April of the year I graduated high school, Mom married a guy named Patrick, whom she'd been dating for some time. I've come to love him, but at the time I hardly knew him. They were moving to Raleigh, N.C., at the end of the school year and taking Luke to live with them. As my life and friends were in Charlotte, I didn't want to go even though I was welcome to live with them. I'd totally scoffed at the notion of college, as I hated school and couldn't imagine continuing to go (I had no idea college was very different from high school). I had taken the Scholastic Achievement Test (SAT) used to sort out college applicants, because Mom insisted. It was given before I wrecked my car and I drove over to take it with a massive hangover, one of only 2 I've ever had, despite my ridiculous amount of alcohol consumption. I made an 800-something. High score was 1,600 and I think they spot you 500 points for just filling out your name. And, I'd never have gotten into a regular college or university anyway, with my abysmal high school GPA. So, W.B. and I decided we'd move out of our respective houses and room together to split expenses. We figured we'd work day jobs and play music until we could make our living from it. Dad co-signed our lease and we moved into a nice apartment in a complex of 3 duplexes right after my graduation.

Chapter 5

Phase III, How Much Worse Could I Get?

Our new place was behind the Park Road Shopping Center which was extremely convenient for me, since I was without a car. I got a job at Constant Carwash not far down Park Rd. and was able to walk to work. Byron also worked there, so that was nice. With all my experience at RingClean, they paid me almost $5/hour, plus tips. I worked about 50 hours/week and that gave me a monthly take of just under $1,000. And, my hours and tips varied, so sometimes I made less. My share of the rent was $250 a month, plus half the bills, for about another $100 a month. I drank even more when I became 'independent,' and had about a $200/ month drinking habit. I also smoked a lot of pot, though W.B. and I often alternated buying it and shared. I spent about a $100/month on weed. I bought all my own food and later when I got a car again, my own gas. All that left me with very little 'extra' cash, which I spent on going to shows and buying musical equipment and guitar strings, and the like. But I was happy, or at least seemed to be outwardly. I had no one to answer to.

The nice thing about working at a carwash, is there's very little shit to take. You wipe down cars, and if you can handle that, you get paid. When "you got nothin', you got nothin' to lose," and "freedom's just another word for nothing left to lose," at least according to Dylan and Kristofferson. It felt great having very little to do other than have a 'good time all the time,' though it was tough at times just to make the rent. The Manager at Constant was a fascinating middle-aged guy, with whom I had some good conversations. He wanted me to work the gas pumps some of the time, and one day he came over to show me how to read the tanks to see how much gas was left. He got the 10-yard-stick and approached the lid to the main tank with a lit cigarette. I said "I don't think you want to open that lid with a lit cigarette in your mouth." He laughed and said "Watch this!" He opened the lid, and threw his lit cigarette into the tank. I jumped back, as if that'd save me if the tank exploded. But, nothing happened. He thought that was hilarious and said "It takes an open flame to ignite gasoline!" So, I worked the gas pumps occasionally, and it was usually quiet. I found a copy of the *Big Book* from Alcoholics Anonymous under the register. With plenty of down time, I read the whole thing. It's full of tragic stories, showing how anyone from any walk of life, could have their life destroyed by alcohol addiction. It made an impression, but I wasn't about to quit drinking.

I got drunk and high all of the time. And, I didn't eat much. I found if you drink enough, you don't have to eat much. Beer calories are apparently sufficient to live on, and when you've got a belly full of beer and/or vodka, you don't feel hungry. I'd usually eat popcorn or peanut-butter-and-jelly sandwiches, which were easy enough to afford. Our neighborhood was very nice, and I could walk anywhere I needed to go or catch rides with friends to wherever they were going. And, I could play guitar or the stereo any time I wanted. I thought I 'had it made.' I was young, full of life, and without a care in the world, except for myself. When you start caring about other things and other people, the world gets much more complicated and harder to handle.

I was very much into the local music scene and I jammed with several bands, starting and ending several musical projects, none of which played in public. As I'd roadied for Power Mouse since 8th grade, I had connections with lots of other rock musicians in the area. My favorite local band was Creature Sack, and I still think they should've made it big. They didn't and eventually disbanded. But that was after a huge number of local shows, a 2-year move to LA, releasing 2 CDs on a major label, a tour of America, and over a decade of commitment to their music. They were very popular locally and the parties that followed their shows were legends of debauchery, which I enjoyed as much as the bar scene. Many local bands partied after shows, but Creature Sack drew the most 'hard core' partying crowd of them all. Most of these massive parties were held at the drummer's grandparent's house, in the basement apartment where he lived alone, and where partying amongst a few friends was virtually a 24/7 event. He was called Spook, though obviously that wasn't his real name. He was one of the nicest people I've ever met (both he and Ian are now deceased). Spook stayed stoned all the time on any drug he could get, and got a lot of drugs. He also got 'laid' all the time with a ridiculous amount of different and beautiful women. He was different from me in that he didn't work (other than to sell weed, which we bought from him, and from which he made plenty of money), he was an extremely talented musician, he was way more successful with women than me, and I didn't use nearly as many kinds of drugs as he did. Otherwise we were very similar and we had a brotherly relationship.

It just so happened Spook's grandparents were quite well off, and were the coolest older couple you could imagine. And, they lived a block from where W.B. and I lived at the time. Creature Sack practiced in the upstairs living room. This made going to parties, getting weed, and listening to great music, very convenient. I'd often get wasted and stumble across the park behind the school that separated our streets, and pass out in the comfort of my own bed. The other Creature Sack members at that time were Ian the guitarist, Obie the bassist (both of whom did harmony backing vocals), and Braüse, the original singer. I started carrying equipment for them and soon became Ian's guitar tech, until they moved to California. Not long after I became associated with them, Luther (Anne's brother) replaced Braüse as the singer. I never had more fun as a young man, than hanging out and working with Creature Sack and our crowd. I never got close to Braüse, but I liked him. All the other members became like an extended family, of sorts. There were lots of people in the Creature Sack crowd and I became good friends with many of them. There was a lot of insanity that went on at different times and one person in our crowd, Krull, was 'crazy' as shit.

When I first met him, we were at a raging party in Spook's basement apartment, and he was verbally abusing everyone in his path. The guys in Creature Sack just laughed at him and loved him. Krull came up to me and insulted me in a loud and ignorant fashion, and I insulted him right back. He started laughing and put his arm around my shoulder. I'd encountered quite a few 'nuts' in my days at the carwashes and other places, and most people considered me 'crazy,' so he didn't bother me at all. It turned out he was way 'crazier' than I was…though I could hang with him at his most absurd. We eventually became very close, again like family. I began to hang out at Spook's all the time, so I also hung out with Krull all the time, because he was there a lot. He raised more hell than anyone I ever knew. While he was always in people's faces, getting arrested, getting in fights, etc., he was the kind of person you had to like, unless you were 'uptight,' in which case he was the kind of person you had to hate.

I didn't work at Constant Carwash long before I started working with my next door neighbor, James. He saw my seedling pot plants on our back porch (they died, as did all I attempted to grow). He'd seen us around but was now sure we shared an interest. His wife was named Sherry. W.B. and I went over to their apartment and got stoned. They were also snorting cocaine and offered us some, but we declined. James was an installer of all type of flooring materials (except carpet) and was looking for a helper. He asked if I wanted to earn $50 a day and get high all the while. I'd make roughly the same amount each month, but I couldn't get high at the carwash, so I said it sounded like the job for me. And, sometimes he wouldn't be able to give me all of what he promised, so again, I sometimes made less than $1,000 a month.

Thus, I took on my first construction job as a helper. A helper does all the 'grunt' work, but gets to learn the trade. Construction is still very much a system of apprenticeship. I swept floors all the time, laid out the glue as 'glue baby,' and cleaned up everything when we were done. James did 'bumps' of cocaine all day and we both smoked weed, which James supplied. We mostly laid sheet vinyl, but occasionally put in parquet (hardwood squares). James initially did all the job layouts and all the cutting of materials. I carried 5 gallon buckets of glue, the 100 pound roller, and all the other tools. Even though we were friends, and eventually also like family (he still calls me "little brother"), I was still a long-haired punk to him. He gave me all manner of grief on all types of subjects on which we disagreed. And I gave it back, all day every day. We'd get in his van whenever the mood hit him, which was often, and take off to smoke a joint. James would get up very early and ring my phone or knock on my door until I woke up out of my 'passed out' state. I'd stumble out to his van and go back to sleep for the 30-minute ride to the shop, out of which we worked. We'd get to the shop at 7 a.m., to clean out the truck and pick up the day's work. We rarely worked past 3 in the afternoon and when we did, James would pay me a little more. I got used to the work quickly, and became good at it, eventually being able to lay out jobs and do the cutting myself. At times James couldn't afford to keep me on as a helper and thus I wound up doing other construction work.

I worked with Krull for several weeks during that second summer on my own. He was a framing carpenter and he was working for his crazier brother, Walker. I've met people as 'crazy' as, but never anyone 'crazier' than, Walker. After I got educated in Psychology, I'd come to realize Walker had Antisocial Personality Disorder (APD), multiple Substance Abuse disorders, and Bipolar I Disorder, all of which are serious enough individually, but are absolutely devastating in combination. Krull was one of the most unique people I've ever known and I truly feel privileged to have become a very good friend of his, though at times he'd strain the bonds of our friendship, as he did with everyone he knew. He idealized Walker and he seemed to strive to be just as 'crazy' as his older brother and in many ways he was, and much later I'd come to realize that while Krull didn't have APD, he likely had Bipolar I. And, he definitely had major substance abuse issues. Krull was as big a drunk as anyone and also loved to get high on whatever drugs were handy. Krull would go to extremes to stay high on some substance or another, but to my knowledge he never ripped anyone off to do so.

When I first worked with Krull, each morning he'd bang on the door and scream, "Off your ass and on the truck!" He'd then break in through the front window and continue screaming until I woke from my drunken stupor and got up. W.B. hated that shit, though he also became best friends with Krull. After about a week of that obnoxiousness, James (who again, lived next door, with Sherry) informed me calmly and seriously that the next time he heard screaming and banging that early in the morning, he would come over with a baseball bat and put an end to it. It was hard for me to explain that to Krull, who had no cares about his effect on others, but I convinced him that if he did it again, he'd wind up with a bat to the head from a very intense guy. He agreed to just break in and wake me up more quietly.

As I said, Krull was then working for his brother Walker, who was at the time stable enough to have steady work as a sub-contractor framing houses north of Charlotte. Very few people could work long with Walker. He was abusive in the extreme and ran off several people I know. Many in the construction industry can be rough in their treatment of others, but Walker was extremely bright and extremely muscular, and he could be brutal. He never got ill with me other than to yell at me about what task I should be doing and how to do it. I hadn't worked in carpentry before, so I was the 'grunt,' of course. After talking over with him my philosophy of restrained drug usage, saying I used constantly but only pot and alcohol, he began to always refer to me as "Duly Addicted to Pot and Alcohol," as if that was my name. Walker drank incessantly and liked heroin and anything else he could get his hands on. He was a lot of fun, if you could stand him. He was very amusing and even won a talent contest in rehab doing stand-up comedy. He didn't have any planned material, he just got up and was himself. However, he was a con-man of the highest order, having no empathy for anyone. Lack of empathy is a core characteristic of APD. As such, he could be extremely charming in order to get whatever he wanted.

I'd wind up working for Walker on several short occasions, never more than a few weeks at a time. I'd get hired when he was somewhat stabilized and working regularly and then he'd flip out and take off to who knows where, and the job was over. To humor himself, he'd yell all types of standard quotes as you worked. Regarding workman's compensation insurance, which he never carried even though it was required by law, he'd say: "You're on the Sure Fire Insurance Program..... as sure as you're hurt, you're fired!" If you were covering a roof in felt paper, he would say something like, "If you fall off, you're fired before you hit the ground!" Or, "If you fall off, bring me a soda on your way back up!" If you were struggling with a sheet of plywood in a heavy wind, he'd say, "Don't let it whip you! You grabbed it first!" If you were taking too long on a task, he'd say "Come on, you're not building a Grand Piano!" Fortunately for me I never got hurt on his job sites. Anytime he was questioned about anything official he'd lie about his credentials, and could convince anyone of almost anything.

He and his occasional partner, whom Krull called 'Weed Monster,' would go to the huge hardware stores like Lowe's and Home Depot, whenever they ran out of supplies. They'd never pay for anything, because they always spent whatever money they had on alcohol and other drugs. Instead, they'd walk in and take what they wanted. Walker would either shoplift it or make up a purchase order number and charge the full amount to whatever company he happened to say he worked for. I saw him do this once, and asked how he got 2 boxes of 16-penny nails, which weren't cheap, when I knew he had no money. He said "I used the purchase order number, dummy!" I said "What purchase order number?" He said, "The one I made up!" He smiled and went on about his business. Weed Monster was a scary fellow who'd been to prison a few times, and dealt cocaine and various other drugs, including marijuana, as Krull's name for him implied. He was big, loud, and mean, but we always got along well.

Walker rarely payed me what I was fully owed. There were several times I worked for people who wound up not paying me for some reason or another, and every now and then I had trouble paying the bills. Other times I had trouble paying bills was when I quit jobs for whatever reason, and stayed on a drunk/high roll until I ran out of money. Usually within 2 or 3 weeks, I'd get another job. The last time I worked with Walker, it was also with Weed Monster as his partner. As a sub-contracting framing crew, we'd build houses with the materials purchased by the General Contractor (minus tools and nails and such, which Walker would steal). Walker was in fact, a master carpenter and truly talented. When half a job is finished, the Crew Chief gets a half-draw (half of the total amount), and is supposed to pay the crew their share. When the whole house is finished, the Chief gets the other half of the money. On this job, we'd worked to the point of getting the half-draw, and the next day I went to the job site to get paid. Rent was due and I really needed my money. But, Walker and Weed Monster never showed up. And, I mean they never showed up again, leaving the house half finished, requiring the General Contractor to find another crew to do the rest of the work; also leaving the crew, including me, unpaid. So, I struggled hard that month with rent and bills.

I saw Walker about a couple of years later. I was living alone in an apartment complex off South Blvd., and there he was one day, just walking through my parking lot. I didn't know of anyone he knew there, except Ian, and was surprised to see him. I yelled and got his attention and yelled back "Duly Addicted to Pot and Alcohol!" He came over and after shooting the breeze a few minutes, I jokingly told him he still owed me money, saying "Man, you really left me hanging on that last job." I said it jokingly because Walker is a very muscular and highly unstable guy, so I didn't want to press anything too far. But he looked at me most sincerely and said, "Dude, me and Weed Monster went to the beach!" So, that's what happened: they got the money and went to the beach to party, without a single thought for anyone on the crew, much less about finishing the house. He then said, "How much did we owe you?" I told him $240. He proceeded to take a huge wad of cash out of his pocket. He peeled off $120 in twenties, gave it to me, and said "There! Weed Monster owes you the other half!" Then he laughed semi-maniacally. I told him I appreciated it very much, because I was short of cash at the time. He then turned and walked off into the woods behind the complex. I didn't see him again for a few years, and still have no idea why he was in my parking lot or why he wandered off into the woods. It was one of the strangest 'professional' interactions I've ever had. I never asked Weed Monster for the money, because he was never in a state of mind where he seemed approachable for such things. And, I only very rarely saw him and didn't hang out with him. The last I heard of him, Krull said he'd been arrested by a Charlotte-Mecklenburg Police Department S.W.A.T. team, who assaulted his house and shot his pit bull. Apparently, he'd been dealing, and using, a lot of cocaine, and developed the customary paranoia to an extreme degree. Krull said Weed Monster had been collecting weapons of all types, including automatic assault rifles, and was telling people the Police Department was trying to "fuck with his head," and that he was going to start a one-man-war against them. So, the cops won the 'war.' At least that's the story Krull told me.

Like I said, Krull idealized Walker. He'd tell wild stories of their adventures together. Krull told a particularly bizarre account of the time he and Walker were arrested after a NASCAR race at what was then known as the Charlotte Motor Speedway. Apparently, Walker had an infield pass. They got there early the morning and parked amongst the recreational vehicles (RVs) scattered about inside of the track. Walker began drinking immediately and by the end of the race, was smashed. At the end of the race, Walker began to do doughnuts on the infield, with his Chevrolet pick-up. Now the winner of races often does donuts on the track, but the fans most certainly do not! Track Security quickly stopped him and forced him to wait until everyone left the track, before they'd let him leave. Drinking isn't uncommon at such races, so they were trying to sober him up before letting him drive. When Walker was released, he pulled out onto the then 2-lane highway that led to town. He was behind a huge line of RVs that Krull estimated to be a mile long. Rather than wait for traffic to clear, Walker crossed the double yellow lines and illegally passed everybody all at once. Krull said he got up to about 60 MPH and was flying past all the RVs, in the wrong lane (where there were fortunately no cars coming the other way). When he came upon the intersection, Walker slammed the brakes and skidded across into a gas station parking lot, in front of several police cars. Krull said a cop hit his blue lights and screamed out the window to, "Hold it right there!" He said Walker looked at the cop, flipped him off and said, "Fuck you!" as he punched the accelerator to the floor. A high speed chase followed that involved several police cars. Krull described the fear he felt as Walker raced down city streets at speeds approaching 100 MPH. He said his brother sped through red lights without so much as a glance to see if anyone was coming through. They wound up turning into a neighborhood where Walker ditched his truck, got out and ran off, leaving Krull alone. With police directly behind them, Krull was quickly apprehended and arrested, even though he was only the passenger on a maniac's joyride. Police Dogs later sniffed out Walker under the crawl space of an unsuspecting person's home.

Walker told me of his manic-depression (Bipolar I Disorder), which again I knew nothing about at the time. He said he was prescribed Lithium for it, but he refused to take it. He told me that it made him feel "too even." He liked the ups and downs and psychoticism appeared to be kind of a hobby for him. Walker had a girlfriend the last time I saw him, and a child. They'd apparently dated the previous few years or so, and he said she was as 'crazy' as him. Years prior, he'd gotten angry with her about something and literally burned down her house. He described the fire with great enthusiasm. "It was so hot that it melted the plastic headlight covers on a car across the street!" he told me. She left him for a while and then forgave him. The time I visited, they were living together with the child, who was about 2-years-old. I'm connected with this kid now on social media, and he seems to be a very-well-adjusted young man. Krull's and Walker's parents were very well-off financially, and did everything they could to help their sons, but they were in many ways, beyond helping. Anyway, that day I came by, Walker was wearing a house-arrest transmitter around his ankle and told me he wasn't supposed to leave the house other than at appointed times, when he was allowed to work. We hung out awhile, and I left. Walker wasn't supposed to leave his house at nights or on the weekends. He certainly wasn't allowed to leave the city, or the state, and yet one day he did just that. According to Krull, Walker decided to go to a South Carolina lake, just past the state line. Walker got drunk and started harassing some people there. Someone called the cops. When the police arrived, Walker started a fight, with all of them. He was arrested, again. He's been in prison many times, often for long periods.

With a 'role model' like that, it should come as no surprise when I say that Krull was arrested many times himself. He had a pickup truck his parents gave him, which he called the "Heavy Chevy." He always drove without a license, without insurance, without a current inspection sticker, and without a care. He'd pick his nose whenever he came to a red light and happened to face a police car going the other way. It was a trick that worked 2 or 3 times that I was with him. A cop would be looking at him as he pretended to be obliviously digging his finger into his nose. Then the cop would drive away, never noticing the inspection sticker was out of date, being distracted by the disgusting display. Once, I was riding with Krull and for some reason or another he decided to push the envelope. We were on South Blvd., a main roadway through Charlotte, with businesses all down its length. We were in a 45 MPH zone when he punched the gas and took us up to 95 MPH. I was stunned as I watched the speedometer rise. Telephone poles and traffic whipped by. I told him to cut it out. He didn't. We entered a 35 MPH zone at the same insane speed. As we approached the turn he wanted to take, he slammed on the brakes and screeched the tires as he slowed down just enough to make the corner. I again told him to slow down or let me the hell out. He just laughed and asked, "Can't you take a joke?!?" I was amazed such bravado was not observed by a single officer, as it was broad daylight and a highly crowded area. I was also amazed he didn't get us or someone else killed.

Krull got into a lot of trouble with the law, but he always avoided any serious punishment. He attributed it to a 'high dollar' lawyer his dad would get him. He said his lawyer regularly had 3-martini lunches with the judge who always seemed to be in charge of his cases. Krull said once he was up on some serious charges, and the Prosecutor was about to enter his arrest record (which he claimed was several inches thick) as evidence against him. Krull said his lawyer walked up and took the pile of papers out of the Prosecutor's hand, stating that they were irrelevant and inadmissible. The judge upheld his action and the case was dismissed. Other times, Krull avoided getting tickets by claiming to be someone else. He did this several times to one fellow who was a friend of his, who apparently never called him on it. Krull memorized this guy's license number, birth date, address, etc., and would totally convince the officer in question that he was who he said he was. The cop would write the ticket in the other guy's name and give it to Krull, who would then throw it away and never tell his 'friend' about the incidents. I'm not sure the fellow could prove it was Krull, because I know he had his license revoked once due to lack of paying fines. Krull could certainly tell a convincing lie, very much like Walker.

Krull would get out-of-control drunk every night, as did I. He either paid for his alcohol himself, 'borrowed' it from others who made the mistake of leaving their beer conspicuously in the refrigerator, or he stole it from a store. He was instrumental in getting my beer/wine when I was underage. When I first started hanging out at Spook's, Krull and I would go on beer runs frequently. If he was awake, it was "Beer-Thirty" to him. He was of age, and I wasn't, so my constantly going with him to the grocery store in Park Road Shopping Center led the Manager and cashiers to believe I was also 21-years-old, though I'm sure I didn't look it. I went in and grabbed a case of beer one day and the cashier rang it up without question. I was in paradise. I lived near an unending supply of alcohol as they were totally unaware I wasn't legally able to buy it. I got to be friends with the Manager, who'd shoot the shit with us. He actually loaned me money one day to buy beer. I told him I was short and that I'd pay him back when I got paid. He handed me a $10 bill. And, I did pay him back. There was one cashier in particular, who'd often ring me up for far less than what I should have been paying.

Krull got us into trouble of one kind or another, many times. Due to his legal issues, he was sometimes forced to ride around on a moped (which he called his "Garelli with Perellis"), although he still drove the "Heavy Chevy" when he got the urge. We were both unemployed at the time of the next incident I'll relate. We had some money and it was 'Beer-Thirty,' so we got on his moped to make the 200-yard run to the grocery store. Krull was driving as I sat on the back. We passed around the back parking lot where a popular nightclub was located. There were 3 guys standing around a truck. One was huge and the other 2 were average size. One of the smaller fellows was dribbling a basketball when we passed by and Krull yelled, "Basketball is for pussies!" They ran after us, but we had momentum and they couldn't catch us. I asked him what the hell he did that for, and he said for "fun." We could've gone back another way, but no. Krull rode us back through the same lot, and the guys were still there and still mad. The biggest one tried to grab us and as Krull swerved around him, he just snatched the back of my shirt which popped out of his hand.

We went back to the apartment I shared with W.B., and Krull insisted we prepare to fight. Figuring they'd seen us make the turn onto our street, and that they'd come after us, I decided to go ahead with his plan and head them off before they found out where I lived. I grabbed a baseball bat and Krull grabbed a fire poker which I had laying around (I didn't have a fire place). We ran back out to the main road that led behind the shopping center just as they pulled out of the lot. The big guy slammed on his brakes and jumped out holding a metal pipe. The other 2 got out of the truck as the big guy slammed his pipe into the ground in a display of aggression. When he did that, the pipe bent 45-degrees or so. He looked at his bent weapon, and then looked at us with our bat and fire poker. He apparently got scared and then asked why we wanted to call them pussies. Krull said he'd just been kidding and didn't mean anything by it. Krull diffused the situation with his mastery of bullshit as I stood by wondering how someone could get so deep into trouble one minute, and get totally out of it the next minute. We all wound up laughing about it together and going our separate ways.

At Creature Sack shows, Krull was totally in his element. He'd harass everyone, much to our amusement. He'd rock out harder and party harder, and longer, than anyone. He was a lot of fun to hang out with in such places. He'd then fall all over Spook's or whoever's house afterward, offending anyone who was unfamiliar with his ways, and even some who were. Then he'd disappear into the night with his 'crazy' girlfriend, Angel. I went and picked him up one evening when he called and said she'd hit him over the head with a beer bottle and smashed a plate glass window at a hotel near the airport. He was hiding out from her and the cops, behind the railing of a bridge on the Billy Graham Pkwy, and when I stopped at the intersection he came running out, and I got him away from there.

Krull and Angel would fight regularly and intensely; thus they drew the police on many occasions. They'd fight, break up, have sex with other people, and then get back together, without fail. Once when Krull and Angel were riding in W.B.'s car, she was on Krull's lap in the front passenger seat and I was sitting alone in the back seat on the front passenger's side. They were arguing as usual, and he picked her up and threw her in the back seat behind W.B., who was driving. He screamed at Angel: "Go ahead and fuck him, I know you want to!" She complained in a whiny voice that he was acting 'crazy,' when he turned on me and drew his fist back. I told him if he hit me, we'd get out of the car and I'd beat him into oblivion, and that I could do it because he was far drunker than me. I wasn't non-violent then, and friendship with Krull often required establishing extremely firm boundaries. He apologized to me sincerely, as drunks often do, and said to Angel, "Get back up here...why the hell are you bothering Sage?!?"

Krull had a highly selective memory. He'd always come around the next day to wherever he'd been the night before, and ask people what he'd done. If they told him something that they or he found funny, he'd remember everything in detail, and it would become his 'story of the night.' If someone told him he did something that made him out to be a total asshole, which was often the case, he'd have absolutely no memory of it, and deny he'd done anything uncool, no matter how many told him otherwise. I think sometimes he really knew the truth, and sometimes he didn't. He could fabricate a spin on anything that had happened and make it sound like the funniest thing ever. Like his older brother, he had a gift for humor. This lifestyle got to him regularly, and he'd cycle from manic phases into severe depression. Again, I'd say in retrospect he also had Bipolar I Disorder. When he was up, there was no stopping him; but when he was down, he often said he'd kill himself.

Meanwhile, W.B. and I continued to have a great time. I don't know how he put up with me. We both smoked a lot of pot. He drank, but nowhere near as much as me. I'd regularly get a fifth of vodka and black out within an hour. He and a woman I dated very briefly (a 31-year-old waitress at a club we frequented –why she wanted to date an 18-year-old, I don't know, but I suppose I could be charming, at times) were hanging out, when I got trashed and ran out of the apartment. They later found me in the bushes in the back, passed out. I know I frequently got out-of-hand in his presence, and as overbearing as I was, it must've been a lot to deal with at times. His much older brother, father, and mother were all alcoholics, and he grew up amidst a lot of chaos and conflict. So, the last thing he really needed was an alcoholic roommate. But he always put up with me, like a true brother.

It was during this period in my life that I did my very short stint as a very small-time cocaine dealer. This was when James had put me on as his full-time helper. Like I said, James and I had a great working relationship. He didn't care that I usually looked and smelled like a drunk ragamuffin, and he'd get us high all day long. And, he bought me drinks and food whenever I didn't have any money. And every day at work, and each night, he snorted his cocaine. We had a ritual of going to load up the van at the shop, and then several of the different installers would go back to Gary's house. Gary was friends with James and James' brother, Bill. Gary was the main cocaine dealer for that crowd. Everyone would go over in the morning on their way to work sites, and get their day's rations. Gary fronted it to them until payday, and kept meticulous records on what was owed. After dealing sessions, everyone, including Gary, would head off to do the day's work.

As long as James had his coke, weed, and Camel cigarettes, he was a happy man. He'd joke and laugh at problems and fix them. When he didn't have coke or weed, he'd lose his temper at some point during the day. It'd just be a matter of time before something would come up as a trigger for a violent outburst. He never hurt anyone, and he never would've unless it was in self-defense, but he was a big guy and he'd rage. Too much mud on the floor, screwing up a cut on piece of material, a power pole not being close enough, whatever. He'd pitch a fit and we'd leave a job unfinished, only to return to it the next day, so we'd get paid. But, that'd also put us behind on our work. When people do lots of cocaine for extended periods, their emotions become highly volatile. Whenever he ran out of coke, he'd call the shop and figure out where Gary was working. We'd then leave our job and drive any length to get another half gram. If we got it, everything was alright. If not, we'd leave our jobs unfinished.

As James would finish his half-gram portions of coke, he'd be left with a small circular piece of cellophane that held the substance. He never pressured me to use coke, and I never wanted to. But after he'd finish it off, there'd be a fine residue on the cellophane and I'd put it on my tongue. If you don't know, cocaine is a powerful anesthetic; a property clinically described by Freud, who was a physician. Novocaine, Lidocaine, and Xylocaine, often used as local anesthetics nowadays, are chemically related to cocaine. Anyway, my mouth would go completely numb. It had a strange taste that's difficult to describe. My tongue, cheeks and lips would tingle and since I was always stoned, this always amused me. After a while of working with James and the people he hung with, I came by the opportunity of selling coke, which is very expensive and highly illegal.

I knew a woman who lived in the apartment that faced ours. She and I were talking one day and she was saying how she wished she had some cocaine. She said she had the money, but she couldn't get in touch with her dealer. I happened to mention I might be able to find some, and she was all over me to get it. Not literally. She was attractive, but she only wanted coke. So I talked to James who put me in touch with his brother, Bill, who'd recently become a bona-fide dealer himself. W.B. drove me over to Bill's house, and I got an '8-ball' which was 2.5 grams, for which I paid $230. Bill told me to charge $280 for it. He offered me some, but I declined. He was astonished at that. Like James, Bill was a very big fellow, and really intimidating. He smiled and asked if I smoked pot. I told him I did and he gave me several joints of very good marijuana. He told me to come back and get more any time I needed it, night or day. The entire process took about an hour and I'd made a nice-looking woman happy, got some weed, and made $50. W.B. and I bought a quarter ounce of weed from Spook, a case of beer, and a pizza. I thought I'd stumbled onto quite the enterprise. I always had pot or beer, but having cocaine was really weird, even though I hung out all day with James using it (it was his, not mine) and had lots of friends who used it at parties. I'd been to jail and certainly didn't want to go to prison, which is what would've happened were I caught with the stuff.

The lady across the yard had a friend, equally hooked on the substance. Cocaine addicts are sad to watch, I've found. This other lady became my main customer for the couple of months in which I sold the stuff. She was a secretary. At first, I didn't think about how a secretary could afford to pay me $560 a week in cash. She'd usually call at night, and W.B. would drive me to Bill's house. Then we'd meet her back at our place, and she'd hand over the cash with great joy and disappear. I enjoyed making an extra $100 or so a week, with no work involved, but it quickly started to bother me. First, there was my own paranoia of getting caught with cocaine. Second, I realized the woman to whom I sold, could not possibly afford to do the amount of coke she did, given her occupation...at least not legally or morally. I began to wonder what she was doing to feed her habit. I got more uncomfortable being her supplier, and decided I couldn't do it anymore, so I quit. She was not happy about that. She called me for 3 months afterwards pleading with me to go get just "one more" 8-ball for her. I always refused and eventually I had to get rude and tell her off, and she finally stopped bugging me.

Cocaine is a dangerous thing, not just because you might give yourself a cardiac arrest doing it, but also because of the black market practices that surround its distribution. The tools of the drug trade are firearms, and the manner of settling disputes, which are bound to occur, is often to intimidate, injure, or kill the opponent or competitor. Once during the short period I dealt, I was at Bill's house getting coke for my customer, when he pulled out a stone-like object that was yellow-brown in color, about a foot square in area, and about 5 inches thick. He handed it to me and was obviously waiting for me to be impressed. I held it with the fingertips of both hands and asked him if it was cocaine. He said it was pure cocaine, "straight from the docks," and this was how it looked before it was 'cut.' He said he was going to 'cut' it up and sell it all himself. I have no idea why he showed it to me, because in his little 'empire' I was nobody, totally negligible in my contribution. I asked him how much it would be worth on the street and he said "$250,000!" I immediately handed it back to him and got an uneasy feeling.

I was ready to go. I was sure neither W.B. nor I wanted to hang out around a $250,000 rock that would be sought by any criminal who learned of its presence. I licked my fingers to anesthetize my mouth like I always did. I said I was late for something and we needed to go, and Bill was cool with that. As I walked out the door, my stomach was seized by violent cramps as the cocaine did its work on the lining. I was shocked. There was no visible residue on my hands from touching the rock and I didn't think it would've even numbed my mouth much. But pure cocaine is not at all the same as powder cocaine, which is typically 'cut' with filler (which makes it look white instead of yellow-brown). It virtually knocked me down and W.B. asked what was wrong. I told him what it was and within a few moments it passed. I then wondered why anyone would want to put that stuff up into their sensitive nasal membranes. I know people whose nasal septum eroded due to frequent cocaine snorting and I've talked at times with users who were unaware of their bleeding noses. After that episode, I also wondered what it did to their brains. Anyway, that $250,000 rock was indeed stolen, in a violent manner. Bill's house was stormed by 3 masked criminals who held him and his wife at gun point. He was ready for such a move, in that he had many weapons of his own, but they caught him asleep and took him by surprise. They didn't hurt him or his wife, but he absolutely lost it afterwards. James told me Bill went over to a friend's house and held the man's wife at the end of a shotgun while he demanded to know if he'd stolen his rock. He never did get it back, and that guy hadn't stolen it anyway.

James continued to do coke in spite of what happened to his brother. He never robbed anyone or stole anything to pay for his habit; he just worked hard and spent all he had left after paying his bills to cover the cost of his addiction. Sherry had a steady job that payed fairly well, so they made ends meet while still maintaining their habit. However, it took everything James made to keep them supplied, which was why he sometimes had to lay me off awhile, or pay me less than I was technically owed. One night James had a terrible experience after smoking some cocaine. The next morning he was shaken and acting weird on the way to work. I asked him what was wrong and he said that he almost died the night before. He said he'd spent over an hour on the bathroom floor feeling like he was literally going to die. He and Sherry always discussed quitting, but couldn't.

He was scared by that experience and he made me promise not to let him do anymore cocaine. I said I didn't believe he'd quit, but that if he was serious, I'd promise to do what I could to keep him from it. He said he was serious, so I made my promise. We didn't get coke that day. But the next day, we were headed to Gary's. I asked why and he said to get "just a half a gram....I need it." I started giving him hell for it, but he drove over and got it anyway. We were almost to the job site and when we got there, he pulled out the tiny baggie and opened it up. I asked him to let me hold it. He asked why, and I said "Just to look at it." He handed it to me and I said "That's it, no more coke!" He laughed and said, "Give it back, you fucker." I told him that when I made a promise, I kept it, and he made me promise not to let him do coke. He got furious and repeatedly said to give it back. When I continued to refuse, he actually pulled a knife on me and held it against my throat. He said, "Now...give it back!" The baggie was already open and I looked straight into the eyes of the man who'd helped me through many troubles until then, and I said, "You can cut me if you want to, but if you do, I'll throw this shit all over, and you won't have anything!" All of a sudden he realized what he was doing, and to whom he was doing it. He put the knife back and apologized profusely. He said I should just give the baggie to Sherry when we got home, and she'd handle it. I agreed and kept it until we got home, and then gave it to Sherry. The next day he said he just couldn't quit. I said that was fine, but that he should never ask me to help him quit again. He agreed and I never mentioned it again.

Lots of good people I knew became drug addicts. Don't get me wrong, there are plenty of bad people who are also drug addicts, but being an addict doesn't automatically mean one can't also be a good person. I should know, because I smoked pot every day until the year 2,000, having a couple of kids whom I adored, and I did everything I needed to do to be responsible for them. Weed's not the same thing as cocaine by a long shot, but those weren't my finest days. Yet before I'd finally quit, I'd obtained several college degrees, including a Masters' degree in Clinical Psychology. My undergraduate GPA was a 3.9 and my Masters' GPA was a perfect 4.0. In my Masters' program, I'd also served as a student government senator, taught a Psychology class, and worked 20 to 30 hours/week while taking a full-load of classes. I was the best husband and father I could be, and I still found time to volunteer to help various charities and I donated blood regularly. I was also certified in CPR and First Aid procedures. I'm not saying I was a great person while using weed every day, but I wasn't a bad person, and in fact, I'd say I was a good person, and a great father. I'm just saying some people can handle some drugs, and some people can't. Some are generally good people, other than what their addictions do to them, and others' aren't good people to begin with. I watched addictions destroy the lives of some otherwise good people, and it's a tragic thing to behold.

Chapter 6

Phase III Continued, Still Broken

So W.B. and I continued to live our happy-go-lucky, albeit penurious, existence. Again, I had total freedom, but I was utterly disconnected from my family at this point. I talked with Dad on the phone every couple of weeks, but I reached out to no one. It was then it happened that I found out about Lee's suicide. Like I said, I was so wasted during that period that he was actually already buried when I heard about it. Dad said he'd tried to reach me for a week, but couldn't. The family was terribly distraught. No one saw it coming. It shook me up even worse to know I was so out of it that I missed my own brother's burial. I loved him, but I'd never even told Lee that I loved him. From then on, every time I end a conversation with a loved one, I make sure to tell them "I love you." Dad and Laura divorced not terribly long after Lee died, where the strain just became too much on top of other difficulties they had. Fred actually asked Dad to adopt him, as he felt no real tie to his biological father. He never did adopt Fred, but he has remained a true Dad to him, to this day. The night I found out Lee was dead and buried, there was a general memorial service coincidently being held in Freedom Park, with candles in bags all around the lake. You could write someone's name on a bag in remembrance of them. I lit a candle for Lee. Krull made fun of me for this, not really knowing the gravity of the situation for me, and I let into him fiercely, until he backed off. At some point when I was alone, I cried, which was something I virtually never did.

And again, that was when I wrote off suicide as an option for me. I'd come close to attempting one time other than the incident on top of the parking garage, but I didn't have any way to accomplish the act, so I desisted in my intention, and soon felt better. Suicide is always a terrible tragedy to those left behind, and people who attempt to take their lives are in great distress, feeling trapped, and not thinking clearly. Now I always say that being in a deep depression is the worst time to make a life-or-death decision, because you're not rational. Since obtaining my degrees, I've professionally helped many people who were suicidal, giving them support and assisting them in seeing there really are lots of alternatives to dying, if they're willing to explore them. Encouraging them to explore the options they may not have known or otherwise fully considered, and follow up on them, can be a major challenge.

Anyway, our general partying behavior was not appreciated by at least one of our neighbors. Remember that aside from W.B. and myself using copious amounts of alcohol and weed, at least 3 of our maybe 10 neighbors were also cocaine addicts. Another unit was occupied by 2 attractive blonde women in their late 20s, who seemed very cool, and who would occasionally speak to us. Our other 2 sets of neighbors we never met. They parked around back and never came into the courtyard. The one directly next door to us, on the opposite side from James and Sherry, was a classical pianist, whom we could hear practicing in our apartment. She was unable to tolerate 2 long-haired, rock-and-roll blasting, hard-drinking, pot-smoking, loud youths. She'd race her car past our back door, when we were on the back porch, and never glance at us. She banged on the wall of my bedroom whenever we were playing music too loud, which was often. Three professionals owned the place in a partnership, and one came by to 'talk' to us. When he did, he found the place full of empty beer cans, cigarette butts, and dirty clothes. He wasn't pleased, even though we assured him we cleaned on an 'almost' weekly basis. So, we got our first eviction notice and had 30 days to find a new place to live.

It was time to leave our very nice neighborhood and find a place where we could be tolerated. We thought we'd found such a place on Wilbrown Circle off South Tryon. It was a brick house with a couple of rooms in the basement. The landlord didn't actually live in Charlotte. We met him at a fast food joint and he expressed reservations at renting to young 'kids.' Once I told him my Dad would co-sign the lease, he lightened up and welcomed us. We executed the lease agreement and moved in. Wilbrown was a very culturally mixed neighborhood. Almost everyone there had a blue collar job and some owned their homes, while others rented, like us. It was a fairly laid-back community. It was also racially/ethnically mixed, which lent itself to my broadening my understanding of other groups. Having a house was much more suited to our lifestyle. We could be as loud as we wanted and no one complained. We set up our instruments in the basement and could finally play without restricting our volume. It was a nice place to be.

Just before we moved out of Arbor Lane, Dad gave me another car. It was a nice Cutlass with plush burgundy seats, power windows, air conditioning, cassette stereo, and all that. Fred had it before me. I was back in business for driving. It was nice to have a vehicle again, because it was hard to find people to work with in construction who'd come and get me in the morning and take me home. I was still drinking liquor and whatever else I could get. I was still broke most of the time and jobs came and went, due to my own volatile ways. I worked for a couple of temporary service companies at times, doing what they called 'light industrial work,' which is just a nicer way of saying "hard or weird tasks no one who works here is willing to do." But, it was difficult to get the bills paid and keep my alcohol and weed habits going. There were several times when there was no food. I lived on rice, popcorn, peanut butter, and alcohol, for many weeks at a time. I learned bar-b-cue potato chips could be placed between 2 slices of bread to make a crunchy but authentic tasting bar-b-cue sandwich. I once took a dozen ears of corn that had fallen out of a busted crate on a refrigerated train car I was unloading as a 'temp.' They'd backed the train car in the wrong direction, and they couldn't get the forklift lined up to pick up the bundles. In trying to move the stacks to where they could pick them up with the forklift, by pushing them around with the forks, they'd punched a hole in one of the crates. Thus, they got 'temps' to come offload the whole boxcar into the warehouse, by hand. As the corn had been on the ground, they told us to throw it away, so I stuffed a bunch into my heavy coat pockets. Since we were going to be unloading a refrigerated boxcar, they told me on the phone before the job to wear a heavy coat. So, we had corn to cook up for dinner that night, which was good, because we were out of food that day.

On rare occasions, I also stole from grocery stores when I really needed to eat. When I did this, I'd put on my heavy coat and go to a store on Tyvola Road. I'd wander around and put some food into my coat pockets then buy a pack of cigarettes, to look less suspicious. I justified it by thinking I wasn't taking from a person (which I'd never do, even then), but rather from a corporate entity that could absorb the loss. And, when I had money, I felt I overpaid them anyway. It was a weak rationalization for immoral behavior. Though I didn't do it often, I got away with it so easily, that I got cocky. Once I was working with Krull, Ian, and Weed Monster, framing apartment buildings in North Charlotte (as well as with Walker, who wasn't with us in the story I'm about to relate). We'd worked a week on the job and it'd still likely be a week before we got paid, and we were all flat broke. Krull and Ian would steal us food from the break truck every morning. Ian would take whatever change we could scrape up and go distract the vendor with a purchase. Krull would slip behind the vendor and take candy bars, drinks, sandwiches, etc., and quickly walk away. By the end of one day, we were out of cigarettes and everyone was bitching as we were driving home. We four were crammed in the cab of Krull's truck. I told him to pull into the nearest grocery store, and I'd get us some smokes. He pulled in and I got out. We all smoked different brands and I walked in with the most arrogant attitude; casually strolling up to the cigarette stand in the front of the store, in plain view of everyone. Weed Monster also went into the store, though I didn't know why. I picked out one pack each of 4 different brands and just walked out. No sneaking, no checking to see if I was being watched; I just got what I wanted and left without paying.

I was a little over half-way to the truck when I saw Ian and Krull making frantic gestures. I smiled and held up the cigarettes. Just then I got tackled from behind and I heard my shirt rip. Some guy was on my back, holding me down, and I knew I was busted. A lady wearing brown slacks and a blue windbreaker was holding a pair of handcuffs in front of me yelling, "I have to put these on you! I have to put these on you!" I didn't want to get anyone else in trouble as accomplices, as there were no accomplices…it was my idea and I took responsibility. So, I surrendered and totally ignored the truck 20 feet from us. I turned and asked the guy who tackled me, "Was that really necessary?" He said, "That's what you get when you're a thief!" I never really thought of myself as a 'thief' before that moment, I just figured I was a likable 'rogue' getting what he needed to scrape by in this world. I said, "You tore my shirt!" The woman put on the cuffs and they escorted me back into the store.

Weed Monster had disappeared and again, I didn't know why he went in. I didn't ask him to help, and he had no money, so he may have been going to steal something himself. But they asked me about my "lookout." I said I didn't have a lookout. The guy said he saw another fellow come in behind me. I said that must've been a coincidence as I had no idea what he was talking about, which was technically true. Then they called the cops. While we waited for the police, we discussed my deed. I told them I was addicted to nicotine and that I didn't have any money, so I felt compelled to do it. The guy, who turned out to be the Manager, asked why I didn't just come and ask him to help me out. I said, "Because I didn't think that would work." I apologized for having stolen from the store and said I knew better, which I did. I wasn't raised to be a thief, but I had habits that needed feeding, and it was hard to come by cash, so I did what I felt was necessary, though clearly it was wrong. I was very polite to my captors and we had a nice, genuine conversation until the cops arrived. By the time they switched me to my official pair of handcuffs, the Manager even apologized for having me arrested and explained it was just store policy. I told him I understood and deserved what I was getting. I was sincere.

I was released several hours later on my own word that I'd show up for my trial, a thing called Pre-Trial Release. Apparently, you can have it once, if you're not a habitual criminal and the charges are minor. I was charged with a misdemeanor, petty larceny. I got a ride home and got stoned. I tried to get a Public Defender since I didn't have money for a lawyer and I didn't want Dad to get involved, but I found even as poor as I thought I was, I wasn't poor enough to qualify for free legal counsel. So, I decided to represent myself and just plead guilty. I went downtown for my arraignment, and sat waiting for my name to be called to get my trial date. After an hour, they finally got to my case. When my name was called the Prosecutor said, "The charges have been dropped; you're free to go." I asked him to double check. He did and confirmed there were no charges against me. I was elated as I left the courthouse. I guess the Manager felt I'd learned my lesson. He was right as I never shoplifted another item. With my flimsy justification gone, I'd never take anything again. Like I said, I never stole from an individual, but I realized taking stuff from companies was also indefensible.

Everything seemed to be going okay. I was fairly happy, though occasionally hungry. I met some of our neighbors and had a good time in our new home. W.B. always worked steady, so whenever I was short, he'd cover my portion until I got paid. Our house was usually trashed. We held more than a few parties and were amazed at how dirty the place could get. Our huge double sink held a mountain of dishes that hadn't been washed since we'd moved in. On pulling a pot out, I found a most intricate and beautiful mold formation inside. Light green and web like, I could appreciate the cosmic beauty contained within, but we decided it was time to clean the sink. We didn't wash the dishes though; rather, we opened the window behind the sink, and threw them all into the back yard. We hosed them off and threw a lot of them away, though we salvaged some. When we got to the bottom of the sink, we realized someone had vomited in it during one of our earliest parties. Neither of us was big on cleaning.

I was getting on well enough, now having a car. I could work at least 3 or 4 days a week with the temp service. I learned a lot working as a nameless 'grunt' in so many places. I did a few days working with the housekeeping staff at an upscale hotel, cleaning rooms after guests checked out. It looked to me as though some of the upscale guests went out of their way to trash their rooms, which made it all the harder for the underpaid workers to get through their day. I never left another hotel room in which I stayed, without cleaning it completely before checking out. Among other jobs, I assembled industrial shelving at a warehouse and shoveled oily debris from under machines at a factory. The nicest thing was I didn't have to accept any job I didn't want, and I could leave any I didn't like. I never did either, but knowing I could was nice. I did every job offered, to the best of my ability.

I still worked with James every now and then, but he'd fallen on hard times and couldn't afford to work me much. He and Sherry still had their coke habits and he'd gotten busted for tax evasion. He didn't file taxes for a long time, but he'd paid the previous 6 years. He figured if he could make it 7 years, a statute of limitations would apply and he'd be off the hook. It was the 11th month of the 6th year when a Federal Marshall came to his door. With interest and penalties James owed over $70,000 to the government. They threatened him with prison, but they settled for garnishing his wages. I'd soon be working a different trade, sheetrock, but at this point I was switching back and forth between temp jobs and a rare day's work with James.

I think I'd have done alright, if it wasn't for my massive liquor habit (though later, I'd realize I had to quit all forms of alcohol). While on Wilbrown, Spook's birthday came up, and there was a major concert that night. I went to Spook's before the show, to wish him happy birthday and tell him we'd all planned a party at our place after the concert, to celebrate. I started drinking heavily while I was there, and continued until we left for the show, where I also smoked a lot of weed. I drove separately, and was so high I barely remember the concert, which was at the Charlotte Coliseum. I was 18 and lived there all my life, but when I left the show, I got lost. I was trashed. In due time, I found my way back home, and the party was already going strong.

I'd put a fifth of vodka in the fridge before I'd gone to Spook's that afternoon, and I gulped it down in minutes. Very quickly, I blacked out. Everything that happened afterwards was told to me by various friends who were there. It seems I got an itch to drive, and everyone tried to dissuade me. But nobody kept me from doing anything I wanted to do. Apparently, I got in my 'new' Cutlass, and W.B. stood behind my car to try and keep me from leaving. They told me I almost ran him over in pulling out. Wilbrown Circle was truly a circle: a single road leading into the neighborhood, breaking right and left through the neighborhood, forming a complete circuit. So for whatever reason, I drove up one side of the circle and was coming back down the other toward the house, at high speed. I ran into the back of my neighbor's work van. He lived 2 doors down. I hit his van so hard that my car went under it, and ran it into his wife's car, which then hit his daughter's car. This was around 2 a.m., and only a few people were still at our party. My remaining friends came out and took me inside, virtually unhurt except for a deep cut on the back of my shoulder. They tried to back my car out from under his van. My car was somehow still running, and they were going to run it into a ditch somewhere and report it stolen. I had some seriously loyal friends. The car wouldn't come loose, and they just dragged the van back a few feet. The car never ran again, and was totaled. They tossed me in my bed, shirtless since someone had the presence of mind to make sure I wasn't going to bleed to death. Then the few people remaining went home, except for W.B., who obviously lived there.

The next morning, around 7 a.m., I guess, I awoke to a thundering and persistent knocking at the front door. I had no idea anything had happened other than perhaps passing out in my bed, so I got up and went to the door. It was a police officer. He was terribly excited and started barking questions at me. He asked who I was, what kind of car I drove, etc., and I told him. He asked if I'd been driving my car last night, and I said "No!" Having blacked out, I really had no idea what he was talking about. He said my car had crashed into my neighbor's vehicles and the whole windshield was smashed out. He saw blood that had dried on my side from the big cut on the back of my shoulder, and he examined the wound. I suppose I'd rolled sideways on impact. From this injury, he insisted I must've been the driver. He said "Who was in the car with you?!?" I said "Nobody!" I was just answering randomly. He said again, "The whole windshield is smashed, so somebody was a passenger." He yelled again, "Who was in the car with you?!?" I said "The only person who could've been in my car was my roommate." He said, "So your roommate was in the car?!?" And I yelled back, "NO! Nobody was in the car with me! I wasn't in the car! I have no idea what you're talking about!" He arrested me as he said the cut was proof that I'd been driving. He cuffed me and led me to the patrol car. I saw my next door neighbor with 2 other cops, clearly talking shit about me, as he was pointing and seething. I knew he didn't like us as neighbors, and here he was trying to get me in trouble. So, I started yelling and cussing at him. I was still quite drunk. They put me in the back of the patrol car, and I kept cussing and yelling at my neighbor from behind the closed window. I was taken downtown and processed. Somebody, though I don't remember who (perhaps Dad), soon bailed me out.

When I got home, W.B. told me the whole story. But, I'd never admitted to anything to the police, as I seriously didn't know I'd done it. I hadn't even seen my car or the crashed vehicles because the police cars were in front of it and them. There were no witnesses to the actual crash. I felt absolutely terrible that I'd almost run over my best friend. I had an epiphany. It finally hit me, hard, that I could've killed or injured somebody with my reckless behavior. I really didn't care if I hurt or killed myself, but the idea, which had never occurred to me before, that I could hurt or kill someone else, was unbearable. I made a decision to never drink and drive again, ever. Even though I still kept drinking heavily, I quit drinking liquor, so I wouldn't black out so quickly. I still blacked out on occasion, but I've no evidence I ever drove again, so something changed deep within me. When I drank thereafter, I never drove, so I always made sure I was well supplied before I began a night's drinking.

I also felt terrible about my neighbor's vehicles. Several days later, I went over and told him what I was told about that night, and said I was very sorry about it. He was a much older, blue collar HVAC worker, and very down to earth. I remember he had a "Born to Lose" tattoo on his arm. I was bigger than him, but I'd have let him beat me up, so I'd feel some absolution. But instead, he said "Don't worry about it!" He also said something like, "I used to drink when I was younger and I did some really stupid shit, too." He told me his insurance was paying to fix all his vehicles, and it'd all be okay. Later, when the trial came, he was the only witness called for the Prosecution. I'd never said I did anything, so there was no confession. They called him up and swore him in. They asked what he saw the night of the crash, and he said "I didn't see anything." They were incredulous and said, "A car crashed into 3 of your vehicles in front of your house, and you didn't wake up and come out?" He simply said, "Nope." And, that was it. With no confession and no witness, they dropped the charges right then and there, and once again I was free from the most serious potential consequences of my ridiculous actions. However, I no longer had a car, and thus couldn't work temp labor gigs anymore.

Across the street lived a lovely family, whom I'd met at some point. General D (his performance name) and Adelana were married and had 3 children of their own, twin boys about age 6, and a daughter about 4-years-old, and D's daughter who was about 13. They were a Black family from New York City. As I said before, I'd rejected racism around 8th grade. I was never taught by my parents or family to be racist, sexist, homophobic, Islamophobic, or to hate any group. However, nobody ever taught me it was wrong, either. So, I'd picked it up from other kids in school and in my neighborhood, during my childhood. I was never really sexist, which I attribute to my Mom being single a couple of times, working and taking care of us, and being a great role model, but I certainly picked up sexual objectification as a young male, through interactions with other males and within the rock music I listened to all the time. I also acquired a serious homophobia, as did most males at the time for whom calling each other 'gay' and 'faggot' seemed the most profound insults. I heard such pejorative terms thrown about constantly as I grew up. I'll get to the other isms later, but racism was definitely something I'd gotten past, and here I was in a racially mixed neighborhood, with a family across the street who happened to be Black, and they became like a second family to me.

D was a former gang member in New York City, as was his brother whom I also came to know. He was in his early 30s when we met. The gangs they were in as youths were largely self-protective in tough areas, and not part of the drug trade that would become a hallmark of inner city gangs during the crack epidemic. He'd left that life and went into the military, and he was a proud veteran after being honorably discharged. He'd gone into the sheetrock trade, and became a master craftsman, especially in metal-stud framing. D was working on a building downtown with a crew, of which he was the leader. Since I was working in such an off-and-on manner, and constantly short of money, and now no longer had a vehicle, he offered to let me join his crew. He said I'd have to start out as a laborer, but that he'd teach me the trade, and when I got enough money for a screw gun and other tools, he'd get me a raise. I needed a hardhat and appropriate footwear. He gave me an extra hardhat he had around, and a pair of his combat boots from the military. And, I became the only White member of an all-Black, Nation of Islam, sheetrock crew.

At the time, I had no idea what Islam was, having grown up Christian as what I call a Methopalian. I went to a Methodist Church at Dad's house, and an Episcopalian Church at Mom's, and was confirmed in both faiths, and was baptized. I'd not learned about other religions at that point, and wasn't against any per se; just ignorant. It was from D that I learned about Islam, Elijah Muhammad, Louis Farrakhan, Malcolm X, etc. As noted, I actually loved learning, I just hated my public school experiences. D, like James, became like an older brother to me. He was mature, responsible, a loving father, and very smart. He and Adelana took care of me, like feeding me when I needed food (as I was no longer willing to steal it). Their kids loved me like an uncle. Their young twins and younger daughter were full of life and always ready to play. Being on that sheetrock crew, and hanging out often with

D's family, I became acutely aware of Black American culture, in a way in which I'd never otherwise be so thoroughly exposed.

D was a rapper, having grown up on Hollis Avenue in Queens, near where Run DMC grew up. He knew both of them, and Jam Master Jay. Rap was just becoming a big thing, especially after Run DMC paired up with Aerosmith and did an MTV video for their combined version of *Walk This Way* (2 years prior). The Sugar Hill Gang (their first album, with the classic *Rappers Delight*, had been released 8 years prior), the Beastie Boys (who released *Licensed To Ill*, 2 years prior) and other groups, like NWA (who released *Straight Outta Compton* that year), were increasing the popularity of rap music. In the rock music crowd in which I ran, most people hated rap, and put it down as a non-talented genre. Most, though not all, of the White people I knew in general, who happened to have any opinion on the subject, seemed scornful and overtly racist in their views of rap and rap artists. Some did enjoy it, as evidenced by the rise of White rap artists, like the Beastie Boys, though I'll not credit Vanilla Ice as wholly legitimate here.

But D was in the New York City scene where rap originated, and he was passionate about music in general. He also loved Motown, Soul, R&B, and African-American Gospel Music. I'd only had passing exposure growing up to the first 3, but had never really heard the latter. Every day, he drove me to work with him, and we listened to each of those genres extensively, as rap hadn't yet broken into the radio mainstream. I'd never have become a convert to Islam, but I did learn a lot about it (particularly the Americanized Nation of Islam version), and about African-American history in general. And, while I didn't become a rap devotee either, I really enjoyed some, and especially Kool Moe Dee, whom D played for me. D was always interested in my playing, and he listened to all I had to say about rock music and heavy metal. We were both open-minded, and taught each other in a kind of cultural exchange. As hinted at above pertaining to the Jethrene story, it was D who had the rap group mentioned, with 2 other guys from Charlotte. And, they had a drummer and an occasional keyboard player, and a female soul singer. They were essentially 2 different bands, who practiced in the same space and played together at block parties. D asked if I wanted to join the group to play guitar, and I jumped at the chance to join an already formed group. We were a 'live' rap 'band,' which was distinctive as almost all rap artists at the time used existing records to form the background for their rapping.

I learned this practice began in the ghettos of New York, because people there couldn't afford musical instruments and PA equipment. However, many families had a stereo and albums, so young people found they could plug a microphone into the input jack, and do vocals on top of any record, kind of how karaoke works. Experiences in those areas were pretty negative for many people, and they typically lacked for a specific and personal artistic expression of their experience. All that was needed was a turntable and a microphone, for a beat and backing music, and one could perform lyrics on top. Thus, rap became the way to creatively express views regarding that unique culture. It then became a successful genre and included the arts of blending parts of different records into a continuous flow and 'scratching' records rhythmically, neither of which are easy to do, I discovered. It also brought about the development of distinct personal rap styles, and free-style rap battles. And it started making some artists serious money, when they were lucky enough to be successful, like Run DMC, who along with other artists inspired lots of people to become rappers. Rap 'battles' between MCs were not initially violent. They were just a match of talents. But as the genre progressed to the point of earning some performers millions, the game changed, and led to rivalries which did create some violent clashes. It also became the vehicle of expression for those in much more fierce gangs than D had been in, as the crack epidemic led to many tens of thousands becoming both addicted and dealing the drug. Such drug dealing inevitably leads to the use of weapons to defend a gang's 'turf' or against competing gangs, and conflicts with the police, all of which led to 'gangster rap.'

Again, what made our group different at the time, was we weren't using records, but were a live band, over which our 3 rap artists would perform. So, I got to write music along with them, and play guitar. It was a lot of fun, and I got to be good friends with everyone in that group, as well as getting to know lots of people they knew. So, there I was, the only White guy in an all-Black band (2 bands, really), and found myself hanging out with all kinds of other people who were into this scene as well. Again, I was getting a cultural experience unlike any I'd ever previously known. And all was great up until I became the 'target' of racism myself. I'd never known what it was like to be put down, or shut out of opportunities, due to my skin color. The group had an opportunity to play on a local cable TV talent show, which was well-known. But a couple of the members (not D) thought I shouldn't be in the group, because they were trying to do a 'Black' thing, and didn't think it was appropriate to have me in the band when it got on TV. This confused me, because up to that point I thought we were all friends, and if so, why would they want to kick me out? I've learned there's no such thing as 'reverse racism.' Racism is racism, and it's all related to in-group/out-group psychology, and dominant and minority group structures, and some members of all groups hate other groups, and some don't. D certainly didn't, and wouldn't stand for my being dismissed from the group. So, the group broke up over it and never performed on the TV show, or ever again. I felt bad about it, even though I'd done my best for them and our music. But I was learning what it might be like for my Black friends to have been life-long targets of systemic as well as personal acts of racism. I also understood that when they got their chance to shine on TV, the other guys (again, not D) didn't want others to think it was because they needed the help of a White guy.

Prior to the breakup of the group, D and his brother, and I, went to New York, to see Jam Master Jay, and give him a tape of our music that we'd made in one of their friend's apartment recording studio. We went to Hollis Ave., and they told me not to go out alone at night, because I might be mistaken for a cop trying to bust people, and might get hurt. I said, "But I have long hair and don't look like a cop." They said that was all the more reason I'd be thought of as a cop, because it would look like I was under cover. D's parents treated me like family. I hung out with D and his brother and their friends on a corner, drinking 40oz bottles of malt liquor and smoking joints. When a cop drove by, I got edgy and asked if we shouldn't move somewhere less obvious. They laughed and said, "If it ain't crack, they don't care." This was when the crack epidemic was reaching its height. D and I walked through the neighborhood one day and he pointed out houses that were either where crack was sold, or where one of his friends lived who'd become addicted to crack. The whole scene was quite sad, which is how D saw it as well.

We went to a block party at Jam Master Jay's house. D gave him a copy of our music at some point (I didn't meet him myself), but nothing came of it. On the way back to Charlotte, D's brother was driving and D and his youngest daughter were asleep in the back seat. We got pulled over for speeding and his brother claimed to be D (who didn't wake up), and gave the cop D's information without producing a license. The cop bought it, and wrote up the ticket in D's name. D's brother was a big guy, and tough, and I wasn't about to question him in front of the officer. D didn't know what happened until we got home. So, when it came time for D to go to court, I went with him to explain what had happened, as a witness, and help him get off of having to pay the fine. It was about a 45 minute drive from where we lived and we had to go several times, as his case got postponed each time we went, as the court also handled other far more serious cases. This led us to miss work, and miss out on getting paid, but I wanted to do what I could to help. Eventually, they dismissed the charges and told D to warn his brother about doing the same thing in the future.

I read the *Autobiography of Malcolm X*, co-written by Alex Haley, at D's suggestion. And I was startled to find out how terrible things had been in terms of racism in the past. I knew a bit about slavery and the Civil War from school, but I really didn't know anything about Jim Crow laws, the KKK's systematic intimidation, abuse, lynchings, or how the justice system usually turned a blind eye to all of it. Nor did I know anything about the Civil Rights movement in the US. So, I started to learn. That's a book that needs to be read all the way to the end, as Malcolm X turned into a racist himself based on his experiences, but toward the end described a significant life event that made him ultimately reject racism. And, it was an unpleasant history, to say the least, but I learned things that weren't really taught at that time in schools. Blacks certainly weren't talked about in ways approaching anything like respect within the White groups within which I grew up. Quite the contrary. Racist views were all too common, I found in schools. I presumed that was just a reflection of an overall cultural inclination, which of course, it was. Eventually, I found other Whites, and members of other racial groups, who weren't racist, and found some understanding and solidarity. It seemed to me if we really wanted peace in our time, at least in our own country, we had to start by attempting to really know one another's histories and cultures, and so that's what I did as an individual. America is the best country that's ever existed. I think we have to acknowledge bad elements of our past, to understand how not to repeat them and keep moving forward positively. One thing of which I'm very proud about our country, is while it was built in part on some terrible issues, chiefly with regard to Native American displacement and slavery, we eventually tried to fix those issues. And, that we've worked toward a more positive and inclusive society, consistent with what was included in our founding documents, especially the *Declaration of Independence, Constitution,* and *Bill of Rights*. We aren't perfect, but we've been moving in the right direction for quite a while now.

D and I kept working together on other crews with another company, as the original crew I'd started with went its separate ways when that first job ended. I'd gotten my own tools, including a screw gun and keyhole saw. As I learned to do metal-stud framing and board hanging, I made more money, which was good. However, it was a tough job, physically. I was young and energetic, but a day of toting and hanging sheetrock is hard work. Doing it every weekday, I was worn out a lot. I still played music, partied ridiculously hard with my friends, roadied for Creature Sack and other bands, and so on. But, for a while I could easily pay my bills, until I wound up having to move again, because predictably, we got evicted. I don't know how the landlord got wind of our lifestyle and the state of general clutter in his house, but nonetheless, W.B. and I got notice that we had to leave within 30 days. This time I wound up going it alone in a one-bedroom apartment, in the low-rent complex I'd mentioned when describing running across Walker in the parking lot. Ian also lived in the complex, just up the hill from me. That was really cool because I got to hang out with Ian personally, in addition to hanging with the whole crowd. I loved the crowd, but Ian was an exceptional and intelligent guy, and getting to talk one-on-one in a non- chaotic environment, was a real learning experience.

After moving, I lost my ability to work with D. With him having to take care of his kids before they went to school and then going to work, he just didn't have time to come get me. Not only was I about 10 miles away, but also off South Boulevard, which was a traffic nightmare, especially during rush hours. D and Adelana (they eventually divorced) and I are still friends to this day, though we don't see each other as they live in other states. While I was still on Wilbrown, I bought Calvin's old moped from Mr. Hill after I'd totaled my car. Thus, I had a way to get around, though not quickly, and hardly safely in Charlotte traffic. But it took little gas to operate, so it was cheap. I continued to work for the company doing sheetrock in buildings downtown. One day, my screw gun was stolen off the jobsite at lunch, when I walked away for a few minutes. That was frustrating because without one, I was useless to the company. I went to the pawn shops, hoping to get it back, since I could identify it. Though I never saw it, I had enough cash to pick up a used one, so I didn't lose my job over it. That someone would take something I needed to hold a job, when I'd never stolen anything from an individual myself, really irritated me. But, I suppose for someone to do that, they must be at a very low place in life. Eventually, I learned to have compassion for others who make terrible decisions, even though I'd rather them do otherwise. I've certainly made myriad terrible decisions. I had a milk crate attached to the back of the moped, and I'd cram my drop cord and tools into it, and head to work each morning, dodging death daily. Rush hour was the worst, because (and I've found this confirmed by research) drivers don't really perceive motorcycles, mopeds, bicycles, the same way as cars. They will drive right into you, if you're not extremely careful.

So, I worked for the company until I got into conflict with the main Supervisor, Slim. Slim had given me and D a hard time when we worked together, because we were always enjoying ourselves, singing while working, engaging in philosophical debate, etc. Slim wanted everyone at work to be miserable and docile, it seemed. He'd orchestrated a split between me and D on the job, so we got assigned to different sites and couldn't work together, even if he'd been able to pick me up after my move. I resented Slim for breaking up my partnership with D. They assigned me to a job downtown, which kept me working as I only lived a few miles away. I'd always been argumentative with Supervisors whom I thought were generally too bossy. If I knew how to do something, I wanted to be left alone to do it my way, not told to do it in a less efficient way, just because a boss 'said so.' I was working a new building which was 7 floors, and which had an overhang about 5 floors above the main entrance, and he wanted me to sheetrock the bottom of the overhang. I'd learned how to erect scaffolding safely and was prepared to get all the 'bucks' and 'platforms' I'd need to make a steady work station that high. Since it wasn't near a wall, but rather out in the open, there was nothing to which I could tie it off, other than a couple of columns 25 feet away. I was going to make it 4 units wide, for stability. Lugging sheetrock that high without a lift, was going to be difficult. But, Slim told me I couldn't do it as I'd planned, as he wasn't going to authorize getting that much scaffolding. He said I should just use one unit as the base, and build the rest up from that. So, we're talking a base of about 8 feet by 4 feet, up about 7 units, about 42 feet up, which I knew would be wobbly and dangerous. We got into a loud argument about it, and drew a crowd of other workers. He questioned my bravery, which offended me and I said "Look, I'll show you!" I built it rapidly as people went on about their business, but some stayed and watched. I put each unit together, until it was high enough. I got on top and said "Watch this!" I started moving back and forth and it rocked visibly. I'm lucky it didn't tip over as I'd have been badly injured, if not killed, hitting the concrete below. It was a dramatic demonstration, and I came down to the ground and looked at him, and said "There you go! It's stupid to ask someone to work on the top of that! I don't care how many ropes you run to the columns. Fuck you, I quit!" I got my stuff and left, with my point made, but without my job.

I was in a rut with money again. I'd started singing and playing my acoustic guitar, together by this point. I was a terrible singer, and I knew it but really enjoyed it, so I kept at it. Now I'm fairly good, depending on the night. But I'd worked up a small repertoire of songs, and decided to go downtown and busk for tips, to make some cash. I strapped my acoustic guitar to my back, with the base in the milk crate, and rode my moped downtown one weekday around lunch. I figured white collar workers would be walking around, and might throw some cash my way. Well, I must've sucked, or they must've looked at me as some kind of vagabond to be avoided, but I only made a few dollars in the 2 hours I was there. This homeless guy came up to me, and gave me a cheese sandwich he'd gotten from the local shelter. That was the same shelter I'd worked my community service. He must have assumed I was homeless, too, even though I had a moped behind me (which must've seemed a luxury to him). He told me I could go there and get a shower, bed, and food, every night. I thanked him for his kindness and information, and headed home. I did have a home, crummy apartment that it was, and for that, I was grateful. I wound up eventually having an interest in helping the homeless, and started doing so formally when I got to my senior year of college. But at this point, I still had no idea I'd ever go to college, and was continually struggling to make ends meet and keep my beer/weed habits going.

Soon thereafter, W.B. was also out of work, so I suggested we go to the temp agency downtown, and get some day work. I couldn't do it alone, because there was no way to secure my moped there, which would've likely been stolen. He had a car, so he drove us there the next morning. The place was crowded with all kinds of guys down on their luck, and addicts who couldn't hold a steady job. We filled out paperwork and waited to get an assignment, which wasn't guaranteed. After an hour or so, they sent W.B. out to take some guys to a job site, since he had a car. They paid him a small amount for doing it. I got sent to another job, where I'd be toting 12-foot boards of sheetrock up a couple flights of stairs in a building being renovated. I was paired with a guy who knew nothing about sheetrock. You can carry 8-foot boards by yourself, though depending on the thickness they're not light. But with 12-foot boards, you really need 2 people. There's an art to carrying them, and this guy didn't know that art. He was constantly jostling me on the other end, as we were going up stairs, and no matter what I said, he never got the hang of it. And, it was hot as hell, so the whole thing was miserable. When we were done several hours later, we had to wait around for a ride back to the office, to get paid.

Once they took out 'taxes and fees,' I'd made $12 for the whole day. I was pissed and thought I should've made at least $20. As W.B. was already gone for the day, I had to walk home. Our mutual buddy, Henry, had moved into my apartment complex, only a building away. I saw W.B.'s car outside his place, so I went over, and they were drinking out of a case of beer and smoking weed. I asked W.B. where he got the money for beer, knowing they only paid him a few bucks for driving, and he told me he'd made $20 just sitting around an hour watching TV, and 'donating' plasma. He'd learned about this opportunity from somebody he'd driven that morning. I was dumbfounded, saying "I worked my ass off for hours, wasted more time sitting around, walked home, and all I got was $12. You sat around for an hour and got $20?!?" He just laughed and said 'Yep!' I now had a new and quick way to get cash, and took up regularly 'donating' plasma. I'd go to the grocery store where they knew me and didn't question my age, and 'cash' my plasma checks by buying a case of beer and get $12 change. Henry was dating Lana at that time. She was as wild as anyone I'd ever met, and they were always partying at Henry's place. So we all hung out there a good deal of the time. Eventually, W.B. married her, and that was a nightmare for him, as her mental health and addiction issues became a constant annoyance, and occasionally got him into some serious financial difficulties.

As W.B. and I both needed work, as did Krull at the time, we decided to become a subcontracting carpentry crew together. Krull could get himself together at times, and he got us a job building a house in a new subdivision in southwest Charlotte. Like Walker, Krull was also a master carpenter, but also unstable like him. So, W.B. and I knew we were taking a risk. Krull knew how to read blueprints, so he took charge. It was a lot of work, so we 'hired' Elvis, a mutual friend and also part of the Creature Sack crowd. Elvis was also a coke dealer and user, and a copious weed user, amongst other things. He'd been arrested and was on probation, and had to do urine tests to make sure he didn't have drugs in his system. But, he always did, as he just couldn't stop. He even tested positive for cocaine, which you only need to abstain from about 24 hours for it to be undetectable. That's how bad off he was: even knowing he had a drug test, he couldn't stop using coke for a couple days before his appointment. Weed takes 30 days or so to clear out of the system, so there was no way he wasn't going to test positive for that. Anyway, he had a car and he picked me up the few days he worked with us. His car smelled like pot, because his ash tray was packed full of 'roaches' (the butt end of smoked joints). They were big enough that they could be re-rolled into joints of the size I'd smoke. I was careful not to 'waste' mine, and preferred using a bong to stretch my bags as long as possible. Being a dealer, he had tons and didn't mind 'wasting' plenty. Elvis gave me some roaches, to supplement my stash. He didn't like manual labor, nor taking orders from Krull. So he soon quit.

A few years later, I went to see him at an attic apartment he rented in a huge house that had other apartments and businesses within it, including the studio where I took guitar lessons from Murray when I lived at home with my Mom. Across the street was a small shopping center. Elvis was smoking crack at that point, and had a glass container with a sheet of tinfoil stretched across the top, onto which he'd place his rocks at one end on holes he'd poked in the foil. He'd light it up and suck up the smoke from a hole he'd made in the other side. He looked haggard, but was in a great mood. He offered me a hit, and I said, "I appreciate the offer, but I don't do coke, so no thanks." A few minutes later, offered me a hit again. I said, "You know it's weird, but

I still don't do coke, so no, thanks." He offered to sell me a really nice camera set, with expensive lenses and a leather case, for $20. My Dad was a photography buff, so I knew it had to be nearly $1,000 worth of equipment. I said I had no use for it, but asked where he got it. He said his grandmother had given it to him. As it turned out, he'd stolen it. I found out later he'd watch cars come into the shopping center parking lot, and target the nicer ones. He'd take stuff out of them, and then sneak back across the street with his ill-gotten loot. Elvis had grown up with money, and really was originally a nice guy. But, his addiction made him resort to stealing to supply his habit. Later, he got into an argument with another dealer, living in a different place, and he shot and killed the guy. He said it was self-defense, but the court didn't see it that way, and he got sent away for life. He also developed a Parkinsonian-type syndrome, likely from all his drug use. It was very sad, but that's the level to which one can be reduced in such situations.

Anyway, back to the job with Krull; he quickly got more and more flaky. W.B. started bringing me to the site, but Krull started showing up late, and leaving early. That was a problem because without him, we weren't exactly sure what to do, because he had the blueprints. After we got our half-draw, he got worse. We had to put 'returns' on the bottoms of the eaves. For some reason, Krull didn't want to do that. He said we should just burn the prefabricated returns, and tell the General Contractor they'd never been delivered. W.B. and I both protested and said there was no reason not to just do the work. But Krull threw them in a pile behind the house, and set them on fire. That was it for Krull, and he never came back. W.B. and I were counting on the other half of the money and needed to finish the house to get paid. He got the blueprints from Krull, and being an extremely intelligent guy, W.B. quickly figured out how to read them, and showed me how. We told the Contractor we'd never gotten the returns, so they had more brought over. It was a clumsy affair, but we got it done. Once we were on our own, and thought we were about done, the Contractor did an inspection and came up with a 'punch list,' which was a detailed description of everything that still needed to be done, and everything that had been done wrong and had to be fixed. We had never been in charge of a job site, so we were woefully naïve about some things, and didn't realize we'd have to do everything on that list to get paid. It was just us, and the list was long. So, we set about it.

One Saturday, my first fiancé, Anne, came up and took me over to work on the house. She had no idea what she was getting into with me, but I'll get to that later. She was literally a model, so she looked out of place on the job-site. I worked with her all that day, as W.B. couldn't make it, with her handing me lighter materials or holding things in place while I nailed them. Eventually, W.B and I got done and got paid, and that was it for our partnership. Neither of us knew how to get more jobs and a 2-person framing crew would never be hired anyway. Because of Krull's antics, that Contractor had enough of us by then, and wasn't offering us anymore work. About a year later, I drove by that house, just to look at the finished product. One of the cool things about working construction is that it's very tangible, and your work stands for a long time. But it's not yours, so that takes away from the satisfaction. As I went past, I noticed a wave in the roof, where we mistakenly offset one of the trusses by a few inches. Other than that, it looked great.

Around this time, James contacted me and said, "You've got to get a van from Uncle Ronald, so we can work." James had lost his van in his tax settlement, along with most of his tools. With his wages being garnisheed and his cocaine habit, he didn't have money to replace the van, but he'd gotten hold of some critical tools. I needed work and James was going to make me a full partner if I could get the van. I don't recall how because I was typically broke, but I was able to scrape up the $800 Ronald wanted for an old burgundy Ford van. Ronald was the head of the cocaine cartel of which Bill (James' brother) had been a part. They whole cartel had been busted by the Feds, and were facing serious jail time. Ronald was selling everything he had to pay for a lawyer. The van was not really worth $800, but James and I were desperate to get back to work, so we went to Ronald's place in the country, and I bought it for cash. In NC you needed to proof of insurance to get a license plate, and I didn't have any more money for insurance. James and I devised a plan. I put a piece of cardboard where the tag should go, wrote in a fictitious license plate number, and across the top wrote "Lost Tag." We figured that'd throw off any cops. We'd work the upcoming week, get paid that coming Friday, and I'd use my pay to get insurance and get a legitimate plate. Everything went as planned, up until that Friday.

I'd had a few cops behind me as we worked that week, but didn't get stopped, and I thought I'd been clever. On Friday, we went to the shop and picked up the day's work, as well as our pay for what we'd already done. It was early and we headed to the job site, just north of Charlotte, and were approaching the hospital near the university on the way. A state trooper got behind me, and I got worried (as usual, James had weed). Still, I thought we'd be okay since the ruse had worked all week. But he hit his blue lights, so I pulled over into the wide driveway of the hospital, and stopped by the curb. As noted, I'd learned to be courteous and respectful to officers, so I immediately got out with my license in hand, hands out front where he could see them, and approached his car. I'd also learned to take the initiative and get out of the car first and approach them, when I had pot in my vehicle, to keep them from smelling anything or looking in my vehicle. I started off saying, "Officer, that's a fictitious tag." I gave him the whole scoop on the recent purchase and the need to make enough money that week to afford insurance, in order to get a legitimate plate. He was cool about it, and didn't even ticket me. He said, "I want you to leave your van right where it is, and don't move it until you get your tags." I agreed right away, and thanked him for his kindness. We called the shop and they sent a company van, and we moved our tools and materials over to it, and did our day's work. We dropped the van back at the shop at the end of the day, and someone gave us a ride home.

Later that evening, I was in my living room, smoking my bong with a bag of pot on the table, drinking beer, and watching a rerun of the *Bob Newhart Show*. A solid knock sounded on my door, and I wondered who it could be, as I wasn't expecting anyone. I figured it must be Ian or Henry. I opened the door, and it was the state trooper who'd pulled me over that morning. I asked if I could help him, and he said "I hate to do it, but I'm going to have to arrest you." I asked why, and he said it was because I didn't have a valid driver's license, and state law required that he arrest me. I told him I did have a driver's license, and reminded him I'd showed it to him that morning. He said "Oh, I know you don't know it's not valid. You didn't pay some tickets and it was revoked. They sent a notice to your old address, but no forwarding address was left, so it came back."

Like I said, I'd gotten paid, and since James made me a partner, I'd made a good bit more than I would've from a typical week. So, I figured I had enough money for bail. But, I wasn't wearing any shoes and didn't have the money on me. I'm sure there was a smell of marijuana smoke in the air, and the open bag on the table was surrounded by a plethora of beer cans, and obviously I wasn't old enough to legally drink. So I said, "I understand, just let me go grab my shoes and some bail money. I'll be right back." He said, "Okay, but I'll have to come in while you do that." I started running my mouth non-stop, trying to keep his attention focused solely on me, and away from the weed and beer. I quickly grabbed my shoes and wallet. It seemed to have worked. We stepped outside, and a crowd of neighbors had gathered around to see the long-haired urchin get busted for something. Some didn't like me for sure, as the company I kept was loud and obnoxious, I played loud music, and looked disreputable most of the time. Others who knew me, liked me just fine. It must've been quite the spectacle for some of them.

Instead of cuffing me and putting me in the back of his car, the trooper motioned me toward the front passenger's seat. I asked "Don't you need to handcuff me?" He said, "Do you think you need it?" I said, "No, I've never thought I needed it." He smiled and opened the front door and I got in, surely to the disappointment of those watching for me to get my humiliating comeuppance. To an outside observer who didn't really know why he was there, it could've looked like we were friends, and he was just giving me a ride somewhere. That was thoughtfulness on his part. As we pulled out of the parking lot, he said "You know, I'm not going to say anything about that marijuana you had in there." I said, "I can't thank you enough for that. Do you mind if I ask why?" He said, "I had you pegged for the kind that as soon as I pulled away this morning, you'd pop right back into your van and drive away. I went and checked before I came over here, and it's still there." I said, "Well, I gave you my word I'd not drive it until I got my license plate, so I left it there." He said, "I know, but I didn't figure you would, and I appreciate that you did." This struck me as peculiar, as my van was a very long way from my place, and this was 12 hours after he'd pulled me over. So, he'd been on a long shift, stayed longer, and got all kinds of facts about me and the situation, and went over to check for my van, before he came to get me. When we got to the jail to book me in, he actually spoke to the Magistrate on my behalf, and said, "I think we can let him go on his own recognizance. He's been very cooperative." I was thus free to go without having lost any money. Later, when I got my tags, and straightened out the issue with my license, the charges were dropped, so once again, I was free of any serious consequences for my poor choices.

I had the title to the van, but it had to be signed in front of a notary for legal transfer, and of course, we didn't do that at Ronald's country home. There was no way he was going to come to Charlotte to help me out, as he had his money. Ronald was a pretty shady guy, being the kingpin of a coke ring and whatnot. I talked it over with W.B., and we reckoned we could go to a shady area of town, find a notary public, and see if we get him to notarize the title, as if it'd been signed in front of him. We went to the shady area we had in mind, and W.B. drove around until we found a notary public sign. We went in and I explained my situation to this guy, and said I was hoping he might be able to provide his official stamp for $20 cash (I had more, just in case). He said "Let me bless your money," and did it right then and there. With a 'legitimate' title, I was able to get insurance and my tag with my remaining money, the same day. Amazingly, they hadn't towed my van, so I put the tag in place. Just like that, James and I were back in business.

One early Saturday morning, Krull came over with Weed Monster to my apartment. W.B. was there as we'd been drinking the night before, and he'd crashed on my couch. When they arrived, he got up and let them in, and woke me up. They'd been up all night (we'd not been asleep long), injecting cocaine. Krull wanted W.B. and me to go out to the 'hole,' which was a low-income housing project, where they'd get another baggie. I'd only seen somebody inject drugs once, back on Arbor Ln. It was a friend of W.B.'s from high school. He'd gone into the Army and had bulked up, so his veins were bulging. He'd come over to have a safe place to shoot up, and in our living room he tied off his arm with a strand of rubber. He tried to hit the vein with the needle, but his vein 'rolled' and he missed on the first attempt. He got the vein the second time, and quickly nodded off, as he was doing heroin. It was a strange thing to witness, and while I never had a desire to do it, that sealed the deal for me. I didn't mind puncturing my arm to donate blood, which I'd done before (and would do again later in 'donating' plasma), but I couldn't imagine needing to get high so badly that I'd inject drugs.

Anyway, we didn't have anything better to do, and were now awake. Krull was excited to have us along. So, we got into the cab of the Heavy Chevy and headed over to watch them make a 'buy.' We got there and a guy came running to the window where Weed Monster was driving. Weed Monster handed over their last $20 bill and the guy took off. As soon as he got out of sight, both of them got very edgy, thinking he'd just taken the money and run. But about 5 minutes later, he came back and handed over a small bag. Weed Monster hit the gas and sped away. He pulled onto Billy Graham Pkwy and drove about 2 miles before he pulled over, to cook up the coke and shoot it up! Now, this was a huge road, a 4-lane with a large grass median down the middle. And Weed Monster pulled over on the left-hand side of the road! This seemed to me like it was bound to attract attention, and I suggested we go back to the apartment. He told me not to worry about it, and proceeded to cook up the coke in a spoon he had with him, using a lighter and water, to turn it into a liquid. He drew up the solution into a needle and injected it into his left arm, using his right hand. He waited about 45 seconds before he started to lose it with anger. He said "There's nothing in it!" He hit the gas and swerved back onto the road without so much as looking for oncoming traffic. We sped back to my apartment, where he and Krull wanted my baseball bat (that Krull knew I had) and anything else they could use to beat up the guy that had sold them the 'fake' coke. They were adamant that W.B. and I should go to watch them beat the shit out of the dealer. W.B. and I declined. We didn't see them again that day. That night, we wound up at Spook's and Krull was there. He said they never did find the guy. There was never a dull moment with Krull.

At this point, I was dating my first wife, Anne. With my van, I was able to drive down to the semi-rural town where she lived with her parents. Again, I don't know what she saw in me, but when I visited, her parents were kind to me. Again, her brother was Luther, the singer of Creature Sack, and that's how I met her. The band played a 2-night stand in a rural bar, and she'd come to see them with her friend. She was gorgeous and I was immediately smitten, and chatted her up. There was a guy who called himself Bob from Hell, a friend of Spook's who was hanging with the crowd, and he was competing with me for her attention. Bob from Hell was an admitted thief by 'trade,' and had a scam he ran at the airport, before the whole shift in security after 9-11. He'd go in the terminal and pick up people's luggage and take it. He was a good-looking guy, and also being a con-artist, was quite the charmer. But, she took a shine to me, and we became an item. On an aside, some money turned up missing from Spook's basement apartment where Bob from Hell was staying. Spook was certain he took it. Bob from Hell was insistent he'd never steal from a friend, but how do you trust the word of a self-proclaimed thief? Spook threw him out. I let him stay at my place a few days, because I actually believed his claim that he'd never steal from Spook. Being that Spook was always high or drunk, it occurred to me he may have misplaced his own money, or spent it and didn't remember. Anyway, Bob from Hell was torn up about the situation, and was sad he'd lost Spook's friendship. After he left my place, nobody I know of ever saw him again.

Anne and Luther's parents had opened 2 stores in their local mall. One was an upscale young women's fashion shop, named after Anne. She was very fashionable and always looked like a rock/metal video model when she went out. She had to work a lot in her store, so I hung out there when I visited. Next door was the one they'd set up for Luther, a skateboarding store. I hung out there more than the ladies' boutique. They set up a local young-person's fashion show, and her mom even had me serve as a 'model.' I think that was because I had the 'long-hair look,' but it was more likely her mom's desire to include me in activities for Anne's sake. I've always been pretty much game for anything, but I wasn't asked to do it again, so I probably wasn't a good fit as a 'model.' Her parents remained kind to me up until our divorce.

Around this time came my last arrest, and this was the only time in which I'd not actually deserved it, because I didn't do what I was accused of, which was indecent exposure and communicating threats. Anne was up at my apartment, and I'd consumed an entire bottle of Mad Dog 20/20, Orange Jubilee, which had become my drink of choice since I'd quit liquor. We were at the playground in the park adjoining the property, at about 1 a.m., sitting on the swings. I had this tom cat I'd found as a kitten, in a dumpster, at the shop out of which James and I did our work. It was with us, when all of a sudden 2 malicious-sounding German shepherds came out of nowhere and started after the cat and scaring Anne into running up a slide for safety. I went into a reciprocal attack mode, yelling at the dogs and chasing them. I guess I was intimidating enough, because they ran away, around a line of tall bushes separating the closest house from the park. As I rounded the bushes, I came upon a woman who let into me, loudly, about 'scaring' her dogs. I was dumbfounded, and we got into an argument with me saying there was a leash law and her dogs had come after us. She was not sympathetic to my cause. Now her husband was right next to us, and he was easily 6-foot-6 and 350 pounds, all muscle. He stood there passively, as she and I argued. Had I actually threatened her, he could've squashed me flat. Apparently he knew not to interrupt her on a rant. And, while I did a lot of stupid shit while drunk, I never exposed myself to anyone, and I didn't threaten her, at all. I stormed off and Anne and I went back to my apartment, where W.B.'s car was parked opposite my place. He was living off and on with his mom, but preferred not to be there, so while I didn't know it, he was sleeping in his vehicle at the time.

Apparently, the woman wasn't satisfied with having essentially won her argument, and called the cops. Though they didn't know where I lived nor who I was, a cruiser came into my parking lot, as that's clearly where I'd exited the park. I could've easily stayed inside and avoided any trouble, but being jacked up on alcohol and in a self-righteous tizzy, I stupidly went out to tell the cop about this woman and her un-leashed attack hounds. As I came out toward the police car, the officer got out and told me to put my hands on the hood. So, it didn't work out as I thought and I wound up in jail. I was placed into a large drunk tank which held 25 people. It was packed, with everyone sitting on the floor with their backs to the wall. One guy was particularly loud and aggressive, accosting everyone else in serial order. He got to me and said "What're you in here for?" I said "For drinking Mad Dog and standing my ground." He said, "Mad Dog?!?" This either impressed him or made him think twice about messing with me, and he thereafter left me alone.

Anne found W.B. in his car and woke him up. They came down to the jail and W.B. tried to bail me out, as he had just enough money to do so. But when the bondsman asked W.B. what his address was, he said 'transient,' which doesn't fly with a bondsman. So, he and Anne called James and he came down and bailed me out much later that morning. When I got in his car, he had a half gram of cocaine in the ashtray, and did a bump right there in the jail parking lot. I was flabbergasted, asking him if he wanted us both to be arrested on the spot. He just laughed and said, "Don't worry about it, little brother." We left without incident. The woman's father was a lawyer, and they started adding ludicrous details to the already ludicrous charges, saying I was standing in front of her with my pants around my ankles, waiving a gun around. I didn't even own a gun, and never had. If I'd been exposed as she claimed, I'm sure her husband would have beaten me to a pulp. But, I was facing charges nonetheless. I asked W.B.'s mom to be a character witness to say that while I was a wild one, I'd never do what I was accused of doing, and to corroborate that I didn't own a gun (which she agreed to do). At some point, the woman must have felt I'd had enough and that the charges were never going to stick, so she dropped them. And she was right, I'd had enough. I never went back to jail again, as I became way more careful about my drinking adventures. I suppose in a way, she woke me up to the fact that while I may have been essentially in the 'right' in this case, I was way too wild for my own good.

Soon after this, Anne and I decided to get married. Our long-distance relationship with occasional visits, was difficult. So, we thought it would be a great idea for her to move in with me. Being together full-time was our goal, but I was 20-years old and she was 19, and her parents were not okay with this idea. So, we announced our engagement to them. In response, they set up our very elaborate wedding in her hometown. It was a regal affair, and as noted, I felt out of place. I did my best to be a good sport, for the sake of all those who supported us, and as a token of my appreciation for their good will. My Mom and Dad kicked in for a nice rehearsal dinner and an amazing hotel for our honeymoon night, with a limo ride all the way back to Charlotte. I got drunk, but it was a pretty good time, all things considered. Lots of my friends came, including some of the Creature Sack crowd, and from what I recall, had a good time.

James and I didn't work together too long this time. He was able to get his own van within a few months (his wife had always worked steady, and had good credit), and I set about to work flooring on my own. I should mention that James and Sherry both eventually did successfully give up cocaine. They also had a kid together, which was a real joy for them. After he was more or less grown, they got divorced. James wound up unable to work flooring anymore, because of the damage that work had done to his back and knees. Without schooling beyond high school, he was stuck without any means of support. He did work for a construction supply company, selling materials and offering his expertise to customers, but a stroke put an end to his ability to work at all, and he had to go on disability. That was a major blow to his self-esteem, as he'd always worked. James tried to get an online education in theology, so he could become a preacher, as he'd become a very devout Christian. But, as you might imagine, there are lots of people qualified to head up churches, and having only an online certificate doesn't really make one competitive to be hired as a pastor. Many others have masters' or doctoral degrees in theology, and/or lots of pastoral experience. We keep in touch, and for the most part, he's doing okay. His experience really echoed for me how important it can be to get a higher education, to make possible other kinds of careers once construction beats one down physically. That often happens, even to the very best of tradesmen.

Without a 'helper' of my own, installation work was difficult. And my lack of any real record-keeping skills meant that when tax time came, I didn't know how to deduct all my supplies, fuel costs, and such. This was a bit distressing, as supplies are costly, and I realized my weakness in this area meant I wasn't really cut out, at least at that time, to be my own boss. So, I overpaid my taxes. Anne was my 'helper,' a few times, and that didn't work out. We argued constantly. She didn't want to take direction from me, and I can't blame her. At least she was willing to try. Eventually, she got a retail job, as she had lots of experience, but even then, money was still pretty tight. On one occasion Luke, who'd moved from Mom's to Dad's and was still in high school, skipped school and came to my place. I told him if he was going to flunk out of school, he was going to have to get a job, so he might as well start that day. He worked the day out, and went back home. He eventually did quit school and got his GED. Eventually, he went to college. He was a good kid, in the same situation I'd grown up in, except he got tons of abuse from me and our step-brothers. He handled it much better, not getting into nearly the trouble I'd been in. He eventually married and had a daughter, and I'm very proud of him.

As I wasn't cut out for bookkeeping, I soon quit being my own boss in flooring and went back to carpentry, working for a complete jerk named Trent. Trent had been a cocaine kingpin himself at one time. He'd gotten married and 'found religion,' and became a self-righteous proselytizer and critic of all things not conservative in the extreme. Having religious beliefs myself, I wasn't against him having his, but he looked at anyone not staunchly in his camp as degenerate. Not sharing his 'cleaned up' appearance, I wasn't his favorite right off the bat. His level of vitriol and negative judgments of all kinds of people and situations, led me to feel he was a major hypocrite. But he was a fairly intelligent guy, albeit narrow-minded, and he was now my boss. I was married and my wife wasn't working at the time, so I had to keep it together around him, as much as I could. However, I wasn't one to take undeserved criticism, nor to stay quiet when I heard bullshit spewed as 'truth,' so he and I had more than a few 'debates.' I was always on time to work, and did my tasks well, and in short order, so he put up with me as much as I put up with him.

About this time, Hurricane Hugo made landfall, and the eye came right over Charlotte and decimated trees and structures everywhere. I remember the night it hit because I woke up to go to the bathroom. I heard the noise, not knowing we were expecting a hurricane, and looked out my back door to see old oak trees bending to angles that seemed completely impossible. Yet, those behind my apartment didn't snap. I awoke the next day to a city-wide power outage and got ready for work. But, I found the road impassable with a tree across it. Nobody was going to work that day nor for some days after. We got by, eating what little there was in the apartment, and finding a restaurant on South Blvd. that had a generator. When I got back to work, I found the prefabricated roof trusses we'd set up on the apartment building we were framing, had been tossed like matchsticks into the woods by the wind. Trent decided we'd make more money doing repairs at other apartments, so I got my first and last taste of roofing. We were replacing shingles and reaffixing faux chimneys blown off in the storm. As it was the middle of summer, it was very hot and humid. On the roofs, I found my blue jeans were no shield from the heat of the shingles, which seemed to burn right through.

I hated it, but I hung in and eventually we returned to our original job site. Having a lot of sheetrock experience, Trent had me hanging boards in one of the stairwells. I was happy to be working alone, and was making fine progress when he and a couple others happened upon me to see how I was coming along. Trent started critiquing my technique, saying I needed to put a T-square on the boards, draw a line, score the boards on the front and back, and then break them. I knew that to be a long and unnecessary process, and we got into an argument. I told him to measure for the next board. He barked the length at me. I stretched my tape measure, and used the tape to guide my knife blade down the front of the board. I popped the board at the scored mark, then snapped it back instantly, and broke it into 2 perfect pieces in under 30 seconds. He irrelevantly shouted, "You're working in a corner, smart guy!" So I went off on him and quit in the same breath. I'd had enough of his bullshit. So, I had to find work again.

As noted, my first marriage didn't last a year. Shortly before we married, I'd been evicted again, from my apartment complex. I assume it was due to complaints from neighbors, even though I got along with my next door neighbors. Though I came close to being late at times, I'd always paid the rent on time. I moved to another apartment in a quad-plex, across from a grocery store on the 'poor' end of Park Rd., which was a block from a road my friends called "Dirtwood," due to the prolific drug trade and constant party atmosphere up and down the street. I'd been on Dirtwood before partying myself, with Krull.

Once, W.B. and I were there with Krull in his Heavy Chevy. He spied an unattended beer truck at the grocery store where the driver was inside making deliveries. Krull couldn't resist the opportunity to steal a keg. We pulled up and he said, "Give me a hand, dammit!" W.B. and I both told him he was 'crazy,' and that he was bound to get caught and arrested. Plus by that point, I'd renounced stealing things, and said there was no way I was helping. W.B. was never one for stealing, so we both refused. Krull got out and grabbed a keg, and threw it in the back of his truck. At that point, the driver came out and saw him, but Krull jumped in his still-running truck, punched the gas, and screeching his tires in reverse. I've no idea what he was thinking, other than the beer guy couldn't pursue us in his delivery vehicle. He backed onto the road and made a hasty right, then another right, and then another. This put us right back on the other end of Dirtwood, facing the very beer truck from which he'd just stolen the keg. The driver was at the other end and saw us, and started running toward us. Krull backed his truck into a driveway, jumped out and popped open the tailgate, and the keg rolled out and hit the ground, and kept rolling down the steep drive. W.B. and I were pissed at this idiocy. We jumped out of the cab and took off running. We eventually got back to my first solo apartment. We later found Krull got away, and the driver got his badly beaten keg. That kind of stuff was just what happened around Krull, and as noted, there was never a dull moment.

Having moved onto that block with my first wife, I was working sporadically at all kinds of odd jobs. I cleaned leaves from gutters at nice houses with Krull in the neighborhood where his parents lived, pawned my burgundy Les Paul (which I only got back with a $100 gift from my Mom, when I realized I was about to lose it), and laid floors for my new landlord, who was an odd guy, to say the least. The guys in

Creature Sack had moved to LA, where after much living on the edge and without steady jobs (except for Luther, who'd gone to work for a large teen/metal fashion outfit), they eventually got signed to a major label. They put out a full-length album, and it was amazing. The record company made a video of one of the songs, which they deemed to be the 'single,' and it got into late night rotation on MTV's *Headbangers Ball*, which was a really big deal. That song then got picked up for the theme of an ESPN show. They'd also been featured in the pilot version of a teenage television drama that became very popular, as the 'band' at a back-yard party, so they'd been on national TV there, too. And, they went on tour of America in support of a hair-metal band that recently had a huge hit. They were having a blast, though with only a $10 per diem to live on and crappy RV to travel in. They didn't care, and were in great spirits when I caught them on a local leg of the tour. We had a great time, and everything seemed to be looking up for them, for which I was glad. I'd never expected to go with them on their journey, and getting married certainly ruled it out.

Like me, Krull was still in Charlotte and he came around and hung out with Anne and me regularly. At some point he'd gotten into a funk, and was talking to us about suicide and his inability to be sober (as he said, "Sobriety sucks!"). He was generally inconsolable, except he'd cheer up when we drank together. I recollect the Berlin Wall had fallen, and Roger Waters did a performance of *The Wall*, in Berlin, to commemorate the event. It was broadcast around the world and we picked it up on a local radio station, which was the last time I drank with Krull. He came by soon after that, in a much better mood, and said he was giving away his stuff, and asked if I wanted anything. I said I didn't need anything. I remember he told me and Anne, that he loved us, to which we responded in kind. That was really unusual, as I'd never heard him say anything like that before. I didn't realize then, that a major uptick in mood in the midst of a profound depression, and giving away one's possessions, often precedes a suicide attempt. It may well mean that the depression has lifted because they've resolved to commit suicide, and believe 'relief' is in sight. I was just glad he seemed to be feeling better.

Two days later I got word he was dead. He'd been in a single-vehicle nighttime crash in the Heavy Chevy, taking out a telephone poll. It seems he was alive and animated when the cops showed up, and he argued with them before being arrested and forced to go to the hospital. Apparently, his lively behavior led the medical staff to conclude he'd not suffered too much in the way of injuries. However in reality, he'd suffered major organ damage, and bled to death internally in the hospital. I was devastated, and later came to believe that he may have crashed intentionally, as a suicide attempt. He drove intoxicated all the time and never crashed, and he'd just been going around telling friends he loved them, and essentially saying 'goodbye.' As they say, hindsight is 20/20; and that's just my interpretation after eventually receiving education on depression and training in suicide assessment. Creature Sack was back in LA, getting ready to record their next release, which was to be an EP of an acoustic-ethereal nature. I got Ian's number and called to give him and the other guys the news of Krull's passing. Everyone was laid low by his loss. Ian and Spook arranged to fly back home for his funeral. Ian wrote a song in tribute to him, and that appeared on the EP that was to be their last official release. As it turned out, the label changed hands, and they were dropped. They had to return to Charlotte, as there was little in the way of prospects for being picked up by another record company. They soon disbanded, which was unfortunate, as I thought they should've been huge.

Being my landlord was an odd guy, and given to not paying for work he had me do, we got into conflict and it was time to move again. I found an old house to rent on the edge of Dilworth near South Blvd, on Euclid Ave, just up the road a bit. It was in shoddy shape, and occupied by a guy named Dan, who worked on pianos for a living. In fact, he had giant letters on the front of the house, which spelled out PIANO. He was friendly when I came to see the place. As he moved pianos a lot, he was large and muscular, and he also worked for a local promotion company setting up stages for events. The place was crammed full of stuff, with only a small pathway leading from one room to another. He also dealt weed, and perhaps other stuff. He had a long mirror set up horizontally on the wall opposite a giant window on the front of the house, so he could work at his bench and see who pulled up. I didn't know why he was moving out, but the rent was low as the landlord apparently didn't grasp his old property was now in a gentrified section of town, and worth tons. So, I got a great deal, and was able to keep living in the area of town to which I'd become accustomed. Anne and I moved in to the Euclid house, and our interpersonal turbulence continued unabated.

Despite his shadiness, Dan seemed a good guy, and got me a temp job setting up for the 4th of July celebration in downtown Charlotte, putting together a large stage. He also introduced me to his good friend Warren, a few doors up the street, and who ran an appliance repair business out of his home, which was also around the corner from a long-standing topless bar. After Dan moved out, I saw him regularly, as he hung out with Warren. These guys were in their 30s, but still quite wild. Yet they managed to keep busy with work. Warren not only stayed high and drunk, he actually built a tap into a refrigerator, so he'd always have a cold keg on hand, and could go to the fridge door to constantly pour another beer.

After we moved to Euclid, I had the other 'out of body' type of experience to which I alluded earlier. I was asleep and about 1:30 a.m., I woke up as I 'heard' the cow-bell attached to the back door (which served as a door bell) ringing loudly. Anne didn't wake up, but I 'got up,' in what seemed to be my full body. However, I could see my body and Anne, both lying in bed. Why this didn't unnerve me the way the previous 2 experiences did, I don't know. But I 'walked' to the back door, and unbolted it. When I opened it, Krull was there looking very much alive, though he'd recently died. He was carrying a case of Budweiser beer. Beside him were attractive identical twins, with brunette hair hanging down across their arms and breasts. They were dressed, but skimpily. Krull said "Dude, let's party!" This seemed as real as could be, except both girls had 'vacuums' for eyes. They seemed 'evil' to me. I looked at Krull and said "You can come in, but they can't!" He said "That's bullshit, man!" He brushed past me, where I felt him knock into my arm. I never took my eyes off the girls, and as soon as he passed, I slammed the door and bolted it. When I turned around, Krull had vanished. I 'walked' back to the bedroom, and Anne was still asleep. That wouldn't have been likely if this had 'really' happened, because the cow bell was loud, as was my slamming of the door. I looked at the clock and 4 minutes had passed. On seeing my own body, I 'snapped' back into it, and 'woke' up in reality. I checked the house and nothing seemed out of order, so I went back to bed. I'd had many weird experiences, including exceedingly bizarre dreams and thus, I didn't get upset by this event. When I awoke the next morning, I remembered it as if it 'really' happened.

I can't say exactly what happened in my seemingly 'real' encounter with Krull after he'd died, because I don't exactly know. But, it was a powerful experience. Given that losing him was terrible, and also that I used a lot of weed/alcohol, there are plausible neurological explanations. I figure it was likely some kind of grief reaction that happened to seem real. I dismissed it as such, and nothing like that has happened since. I miss Krull to this day. Memory can be a very powerful thing. Dreams (if that's what happened in my meeting Krull after he died) can also be very powerful things, as well the source of artistic creativity. Ian and I had worked together a few times. He told me of a vivid dream he'd had, where hundreds of exact replicas of me, had climbed trees in a forest. Each replica was blue, wearing a tool belt, and pounding on trees with hammers. He called it "the Dream of the Blue Sages." Soon after, I went to Spook's where Creature Sack was practicing. They were in the midst of a 'groove' type of song, with a looping vocal pattern of what could've been "doo-wop." Ian, Obie, and Luther (Spook didn't sing) were singing "Doo-lah," over and over in harmony. It was surreal. Ian told me it was the "Song of the Blue Sages."

Chapter 7

Phase IV, My Pathetic Pattern Persists

Just before Anne and I moved to Euclid, I auditioned for a band made up of 2 cousins on drums and guitar, Ziggy and Reeves, respectively, and their friend, Bob, on bass. They practiced in a shed full of lawn equipment and other industrial tools. We clicked. The guys let me join them, and it was to be the band with which I felt the most personal commitment and in which I grew the most, artistically. As stated, I wasn't much of a singer back then, but here I was trying out as their vocalist, and they accepted me. They had very eclectic tastes and were quite talented. We played some cover songs and wrote many originals. I suggested our name, which I'll call Meadow Magnet here. I had my forceful personality, and they were incredibly kind and indulged me a lot. For the most part my performances on cover songs were endurable. But for our own music, I'd tailor the melody and tonality to my abilities, so I sounded fairly good on those. I'd finally found my element and was proud of the music we created and performed. We managed to put together enough money to record a demo. The guy who recorded us had a home studio. He certainly didn't make what he was worth to us, but didn't care as this type of thing was his passion. We had our first original EP and used a logo created by Anne who was also an artist, for its cover. We played out live with several other bands who were comprised of our friends.

It wasn't long after moving into the house on Euclid, that I completely split with Anne, at my request and thinking of her safety as I couldn't control my drinking. She went back to her hometown. I only saw her again once, backstage at a Creature Sack show, when they were in town and had another band I was in at the time, open for them. She was friendly, though we didn't speak much. I didn't feel I had any right to bother her as she was also with a guy, whom I believe she eventually married. Truly caring for her, I was glad she was free from me, picking up her life and moving on. She was a beautiful woman inside and out, and deserved so much better than what she got from me. Though I was never part of AA, I agree with their philosophy of making amends for the wrongs done under the influence of alcohol. Years later I asked Luther, whom I'd seen at Spook's funeral, to convey my sincere apologies for what I'd put her through.

Also, being tired of the constant tiredness that came with construction work, and my inability to stay employed consistently due to my own cantankerousness, I wound up responding to an ad in the paper for a floral shop delivery driver. It was in the very upscale Myers Park neighborhood. The owners were a married couple and had been there for some time, and they were very successful. I made afternoon deliveries from a pool of florists who'd send their filled orders to a downtown warehouse, where drivers from all the shops divvied them up into specified routes. I was also in charge of taking care of plants at local restaurants and the Myers Park Country Club, which contracted with our shop to maintain live decorative vegetation. I soon found I could trade shabby plants which I'd otherwise have to throw away, to restaurant staff who'd give me food in exchange. I often got free meals this way. I also kept some plants destined for a dumpster. At one point, my living room resembled a jungle of recovering plants, which I'd give to anyone who wanted them. The owners were kind to me. They had a couple of long-time staff members, Trina who worked the front counter, and Gregory, their floral designer. Trina was in her 50s, and was sincerely complementary when she heard Meadow Magnet's demo and read my lyrics. That made me feel fairly accomplished, in a way. She also seemed to like me as a person, and likewise made me feel valuable, as she had no reason to be insincere. Gregory was openly gay, and also very accepting of me. It was at this point, I had another epiphany, this time about my long-standing homophobia.

As I've pointed out, that kind of hatred and bigotry was woven into the fabric of the society in which I'd grown up, and I'd adopted it uncritically. Here I was faced with a man who would've gone out of his way to help me in any way, and I couldn't reconcile the negative stereotypes with this person with whom I quickly became friends. There's a concept in Psychology, called the Contact Hypothesis, which posits that getting to know individuals within stereotyped outgroups, promotes understanding, erodes hatred, and facilitates improved relationships between members of otherwise opposing groups. I just couldn't figure how Gregory's sexuality had anything to do with me, and that if I was the American I believed myself to be, feeling every citizen has a right to be who they are, and engage in any behaviors they wish (assuming they're not hurting anyone else), how I could continue to hold those negative views. So, I dropped them. I eventually became an LGBT ally, where I work frequently on my campus with students, staff, and faculty from that group, as well as other minority groups, to promote their acceptance by members of the majority, help secure their civil rights, and help all people see one another as equals not only under the law, but also as fellow human beings.

Being now single, living alone on Euclid, completely engulfed in alcoholism and chronic pot usage, I was untamed to say the least. I remember hanging out drinking at Warren's one night and him wanting to go to the topless club around the corner. I'd never been to one, but knew it was customary to give dancers money and I had none. I was also underage and figured they'd card me, so I told him I wasn't sure about it. He said getting in wouldn't be a problem and that he'd pay for everything. We went over already quite drunk, and he bought round after round, at the almost empty bar. The strippers were performing anyway. It was a virtually private show, and Warren was doing all the tipping. We wound up playing pool with some of them, and I thought it bizarre to be hanging out with topless and beautiful girls, without any sexual expectations. He then passed out in a chair in front of the stage. I was so wasted by the time I left, I really don't remember walking home. I woke up the next day, groggy but still on time for work. Warren later told me that the girls and Manager had revived him, and he'd stumbled home. He was a regular, so they'd expected nothing less. I'd later find it rather sad for young women to feel this was their only way they could make any substantial money. My second wife worked awhile as a bartender in a strip club, so I hung out a couple of times after-hours at another club talking with her stripper friends, again where there was nothing sexual about it. I found many suffered from addictions that led them into a lifestyle that supported their 'needs,' but where the clubs and patrons also somewhat took advantage of them.

Meadow Magnet had taken to practicing at my house, as the other members then shared an apartment where we couldn't play. I was always drinking after work, but wasn't drinking liquor anymore, so I stayed in relative control. But I was still obnoxious, and controlling in ways I didn't even realize. This wore on the guys, over time. We prepared to record another EP, and were able to raise enough money to book the same studio. I felt our music was outstanding and eclectic, but it wasn't in any way commercial. We'd gotten our first demo to a disc jockey at a local radio station, and he played one of the tracks on air, and found out we were playing a show at Ezekiel's, a bar on Independence Blvd. He wanted to come introduce us. Both of these things were a pretty big deal to us, but we didn't want to 'sell out' in any way. He introduced us with enthusiasm, and we then launched into a weird rock instrumental. He looked at us like we were from another planet, and left in disgust.

We'd taken to trading headlining slots with a few bands, playing at the World Famous Tombstone, Ezekiel's, and Apostate's, regularly. We played other places as well, including a new bar, where they'd booked Defiant Scene, a hard core punk rock band from Charlotte, who'd made an international name for themselves. I'd only seen them once before, years earlier, in a mall parking lot where Power Mouse was playing a battle of the bands. The singer, known for acting riotously and cutting his forehead and slinging blood all around, was in true belligerent form that night. I wasn't a fan of punk rock to begin with, but there'd been a pedestrian hit by a car not far from the crowd and the singer said some pretty morbid things about it, which I found offensive. This new club booked Meadow Magnet to open for Defiant Scene, even though our music was anything except punk rock, and I've no idea why we were paired. We came for sound check and Defiant Scene was there. They'd secured a $500 guarantee plus a cut of the door, a 20-person guest list, as well as free food and beer. When they sound-checked, the singer started poking holes in the drop ceiling tiles with his mic stand. I'd known their guitarist through his work in a local record store, and he was a really nice guy. And Henry was a huge punk rock fan, and had been trying to sell me on the genre's virtues, where I disagreed on most points. He said the music was supposed to be simplistic and aggressive, as it was really just an unbridled expression of rebelliousness. When I heard Defiant Scene play this outrageously simple song at sound check, with total gusto, coupled with the ceiling damage, and being of a rebellious ilk myself, I went up the singer when they finished and said, "You know, I really used to hate y'all." He said, "You probably still do." I remarked, "Yeah, musically it's not my thing, but I think I get it now...y'all just don't give a fuck." He said, "Bingo!" When we went on, the crowd were all rabid Defiant Scene fans. I was sick and taking heavy doses of cough syrup and drinking, and so while our band sounded great, I didn't. The crowd hated us, which made me feel pretty good. I've always felt my job as an artist is to make people 'feel' something, and if they like it, that's fine. If they don't like it, that's fine, too. So, I actually enjoyed the jeers and boos. When Defiant Scene went on, the place was packed. Most in the crowd were prone to moshing, which is a form of violent 'dancing' where people run into each other at full force, which often causes injury to some. There was a line of about 20, probably those on the guest list, who linked arms from the middle of the room and mowed down everyone as they rushed the stage. The singer was bleeding profusely, the music was loud, and the place was a madhouse. The owner got so nervous, he called the cops. I was waiting around to get paid what little we were owed. When 2 cops arrived, they wouldn't step foot past the door. I looked at one and he stared at me a second, and said "I don't get it." I said, "Me either." I got our band's money and left.

There were a lot of talented rock musicians in Charlotte then. I'd met the singer of one of the most popular local rock bands, Deity Aquatic, while working my flower delivery job. He worked with a floral supply warehouse. As I came in to pick up something for the shop, I heard him singing *Jane Says* to himself and recognized him from one of their shows. I introduced myself, and eventually Meadow Magnet played several shows opening for them. The other members were also friends within the Creature Sack crowd, so we got along very well. They were extremely creative and had a huge live presence, and even recorded a full-length CD at a famous studio in Charlotte. Like so many bands, they broke up before they ever made it out of the local scene. That was another band that really deserved to make the big time.

I got fired from my delivery job, for good cause. Had they actually checked my driving record before hiring me, they never would've. On the only day in which I hadn't smoked pot prior to going in, I was pulling out of a gas station to go home for a quick toke, and barely touched another car with the van. I was against drinking and driving at that point, but hadn't made the parallel connection to driving while high on weed. I considered myself a great driver, high or not. It literally only pulled off the raised decorative strip on the back quarter panel, and didn't even scratch the paint. The driver wanted the company's insurance information. I knew this would mean I'd lose my job and asked if I could just give her $50 in cash, to have the strip glued back on. She insisted, so I gave her the information. When I got back to the shop, I told the owner. He said it wasn't a problem, and that was what insurance was for. I said, "It's going to be a problem." The next day I came in, hoping he might not have looked into my driving history. He said, "You have a horrible driving record!" I said "I know." He said, "Well, I didn't know." I said, "You never asked." He said "I have to fire you." I said "I know." He said, "But, you're the best driver we've ever had!" Again I said "I know." He truly felt bad about firing me. I assured him I totally understood and it was okay.

At that point, I was hating life. It was clear I'd never make a living in music, as Meadow Magnet was committed to making non-commercial music, which by definition means you're not likely to make money. I was still single and feeling pretty lonely. I'd destroyed my marriage due to my drinking and inexcusable behavior, and also felt guilty about it. Now I was out of my low-paying but steady job. I'd not given up 'donating' plasma for money, as my pay only barely covered my bills and rent. But, plasma money alone wasn't going to make it, and I was faced with either going back into construction or more temporary labor work, both of which I now loathed. To make matters worse, I got thrown out of Meadow Magnet about the same time. We'd gone into the studio a second time. We'd thoroughly practiced our songs so we could pull them off in a single take, to keep costs down. But I was also a cigarette smoker, as well as pot smoker, and I obviously had the drinking problem to boot. And, I got sick. Dad married his third wife, Gwen, the day before we were to record and I went to the wedding. Gwen's a great person, and was my Mom's best friend growing up. I was happy to be part of the celebration, but I went and partied with my brothers Fred and Luke after the reception. We stayed up most of the night. The next day, I was a mess in terms of my 'singing' ability, which was shaky to begin with.

There was one song the guys really wanted on the EP. I tried to sing it, but I sounded terrible. I did several takes and still couldn't pull it off. They were willing to go with the best take, but I insisted we not include it, as there was no way we could afford to come back when I was better off vocally. The other songs sounded okay vocally, and I said that was enough material and we should leave off the one on which I'd sung so poorly. We didn't actually argue, but there was tension, and as usual I thought I'd won out. Not too long after that session, we had a final version and were in the process of having copies made, when they came to my house. They sat me down, and very gently but firmly, told me they were going to stay together as a band, but without me. I didn't realize until much later, that I'd been too controlling in general. My cutting the song I'd screwed up was likely the last straw. I couldn't believe it. I thought we were coming along so well, and we were on the verge of 'releasing' what was overall a solid piece of work. But that was it, and I was out.

It was a truly depressing situation, to be thrown out of the band I loved by people I'd come to love, being wracked with guilt over wrecking my marriage, being lonely, and to also lose my meager source of income, and now faced with I didn't know what. As it happened, I'd recently become somewhat infatuated, as was fairly common for me, but in a more platonic sense than usual, with a young woman by the name of Sophia. She was older than me, and radiated some type of 'old-soul' wisdom. I'd met her at one of our shows where we talked afterwards, and it turned out she didn't live far from me. We hung out semi-regularly, though she had a long-time boyfriend who lived out of town. I just loved talking with her. Her perspective on life seemed well beyond her years, and I appreciated the depth of our conversations. When I told her I'd lost my job and was planning to go to the unemployment office to see about benefits, she handed me a copy of *The Tao of Pooh* by Benjamin Hoff, and said to read it while I was in line (noting I'd finish before they ever saw me), and to let her know what I thought.

When I arrived at the Unemployment Office, the line was down the block. I read the book before they ever saw me, like she said. It relates the principles of Taoism through characters in the *Winnie the Pooh* stories. The main message was: don't force things which don't come naturally, roll with life's punches without over-interpreting them, and keep a positive attitude. When I got to the desk of the person reviewing my application, she said they could give me about $125 a month. I said, "That's not very much," to which she replied, "You weren't making very much." I said, "True enough, but that won't even cover my rent; just scrap my application." So, I left and told Sophia I didn't totally understand the book, but that I liked it and would consider what it had to say.

I spoke with Mom on the phone that night. She invited me up to the mountain home she and Patrick bought to get away from city life on weekends. I agreed and went, not knowing what I'd do. She'd talked with Dad, and he called while I was there and offered to help me with rent and bills, if I'd consider going to Central Piedmont Community College (CPCC) in downtown Charlotte. Both my parents went to college and told me growing up that I should go. But they never gave me a clear idea as to what it was like, or *why* I should go. I didn't know college was much different from high school, and I hated high school. But, Dad offered to send me enough monthly to cover basic living expenses, if I'd give it a try. I was fiercely independent, and the last thing I wanted to do was to become a dependent again. Yet, I was pretty desperate. And, I'd just read this book that essentially said to 'roll with what happens,' so I figured, why not? I realized I'd never make it in music, no matter how long I pursued it. Hell, if Creature Sack couldn't make it, as talented and dedicated as they were, there was surely no hope for me on that front. I considered that if I didn't like college, I could quit and go back to construction. Again I had these privileges and opportunities most didn't get, but was still unable to perceive that or understand what it meant. I swallowed my pride and accepted Dad's offer. Mom came back to Charlotte with me (even more pride to swallow, as I'd no idea how to enroll). We went to CPCC and she helped me get enrolled. That was the summer of 1992.

Chapter 8

Phase V, A Light Emerges in
the Form of a Child

Much to my surprise, I really liked college. As noted, while I hated high school, I always loved reading and learning about various things. The first quarter (they weren't yet on a semester system), I took a philosophy course, taught by a woman with a doctorate in the subject. I was fascinated. While I didn't know it at the time, community college draws different students than the typical university. Lots of working-class people, many also working full-time jobs, were there trying to improve their lots in life. That was pretty inspirational. There were also younger, traditional college-aged kids there, who wouldn't have been accepted into universities. That would've been the case for me at their age. So not only was the curriculum fairly interesting, there were lots of people doing what I was doing.

Reeves sometimes gave me a lift when I was drinking, since I'd sworn off DUI, and yet still drank heavily. At that time I wasn't going anywhere while drinking, which was nightly, unless somebody drove me. He was sweet on a girl who went to CPCC, and who I'd met there, and she was going to a party at an apartment complex clubhouse. He wanted to go talk with her, but didn't want to go alone. He said there'd be a keg with all the free beer I could drink, so I enthusiastically agreed to go. We got there early, before any other party-goers had arrived. I walked into the clubhouse and there was this darling little 9-year-old girl, with long blonde hair, playing a piano. I've always found kids to be fun, because in many ways I'm a lot like a kid myself. I roll with 'make-believe' topics easily, and kids don't 'talk about the weather' or other silly 'small-talk' stuff, like adults do whenever they get together. I went over and asked if I could play alongside her, having enrolled in a piano class at CPCC.

Mom 'made' me take piano lessons when I was little, and I complained until she let me quit. Now I was an adult who loved music and wished I could play piano. It was one of the first courses I took. I realized the irony in having given up lessons, knowing if I'd kept on, I'd probably have been a good player by that time. I'd learned a few major chords, and this child just lit up when I joined her. We had fun making up 'songs,' and her name was Valkyrie. After about an hour, she said "It was nice to meet you, but I have to go home now." I said it was likewise a pleasure to make her acquaintance, and off she went. Around then the place started to fill up with adults, who began partying full-force. I started in on the keg, and was glad to be drinking for free. After another hour or so, this cool-looking woman came in, with heavy makeup and draped in jewelry. She wore a baseball cap backwards, which is how I wore mine and still do. She was being trailed by a clean-cut muscular guy who was clearly bothering her (I found out later she'd actually invited him). I went up and said "Dude, stop bothering my wife." She played along, and he got nervous and said, "I didn't know she was married!" I said, "That's cool, but you can run along now," and he did.

She said, "Thanks, he was really getting on my nerves." She introduced herself as Michelle, and said she lived in the complex, and that the birthday party was for the husband of a friend of hers, so we struck up a conversation. I told her about the cool little girl I'd met who was playing piano, and she said, "That's my daughter!" We got talking music, and it turned out she was a singer who'd been in several rock bands. She'd moved to town recently with her best friend, Jan, who was also her roommate. They'd come from Florida, and apparently she moved frequently, being from Tennessee originally. I'd later find out she'd either take Valkyrie with her, switching schools each time, or leave her with her mom, who I'd also later find out had an alcohol problem herself. Michelle was a hard drinker, which matched my behavior. I met Jan at some point that night. Reeves never got the date he'd hoped for with the young lady he'd come to see, but it turned out to be a fateful night out for me. As Michelle and I hit it off big time, I got her number and called her regularly. She didn't have a car, relying on Jan for transportation. I wouldn't drive drunk, and drank every night, so we didn't see each other in person. After a few weeks, she mysteriously disappeared. It turned out she and Valkyrie had moved back to Tennessee. So that was that, or so I thought.

I met this cute red-headed young woman, Olivia, at CPCC who was a feisty and interesting person. She was into music as well as sex and drugs, over which we'd soon bond. It seems I have a thing for blondes and red-heads, but I've found women attractive in almost every shade and shape, depending on various characteristics, either physical or personal, especially intelligence and personality. The first night Olivia came to my house, we were sitting on my couch, and all of a sudden a brick came flying through the large window behind us, and sailed over our heads. She said that was probably her ex-boyfriend, with whom she'd only just broken up, and she also said he was psychotic. I said "I speak psychotic," and we went to her apartment to find him. As it happened, she lived just down the road on Dirtwood. I found him cowering below her second-floor apartment. I told him that if he didn't leave her alone, I'd beat the shit out of him. That was enough for him. Throwing bricks through windows was no big deal to him apparently, but one-on-one confrontation wasn't his thing. We never saw him again and began dating. She was from Atlanta, and her mom was an Executive for a major beer company and was sometimes in Charlotte. She paid for Olivia's schooling and apartment, and stayed there when she was in town. Her mom was very cool and seemed to like that Olivia had taken up with me. She wasn't around much, so we usually had the place to ourselves. She also brought all kinds of beer and left it by the case at Olivia's, so that was another benefit. Olivia had a nice car and didn't seem to mind driving me around when I was drinking.

Around this time, I'd asked Henry if he wanted to move into my second bedroom, as Meadow Magnet's gear was gone, with me being tossed out of the band. He lived with his mom, another truly cool woman, off and on. He was living with her then, around the corner. I figured if he paid $100/month and half the bills, I could use the extra money to eat better, drink more, and get more weed, and I was happy to share that bounty with Henry. Like I said, he was really into punk music as well as all kinds of other music, and was a guitarist himself. He's also one of the kindest people you could meet, and it was a breath of fresh air to have him living there. It took the edge off my financial strain as well. Even though I liked Olivia a lot, I didn't love her, and our relationship was one of mutual partying, and was monogamous, or so I thought. And, I often stayed at her place, where there was often free beer, and central air-conditioning.

Henry and I had a mutual friend, Alec, who'd lived with the Creature Sack guys in LA, and was back in Charlotte, and a huge sports fanatic. He was way into street hockey, played on roller blades. I didn't know anything about hockey, but was willing to stand in (without skates) as goalie one day on a city tennis court where the net had been removed. I had no gear, and they were playing with a hard ball. A guy on the opposing team got past the defense, and stood about 15 feet from me, and took a hard shot on goal. I got nailed in the eye. I had to take a moment to recoup, and the guys on my team said the whites of my eye were bloody. I got a major black eye on top of that. After a few moments, I got back in the game and kept playing. That got me some cred with Alec and when he formed a city league, he let me join his team, which also included a couple of guys from Deity Aquatic. Somehow he got the city to provide insurance for only $25. We'd go to Alec's before and after games, get high and have a generally great time. Roller hockey seemed to me to be essentially like moshing, where it was highly aggressive, but where everyone agreed to the violence. It was fun, as long as you weren't easily ruffled, which I wasn't. I bought the cheapest roller blades available, and couldn't skate for anything, though Alec tried to teach me. I ran into other teams' players on occasion, and pleaded 'incompetent,' assuring them it wasn't intentional. Nobody ever got upset with me. There weren't a lot of teams and we made it to the league 'championship.' That was the day of the 'spring forward' time change, and I'd stayed the previous night at Olivia's. I woke up without having moved the clock forward, and realized I was late. I take seriously anything I commit to, so off I ran to my van, and drove down to the rink. It was the best of 3 games, I think, and I got there well into the first game. And, who should be there but Lynne, a 'goddess' from high school, with whom I'd been totally infatuated.

She'd had a daughter, Addison, with Obie from Creature Sack. They'd started dating just before he and the other guys moved to LA, and she moved out there and lived with Alec who had a steady job, unlike Obie, who was totally devoted to his music. Obie lived in their rented practice room along with Spook, getting by on next to nothing and showering with a hose in the alley outside. Spook still sold weed, which made them enough to eat and party on. Lynne got pregnant and realized Obie was in no position to be a devoted father, given his commitment to the band and his partying ways. This was just prior to the band being signed to the label, and she'd moved back to Charlotte. Obie certainly loved Addison, but he was soon on the road touring around the country with the band, and there was no chance of rekindling his relationship with Lynne anyway, as she was fiercely independent herself. She'd grown up in some tough circumstances regarding her parents, though on the surface, growing up in Myers Park, it looked like she was fairly well off. But she essentially raised herself during her teen years, with the help of close friends and their parents. She was not one for making herself dependent on anyone, much less a guy who wasn't around and not able to provide. Again, even though Creature Sack signed with a major label, they only got $10/day on which to live, as they toured the country.

I recall going to Addison's first birthday party, with Olivia I think, at a restaurant, and she was the cutest baby (as they all are, I suppose). I'd also gone to her second or third birthday party at a mutual friend's house, and wound up playing with her, as that was more fun to me than hanging out with the 'adults.' I remember Addison in a little kid's jeep, and we pretended we were driving to Myrtle Beach. But other than that, I'd not seen Lynne, except for talking to her outside a Creature Sack show in Atlanta, where she'd been through a pretty hard time with something, and I was just lending a supportive ear. She still had 'goddess' stature in my eyes, and I didn't speak of my feelings for her. She was dating some other guy anyway, but it was really nice talking with her face-to-face, about meaningful stuff.

Regardless, she was at the roller hockey 'championship,' for which I was late. I was happy to see her in the modest crowd. Like I said, I didn't love Olivia and was always honest with anyone and everyone, about damn near everything, so she knew I 'loved' Lynne from afar, as well as having other infatuations. I wasn't going to be hitting on Lynne, but here I was getting to 'play' hockey in front of her, and I was hopeful to at least not fall on my ass. The second game started, and I was in the face-off. For some reason, I was good at face-offs, which I suppose was random luck. As soon as the 'puck ball' was dropped, I knocked it back to one of our guys, and turned hard to my right. As I turned, my skate did not and I heard a cracking noise and went down. I'd never broken a bone before, and decided immediately that wasn't what had happened. I got back up and started skating, playing with all I had. I sat on the bench at some point, and an older guy who played with us told me to take off my skate. He looked at my ankle, which was swelling severely. He said I should sit out the rest of the game. I said, "No way am I doing that!" He wrapped my ankle in an Ace bandage, and helped me cram my foot back into my skate. I got back into the game and continued playing my hardest. I doubt Lynne ever looked my way, or cared I was there, but I was also committed to my teammates, and didn't want to let them down. In the end we won the championship, and everyone on our team (Lynne not included) went back to Alec's house to celebrate.

Several people looked at my ankle, and said I should have it checked by a doctor. Since I'd paid for my $25 insurance policy, I figured I'd get my money's worth. The next day I drove to a doctor's office. I had to press the gas and brake with my left foot, as I couldn't really move my right foot. The doctor x-rayed it and said I'd snapped my fibula. He put a cast on it and gave me crutches. He was on his way out the door, when he turned and said "I don't guess you need any pain medication, do you?" Having not complained of pain, he assumed I was okay. But, I said, "I don't know about that, what've you got?" He asked if I was allergic to codeine, and I said, "Absolutely not, that sounds helpful!" So, he wrote me a prescription and I got it filled. I loved codeine. I knew this from when I got my tonsils removed in high school, and they'd prescribed me Tylenol 3 with codeine. My Mom had previously had some minor surgery and had Percocet (oxycodone) left in her medicine cabinet. Since she worked then, I was on my own during the day. I got her pills, figuring she'd never know they were gone. I'd wash down several with my Tylenol 3 liquid. I was in a daze for hours at a time, listening to nature sounds on a cassette, as that's all I could stand to hear. When I'd come down, I'd just take more of both and go back into my daze. So, I now had a bottle of codeine pills and wasn't having trouble managing the pain from my broken ankle. I had to navigate driving to school, walking from the lot, and up and down stairs. I didn't miss any classes, but I dosed up heavily as soon as I got home. Within 3 days, I'd gone through the bottle and called in a refill. They said, "You should still have quite a few pills left." I demurred and said, "Well, I'm in a lot of pain, so you know…" They refilled it, and I went through that bottle in few days. It's remarkable, that I didn't get addicted. When it was all gone, I was fine. It just seemed like a great week of partying to me.

When the summer came around, I essentially moved into Olivia's apartment, because she had central air conditioning, and all Henry and I had was a window unit that never cooled the place off enough for comfort. Besides, we had her mom's beer stash. And, Olivia always had weed, and other pills I'd later find out were used for mental health conditions. I took a couple of her Klonopin once and slept for 24 hours, and never took them again. Beer, weed, air-conditioning, and sex were all I wanted or needed, so I felt things were going fine, other than our arguing. I'd always had arguments in any serious relationship, so that seemed nothing new to me, and I thought it was perfectly normal. When fall came, I was out putting up flyers at Ezekiel's, advertising a show for the band I'd joined after Meadow Magnet kicked me out. This attractive blonde and her brunette friend were sitting at the bar, giving me the serious eye. Eventually, I wandered over and opened up a conversation. They looked at me, then at each other, and laughed. The brunette said, "You don't know who this is, do you?" I said, "I'm sorry, I don't. You see, I drink pretty heavily and get around a lot, so I meet a lot of people I don't remember." Turns out I was talking to Jan, and she said "This is Michelle, you idiot!" I'd not talked to Michelle in about a year, and we struck up our conversation right there, as though no time had lapsed. She and Jan had moved back to Charlotte again, and this particular night I'd not been drinking because I needed to get those flyers put up. I'd planned to drink when I got home. We hit it off so well again, that Michelle came home with me, and we started making out. Before it got too far, I said "I'm dating someone, so I can't go any farther, until I break it off with her." She was a little taken aback, but could tell I was serious.

The next day, I drove to Olivia's and told her, I'd rekindled a relationship the previous night with the woman I was going to marry, so that while I was sorry, we were done as a couple. I said "I didn't have sex with her, because I didn't want to disrespect you by cheating, but we did make out a little. Anyway, I wish you the best." She lost it and told me she'd been cheating on me, so that the joke was on me. I'd made out with Sophia's sister once after I'd started dating Olivia, but we didn't have sex and I'd told Olivia about it. We'd both been drunk and she was very attractive, but like me she had a partner, and we never progressed past kissing. I thought I'd done the right thing, not only in not having 'actual sex,' but also in being honest about it with Olivia. But she was pissed about that when it happened. Thus I took no offence when she said she'd cheated on me, and went on my way. In fact, I did marry Michelle a few months later.

Again, Michelle had no vehicle and was a hard partier, as was I, so I didn't think anything amiss when she never left my house. Jan brought over her stuff, and it was now me, Michelle, and Henry, living in the little 2-bedroom house on Euclid. We talked about Valkyrie, who was staying with Michelle's mom in Tennessee. She said her mom had lots of problems, especially with alcohol, but was sober when she left Val there. Michelle would call her mom's house on occasion, and talk with Val. She gave my phone number to their next door neighbors, a young couple. The wife of the couple called one night and said Michelle's mom had been on a prolonged drunk, and was knocking out more than a fifth of vodka a night, passing out on the couch, leaving Valkyrie to run around the neighborhood all night long. It was a trailer park except for their duplex. Val was just 10-years-old, and nobody was watching her. Michelle was upset, and asked what we should do. I said, "We go get her!" She said, "When?" I said, "Right now!" We literally left within minutes, jumping into my van. We went over the mountains to East TN, and were at the duplex within 3 hours, as I sped the whole way. I didn't know what to expect, but I remembered Val and hated the thought of her running around all night by herself, with a drunk grandma as her only guardian. Michelle had a key, so we went right in. Her mom groggily looked at us, like a strange man coming in with her daughter was nothing out of the ordinary. She said, "What brings you by?" I said, "We've come to get Valkyrie, where is she?" She said, 'She's asleep in the bedroom; is anything wrong?" I said "Nope, we've just come to get her."

I took the lead and went in, and Val was asleep in her bed. I put my hand on her shoulder and gently roused her. She looked at me and said, "Hey!" I said "Hey! Your mom and I have come to take you back to our house in Charlotte." She said "Yay!" She stood up on the bed and hugged me tight. Though having only met me briefly once, a year earlier, she immediately said "Can I call you Dude?" I said, "Why would you want to call me Dude?" She said, "Because it sounds like Dad!" My heart was blown open, and I said, "Why don't you just call me Dad?" She said, "Okay!" And, that's what she's called me ever since. I'd become a father. We didn't stay any longer than it took to get all her important stuff, and we headed to Charlotte. So, now it was me, Michelle, Valkyrie, and Henry, living in the little 2-bedroom house. It was in better shape than before, because the landlord had gotten hit with a citation from the city the previous summer, which 'Condemned' his house. The city was essentially going to take over the property, if he didn't bring it up to their standards. I told him I'd do all the work needed, for just the cost of supplies and $10/hour for my labor, which he could take off the rent, which was fine by him.

They sent out a young man to 'inspect' what I'd done, when I'd finished. The house had a drop ceiling, with about 2-feet between it and the original ceiling. The attic (which was full of bats; it was fun to watch them leaving the attic vent at dusk) couldn't be reached without going through an opening in the drop ceiling and original ceiling. I'd knocked off the 'hanging chimney' and sealed up the roof where it'd been. I took out a long ramp Dan had built to make moving pianos easier. I put a new floor in the kitchen and built a rail around the front porch, among much else. The guy who came to 'inspect' poked his head into the attic and declared we needed to add insulation. I asked him what his qualifications were, and he said he was in an engineering program at the university. He related that they'd partnered with the city to do drive by inspections of neighborhoods, and make reports on substandard houses. I asked him what amounted to 'substandard,' and he said "Oh lots of things, like not having screens on the windows." I said, "Y'all condemn houses for something like missing screens?!?" He said it was usually more than that that led to condemnation. I told him everything I fixed on their list was essentially cosmetic, and it seemed like a blatant land-grab by the city, since it was becoming a gentrified and valuable neighborhood. He wouldn't comment on that theory. I asked him about his background in construction. He said he'd worked on a 'couple' of crews. I asked if that meant he'd toted lumber for actual tradesmen, and he said, "Yes, something like that." I further asked if his college program taught him what the best insulator was, and he said "Yes! It's air." I said that's what was between the original and drop ceilings, and he reluctantly accepted that was probably sufficient insulation. Thereafter, the city left my landlord alone.

Anyway it was now pretty crowded, and Valkyrie was used to having the run of her grandma's place back in Tennessee. And, I'd no idea how to be a parent. Frankly, Michelle wasn't great at parenting either, but she loved Val and did her best. But, she had lots of serious issues that made her parenting quite problematic, at times. One day early on, Val was asleep in our bedroom when Henry and I did what we always did, which was get high. We totally forgot about the kid in the next room, got hungry and decided to go get some food. Michelle had taken my van somewhere, and we were on the front lawn headed to Henry's car, when she pulled up. She said, "Where are y'all headed?" I said, "To the store, do you need anything?" She said, "Where's Valkyrie!?!' Henry and I looked at each other, and I said, "Shit, I totally forgot. She's sleeping in our bedroom." That was a serious wake-up call for me, as I'd never had a kid, and hadn't planned to have any. And yet there was some serious paternal instinct awakening within me, where I felt I had to step up for this child. I told Henry I hated to do it, but I really needed him to move out as soon as he could, so we could give Val his room. He was as cool as he always was, and told me he totally understood. Within a couple of weeks he cleared out, and it was just my new family living there.

Shortly thereafter I married Michelle, and we did so on the cheap, having no money to speak of. I got cheap rings for us both by selling the wedding ring I had from my first marriage. While there was no honor in that, it served the purpose. Val was very enthusiastic about it. She'd never known her birth father, and her mother had dated a long series of men, most of whom weren't bad guys. But they didn't stick around for what would later become to me, obvious reasons. Those reasons had nothing to do with Val, other than she came as part of the package. So, we got married in the courthouse, which was the easiest and least expensive route, and then held a 'ceremony' of sorts on the little island in the lake at Freedom Park. My brother Luke read a poem. My new friend Ribs, who was buddies with Jan and Michelle, and who was very drunk, spoke a few incoherent words. Later W.B. would marry Jan, after his divorce from Lana, and I performed their ceremony. I wasn't ordained in any way. They got married in the courthouse as well, but wanted a ceremony. I was honored to preside over it.

After our ceremony, we all went back to our house for a 'reception.' It was a fairly tame affair, though it contained some wild people. This one dealer, who'd been friends with Jan and Michelle, dosed me with some acid as a wedding gift. He came up and said, "Congratulations, stick out your tongue!" I did so, knowing what was to come, but it wasn't a big deal to me at the time. I lost no coherence, and had a fairly good time. Val found a piece of Styrofoam out back, which resembled a tombstone a bit, and wrote "Here lies Spook" on it. She thought he was a funny guy, and I don't know what motivated her to do it. But when she showed it to him, he totally freaked out, saying "Why did she write that!?!" He was very uneasy with anything that had an occult or ghostly feel to it, despite his nickname. I told him, it was the gesture of a creative child who probably associated his nickname with ghosts, and that it meant nothing. He cooled out and the night otherwise passed uneventfully.

Michelle had this thing about believing she was in touch with the 'other side,' and thought she had 'spirits' following her around. She was a very convincing story-teller. She'd claimed to have seen ghosts on numerous occasions, and others who were prone to such experiences, or believed themselves to be, chimed in on that kind of conversation whenever it came up. Ian was very much into magick and was well-versed on the occult, which had led me to read up on the subject in the CPCC library. Ian practiced 'white' magick, meaning nothing malevolent, just 'raising' energy, while also taking occasional hallucinogens and having a good time with his 'coven.' That was a small group of like-minded 'witches,' who got together at a rural property in upper South Carolina. As best I could tell, they just partied and had sex with one another. I never went, but talked with Ian about it. He always made sure to tell me, "Don't tell Spook about any of this; it really freaks him out." Of course, I didn't.

I never took to any of that stuff, other than having a general interest in the fact that lots of people had been interested in those topics for eons. It came in handy speaking with people on such subjects, and in dealing with the 'spirits' that 'followed' around Michelle, especially when she seemed to believe an ex-boyfriend into the 'black arts' had sent a malicious spirit to intimidate her. I did a 'ritual' that seemed to 'calm' the spirit, which calmed her down considerably. I didn't let on to her that I didn't have any belief in such things, but she thought it worked, so that was good.

This knowledge was also useful later when I was working as a graduate student in the State Mental Hospital. A teenager had been admitted who believed he'd been confronted by the 'devil' while huffing paint. He'd passed out and woke up convinced he'd been visited by Satan or some serious demon, and his concerned parents brought him in for help. He wouldn't talk to any of the staff. He was a 'practitioner' of magick, and believed he'd brought 'evil' in through some cosmic portal he'd created, but that's all they could get out of him. I asked if I could talk to him, and they skeptically allowed me, saying I'd do no better. I started in with some customary occult language, and when I asked if he'd 'consecrated a circle,' prior to contacting spirits, his eyes lit up. All of a sudden he had lots to talk about with me. So, I was able to relate some of his relevant drug and mental health history to the staff. They sincerely wanted to help him, but didn't otherwise know how to get him to open up.

Val probably picked up some of that 'other world' lingo and imagery from her mom and her friends. I was starting to realize this child had spent most of her now 10 years, hanging out in the presence of partying adults who talked about all kinds of things that probably weren't appropriate for her ears. But Val was as resilient as they came, and always cheerful, and never seemed to pick up any bad tendencies. She was somewhat obstinate, which was likely the result of having just spent months doing whatever she wanted with a frequently passed-out grandma. She was a great kid, but she definitely wanted things her own way, and had been used to a mom who was alternatively overly-indulgent and overly-critical, without consistency. As a new dad, I took that role very seriously. When I needed her to do something, I expected compliance, which I didn't always get, though she was never particularly mean about it. But Val was dramatic and could be quite defiant and get quite upset.

I had to do something about this tendency. I'd a bit of knowledge from my Introductory Psychology class, which I found helpful. All I'd really picked up at that point was that a punitive disciplinary approach should be accompanied by clear rules, age-appropriate explanations, specifically designated consequences, and a very consistent application. It wasn't hard to get her to calm down and start listening to me, as an authority figure, but it did take some persistence and creativity. I created a 'strike' chart, and put it on the refrigerator, and talked to her frequently about what was expected. She was allowed to 'debate' me and propose alternatives, though I had the final word. If she did something she wasn't supposed to, or didn't do something she was supposed to, I'd give her a verbal warning and a count of '3,' to correct her behavior. If she persisted after "3," she got a 'strike.' A certain number of strikes was associated with certain penalties, such as an earlier bed time, loss of phone privileges in cumulative hour-long increments, being grounded to her room, and the like. If she was able to bring herself under control, and particularly if she would take responsibility and apologize, I'd deduct penalties from the total, as a reinforcement for her positive behavior, instead of having only punishments for negative behavior. I'd learn a great deal more about operant conditioning, observational learning, and child development as I continued my schooling, such that my son, Hunter (soon to be born at this point), received a more balanced approach from me.

One particular consequence I used with Val a few times, which I thought was rather funny as I was a fan of the movie *Cool Hand Luke*, was to have her dig holes in the back yard and then fill them back in. As she got strikes, this would result in accruing 10-minute 'hole-digging' increments, up to 40 minutes. It was a pointless activity of obedience in the movie, but a harmless enough thing for a kid to do. She never dug 'hard' anyway. While she did this activity, I'd read to her out of Stumpf's introductory philosophy text. She'd start complaining, "Dad, I don't want to dig holes and fill them in!" To which I'd reply, "I don't want you to dig holes and fill them in either, so next time please do what I ask you to do, within the count of 3, and we'll both be better off." Like I said, she was a good, smart, and resilient child, and I think it really helped her to finally have a consistent, boundary-oriented, loving parent around.

About 6 months into the marriage, I had the conflict that led me to quit drinking. Again, Michelle wasn't 'hurt' in the altercation, but it was totally inappropriate on my part to strike back at a woman (or any person for that matter) who struck me. She said she was going to leave and take Val. That latter part was what did it for me. If it hadn't been for Val, I'd have probably told Michelle, "Goodbye, good riddance, and don't let the door hit you in the ass on the way out." I was always good at emotionally distancing myself from virtually anything, and letting go of people who wanted (or needed) to let go of me. This time was different. I'd finally found a purpose in life: to help this kid have a better childhood, and hopefully as a result, a better life as an adult. I quit drinking, but didn't quit smoking weed, as I've mentioned. But smoking pot never altered my behavior in a negative way, while alcohol certainly did. I smoked so regularly that I couldn't say it did much to me, or for me. Michelle stayed and I never drank again, to this day. But we were in near constant conflict of one sort or another, punctuated by more tender moments of making up, and some really nice times, especially as a family with Val. We took walks, went out to eat when we could afford it, and watched TV together, so it was certainly not all bad. But it was often bad enough with Michelle and me, and loud, as she was as strong-willed and obnoxious as me. So while we'd typically argue in the bedroom away from Val, there's no way she didn't hear a lot of our arguments.

One regular point of contention was Michelle's drinking. While she'd put her foot down about mine, and was right about it and I quit, she had major alcohol problems of her own. And, she couldn't quit. This was compounded by anxiety, depression, and some physical health issues as well, amongst a history of trauma, strained relations with her parents, regular insomnia, and so on. She'd go on drinking binges, exacerbated by not sleeping, and she'd get rather scary. 'Crazy' was the best word I could use at the time to describe her behavior to her. Of course, she fought such assertions tooth and nail, and would throw in my face the fact that I smoked pot every day, saying there was no difference. I told her there was a world of difference, and that smoking weed didn't make me violent or threatening, both of which she did when she drank.

This argument was of course never resolved, but I realized Val could hear it on a regular basis, so I decided I needed to talk to her about it. I sat Val down on the front steps one afternoon, after school. She was in an elementary school not far from the house. Since my work was sporadic (Michelle worked sporadically then, too, but always quit jobs within a month or so, because of things that were always someone else's fault, which I tended to believe back then), I was able to get home before Val got out of school, and meet her as they dismissed. I'd walk her home most days, and Michelle got her on other days. We'd sometimes walk over to Mr. K's for some soft-serve ice cream, as a treat for us both. It was truly a beautiful thing, being a father.

So, knowing she'd heard the constant controversy, and not wanting to play her for a fool, I just came out and told her what was going on. She'd just completed the 'Just Say No to Drugs' program at school, and was wearing that t-shirt the day we had our conversation. I told her I was proud of her for doing the program, and that a lot of people have real problems with drugs, which included alcohol. I said I knew she knew her mother and I were such people. She knew I'd quit drinking successfully, and I told her that while it had a lot to do with my caring for her, I also had to do it for myself, or it wouldn't be right. She knew her mom couldn't quit drinking, and when we fought, she'd heard the "but you smoke pot" rebuttal from Michelle, repeatedly. I told Val I had a problem with marijuana. I said "I smoke it every day, and it's kind of expensive, so I shouldn't really be spending money on it, but I can't seem to stop t."

Val said, "I can't tell you smoke pot." I said, "I know, because I'd never do it in front of you, out of respect for you, and it really doesn't change how I think or behave, probably because I do it so much." She said, "Why do you do it, then?" And, I said, "Honestly, I don't know. It just seems like something I have to do, in order to feel normal and that's kind of what addiction is like." I told her that if it ever caused me to not be a good father, a good worker, and/or a good student, I'd quit. But I said it seemed to help with stress, and I'd probably keep doing it, so long as it didn't cause me problems. I also told her many of her extended relatives, some in her direct lineage (especially her mom and grandma), had serious issues with alcohol and/or other drugs, which would place her at greater risk for becoming an addict, if she were to use substances. I was already learning stuff at college that had very practical impacts on my own life. By being honest with my child, I felt I was better preparing her for the increasing pressures she'd face as she grew older. Likely not because of that talk, and perhaps just due to her own good sense, she never tried drugs (other than one beer in high school, I think), even though she had access to drugs, like most teenagers.

I also quit smoking cigarettes again around this time. I'd tried to quit once before, during my first marriage, but was cross-addicted with tobacco and alcohol, where I wasn't going to give up the latter. Anytime I drank, I 'had' to smoke. But I did give up smoking and could eventually drink without feeling I needed a cigarette. I was off cigarettes about a year, when Spook came back into town after the Creature Sack record contract collapsed. I'd gone to his basement apartment in his grandparent's basement and we were hanging out drinking as we used to do. He was chain-smoking Marlboro lights. The more I sat with him, the more I wanted a cigarette. This made no sense to me, as I'd thought I was well past having any cravings. I said, "Let me get one of those from you." He said, "Have all you want!" I said, "No, just one, because I don't smoke." About 15 minutes after the first one, I 'needed' another. The next day, and the only way I can explain it was that I 'found' myself at the convenience store buying a pack. It was robotic, like I'd never quit, and just like that, I was a smoker again.

I'd later learn in a class on classical conditioning, that what happened was that I'd 'extinguished' all the former cues to trigger cravings. Lots of people who smoke (or who do any drug), feel an urge to do so because smoking has been paired with other things in their environments. When they're around those things, they go into a pre-emptory withdrawal syndrome, anticipating the delivery of the drug (nicotine in this case), so the drug will have less of an impact and not move them so far from homeostasis. It's the same with other harder drugs, like cocaine, alcohol, opioids, etc., but this of course includes caffeine and nicotine. For example, some people feel a need to smoke right after a meal, or when they get in their car, or particular times where they've established a habit of smoking. Anyway, while I'd 'extinguished' all the other conditioned cues prompting cravings, like drinking, meals, and driving, Spook hadn't been around when I quit. So I'd never 'extinguished' the cues of Spook or his apartment where we'd partied so often prior to his moving. Being suddenly around him and the smell/sight of cigarettes in that basement, kicked off a strong craving. Once you experience the unconditioned stimulus again, nicotine in this case, you essentially go back to the state you were in before you quit. Had I not smoked that cigarette, I'd have extinguished the cue of Spook and his apartment. But by administering nicotine on that spontaneous recovery of the craving reaction, I was instantly re-addicted.

This often happens with people in recovery from alcohol and other drugs, after they get out of rehab. People in rehab are told when they leave, they should stay away from 'old haunts,' and 'old friends' who are still using, because they'll be big temptations. They never tell people the classical conditioning mechanisms behind these temptations, so they're left with platitudes that aren't very helpful. Who coming out of rehab, can't go back to their 'old haunts,' which would include anywhere they'd used substances before, including their homes, which would be 'unextinguished' triggers for cravings. And who wants to abandon true friends, even if they have addiction issues? Even if you could afford to move away, leaving friends/family and moving itself, are major stressors, where increased stress also predicts relapse. Thus they leave rehab, usually wanting to get their lives in order, and feeling pretty stoked about having gotten 'clean' in rehab. They go home and when they do, the 'unextinguished' craving cues are waiting for them. Seemingly all of a sudden, they'll encounter an overpowering urge to use their drug. Most will try to resist, but sooner or later say to themselves something like "Well, I'll just have one drink (or hit, or bump, or whatever), to get past this rough patch, and then I'll be okay." But if they do that drug even once, all of a sudden they'll be hit with the same levels and frequency of cravings they had before going into rehab, and will be re-addicted in short order. And, they'll feel like 'failures' and get down on themselves, believing they have some major moral shortcomings. That then often becomes a justification for giving up on being sober: "I guess I'm just doomed to be an addict." Getting re-addicted, they'll go back to having all the problems they'd had prior to rehab. We could really use a lot more Psychological Science education in our junior/senior high schools, and certainly in our drug/alcohol rehabilitation facilities.

Anyway, I was still smoking cigarettes when Val and her mom came to live with me. And Val had asthma, so I'd never smoke around her and had given up smoking in the house altogether. It was cold that winter, so smoking outside alone was not fun, and I decided if I'd quit before, I could do it again. Within a few months, I'd quit smoking again, which was good for me, my budget, and Val.

Chapter 9

Phase V Continued, The Light Grows Stronger

Time progressed, and Val's mother's anxiety peaked again, and she was having multiple panic attacks each day. I felt helpless as I didn't really understand them, and didn't know how to help. I took her to a local public mental health facility, and she was prescribed Xanax, and told to take a specific number of pills each day. They made an appointment for her with a Therapist, but were so backlogged that it would be almost 2 months before that would happen. And, the most she'd get to see a Therapist was once a month. That seemed woefully inadequate to me, but I didn't know anything about mental healthcare then. So, that's the route we planned to take.

I'd had one experience with Xanax myself, and it wasn't good. I was living at the crummy apartment alone when Krull and W.B. came by. Krull had a bunch of pills he was looking to sell. He said, "Man, you're going to love these!" I bought 10. I knew nothing of Xanax nor pharmacology, and so I took 4 and washed them down with beer. They seemed small to me, and I'd taken a lot of codeine pills when I had those. I incorrectly thought this was pretty much the same thing. Not feeling anything after a half hour, I thought they were weak, so I took 3 more, for a total of 7. And then, it hit me. I blacked out for the next 24-hours. Krull took off after I downed the second round, according to W.B. Everything else I know of the night was what W.B. told me, as he'd taken only one, and had a perfect memory of the night. He said we went to the convenience store, where I walked around taking whatever I wanted, as though it were mine, and walked out. At this point, this was very much counter to my moral stance against stealing, which just goes to show how much certain drugs, in certain dosages and/or situations, can take you out of your 'right' mind. W.B. paid for some portion of it, though they couldn't tell what all I had as I'd left. That seemed to be good enough for the clerk, who let the whole thing slide. We got back to my apartment where I soon passed out entirely, for about 18 hours. When I woke up, W.B. told me what I related above. I was dumbfounded. I said, "I only took 7 pills, right; how could they've had that kind of effect?!?" Not knowing about the 'half-life' of pharmaceuticals, and as I didn't think I was any longer under the influence of the Xanax, I said, "All I have left is 3. That's less than half of what I took last night; so, I guess I'll just take them." So I did, and again washed them down with beer. And, I was "gone" again. I completely blacked out within the hour. Apparently this time I didn't go anywhere or do anything ridiculous, but I certainly could have, and I'd have never known what I was doing, nor remembered it. I woke up again, about 24-hours later, and never did Xanax again.

But, here Michelle was being prescribed the same drug. She took it as she was told to by the doctor, to help with her panic attacks, which clearly involved a lot of anguish. I assumed it'd be fine, but I was wrong. While she did drink a lot in general, she didn't drink much while taking Xanax. But within an hour or so of having any alcohol, she acted as though she'd knocked out a fifth of liquor. Alcohol and Xanax have a multiplicative effect. She was obnoxious and boisterous to the point she'd have been embarrassed if she'd any idea or recollection of what she'd done. At friends' houses on a few occasions, she cussed out everyone. In 2 cases she fell, and once knocked everything off a coffee table. I couldn't understand why this was happening. I'd learned to unobtrusively note how much she'd been drinking on any given occasion, and on these nights, she'd literally had 2, or at most 3, beers. Normally that quantity wouldn't have had much, if any, effect on her behavior. So, I'd tell her in as kind a manner as I could the next days, what transpired. She had trouble believing she'd lost control so completely, but she admitted she had no memory of these events.

Soon, she finally became convinced something was wrong, and quit taking the Xanax cold turkey. I'd been with her when they wrote the prescription, and nobody said anything about *not* stopping Xanax cold turkey. I was elated she was quitting them, and gave as much support to her as I could, because I knew she'd shortly be battling panic attacks again. A week later we were up at Fred's house, visiting with him and his wife, Bethany. They lived in a small farmhouse in the middle of nowhere, about 15 miles from where Dad lived. In the course of sitting around talking, Michelle's body contracted and her face contorted, as she started having a seizure. We whisked her into Fred's car and took off for the hospital; a pretty long drive. She wasn't able to talk or react to the physician, so I gave him her medical history, including the recent starting and stopping of Xanax, and he said "That's it!" I said, "What do you mean, that's it?!?" He said, "People taking Xanax on a daily basis should never quit abruptly; they have to titrate down, or they'll have a seizure about a week after the last dose." I was livid, as nobody'd bothered to tell us that, and the ER doctor said it could've been worse. All this probably played a part in my own eventual choice of professions. Eventually, I literally became an expert on anxiety.

Several years later when I was in my Clinical Psychology master's program, a mutual friend of mine and Luke's, who referred to himself as "The Freak," would call me to ask about various drugs he'd acquired. That was because I had a used copy of the *Physician's Desk Reference*, which described all manner of pharmacological agents, in detail. This was way before the days of Google. The Freak was a really good guy and an absolutely brilliant sculptor, painter, and general artist, as well as an outdoor adventurer. On one occasion, he called and said he'd been using Xanax recreationally for about a month, but had run out, and was getting antsy. He wanted to know what he should do. While I was no expert at that time, I was a voracious consumer of mental health information, and had the experience of Michelle and her seizure. So, I told him, "You have to go to a doctor right now, and admit what you've been doing. Don't worry about any legal implications. They'll need context for what's going on. And, you'll need them to prescribe you enough to ween yourself off of them in a progressive fashion. If you don't, you'll likely have a seizure a week after you last took the pills." He went to the doctor, and was fine.

As an aside, The Freak was really interesting. He was very talented, but also quite intellectual, and as noted, adventurous in terms of exploring the outdoors and his own consciousness. Once, Luke and he and another friend of theirs, Randy (whom I was familiar with from a nitrous oxide party at his rural home, something I'd never experienced before), were going spelunking in a cave. They invited me, and despite my not being inclined toward such things, I went along, as did 10 other guys. It was basically going to be an underground drinking party. We were careful to keep all the empty cans with us, and not litter this natural treasure. The leading trio (Luke, The Freak, and Randy) were very qualified, having done this sort of thing often and having been in this particular cave several times. It was fascinating, and I'll not go into all the details other than to say there was one point at which if I'd made a single misstep, I'd have certainly been killed or severely injured. It was a tunnel with a break in its floor, where the next floor section was about 6 feet ahead, with just a small protrusion about halfway between the edges. The opening plunged down so far, you couldn't see the bottom with your headlamp. They said it was an easy "one- 2-3 jump." I had to push off with my right foot, land my left foot on the protrusion, and propel myself forward to the connecting floor. That gave me a bit of an adrenaline rush, but it was easy enough and everyone made it across fine. However, it highlighted to me how dangerous spelunking really was. There were a couple of other really vexing spots. Yet it was easy enough to get through, as I did exactly what our guides said.

Our guides were also, except for Luke, doing heroin the whole time. I found out when the rest of the group went ahead with Luke, and I was bringing up the rear with The Freak and Randy. They took out a small envelope of brown powder from which they took turns having 'bumps,' snorting it vigorously. They asked me not to tell anyone, though Luke knew. They were worried the others would be terrified to know they were on heroin. It didn't bother me, and I kept it to myself. Knowing they both had some serious drug habits, I'd rather have had them well-supplied than going through withdrawals in the treacherous bowels of the earth. I never did spelunking again, as that type of thing really isn't an interest of mine. But, Valkyrie has gotten into the practice in the last few years, along with a lot of other enthusiast friends. She finds it to be a wonderful way to spend time in an otherwise unseen splendor of nature. With an experienced guide, anyone in good physical shape can do it safely.

While I was doing my graduate practicum at the State Mental Hospital, The Freak happened to also be dating the niece of the

Adolescent Ward supervisor. He was a 'tough guy' with the kids on the ward, being a big fellow who liked bossing people around and intimidating patients under his 'care.' I found that a very odd attitude to have in his line of work. Once I approached his office door, needing his signature on something, and I heard him excoriating someone on the phone. I waited for his tirade to end, then knocked. He answered and was perfectly calm, as though nothing unusual was afoot. He'd once told me that one of the biggest juveniles had punched him in the face. I thought that weird, as I never had any conflict with any patients in any ward. I wondered if he hadn't done something to embarrass the kid, and make him feel forced to 'save face' in front of the other patients. After observing his unruly behavior, it didn't surprise me that he got punched. The Freak said he and his girlfriend (again, the guy's niece) supplied him with weed on a regular basis, and that he was indeed, an odd guy. It's customary to smoke a bit of the weed one buys, with the seller, to be social, if that's something the seller's interested in doing. The Freak said he figured they'd hang out and smoke with her uncle when they sold him pot. But as soon as he'd get his bag of pot, The Freak said he'd disappear to smoke alone. He'd then come back and make them uncomfortable until they'd leave. It made me wonder again, how some people get to be 'in charge' of others' mental healthcare, having serious issues of their own.

Several months later, The Freak was driving through the parking lot of the store where I got our groceries. He pulled up to me and was clearly in distress. He'd just broken up with his girlfriend, having found out she'd been cheating on him. He had a loaded pistol and wondered aloud whether he should shoot her, or the guy she'd been with, or both, and/or himself. So, we talked it out. I asked him to let me keep the gun, so he wouldn't do anything he'd later regret. He said our talk helped a lot, that he wouldn't do anything drastic, and he agreed that if he shifted back toward that type of thinking, he'd come leave the gun with me until he felt more stable. He seemed to go through regular bouts of extreme ups and downs in his mood, in general. As an unprofessional observer of human behavior at the time, I found this roller coaster of emotions to be characteristic of a few people I'd met before, like Walker and Krull, and he likely had Bipolar I Disorder, too. Anyway, The Freak never came to any harm nor did he harm anyone else.

So back to life on Euclid Ave., where one of the physical health issues Michelle had was a rather extreme case of endometriosis. This caused her to have menstrual periods so severe that she'd literally become anemic. She'd also have paralyzing cramps, adding substantially to her mental suffering. A doctor had told her she'd never be able to get pregnant again. Thus, we took no birth control precautions. I found out that medicine is as much an art as a science, when she got pregnant. We were not prepared for that in any way. As I'd never planned to have children, and given Michelle's diagnosis, I'd initially figured Valkyrie would be my only child. As such, I decided to adopt her, and make her truly 'my own' in a legal sense. She was already 'my' kid in a spiritual sense, but legalities matter, too. Dad helped me, as he did so often, with legal fees, so I could start the adoption process. I had to call her birth father, and get him to relinquish his parental rights. As I understood it, Val was the product of a one-night stand on the beach, when her mother had been living there. While he was listed on the birth certificate, her biological father had only seen her once when she was an infant, and had no interest in being involved with her.

In fact, he'd never paid any child support. So, I had knowledge, should he make any fuss about giving up his rights. I got his number from Michelle, who still had it. I called and he was friendly enough, but was trying to keep quiet, as he had a wife and 3 kids, as he explained in a whisper. I could hear them in the background and clearly he'd never told them about his 'other' child. I explained how I came to be Val's stepfather. I told him that since she'd be my only child, I wanted to raise her as my 'own;' and that all I needed was for him to sign and notarize a form, and everything else would be taken care of. He readily agreed. Beyond this request, I asked only that he not try to contact Val until she was at least 18-years-old, if he wanted to at all, so I'd have the opportunity to be her 'only' father until she was an adult. He readily agreed to that, as well. To my knowledge, even though she's now in her 30s, he's never attempted to contact her, nor to connect her with her half-siblings by him. As far as I know, this is fine with Val, and she's never brought it up. I did of course, tell her everything I was doing, and why I was doing it. She was enthusiastic about being adopted by me, and even took my last name (she had Michelle's maiden name as her last name on her birth certificate). The adoption was finalized, and

I was then in every respect a father. As it turned out, I was about to become a father a second time.

I'd been moving along in my studies at CPCC, obtaining an Associate's Degree, with plans to transfer to the local UNC university at Charlotte (UNCC). In the process, I'd also taken Abnormal Psychology, which covers mental illness diagnoses and methods of treatment. It was a fascinating course, and many times I said to myself, "I know someone like that!" Or, in the case of addiction issues, saying, "That's my problem!" I didn't then intend to pursue a career in Psychology, having no idea how to start a career. When I transferred to the local university, UNCC, I had Philosophy as my major, having loved the course in my first set of classes.

In my last year at CPCC, I took an introductory Theater course, for general credits. The guy teaching it was very into the topic, and the head of the CPCC Theater department. It was a very active program, with an annual professional 'summer stock' season, and plays/dances in the fall/spring. Around this time, a very wild guy and his wife, Ned and Mona, moved into the house 2 doors up from us, and made themselves at home, popping in regularly. They had some serious addiction issues themselves, and Ned was 'crazy.' They were both older than me by about 10 years. He worked as a handyman and had a van out of which he operated. Ned established a weird pattern of showing up when something was wrong with the plumbing, gas, or electricity in my house (I'd learned different trades, but never took up those), and fix a problem in no time and declare it was "Neddy Magic!" Once my van broke down far up South Blvd. I didn't have AAA coverage or any money, and didn't know what I was going to do. Out of nowhere, Ned pulled up and raised my hood. He fixed my van in about a half hour, and I was good to go. He said it was "another example of Neddy Magic!"

The only time I ever missed a class was the Monday following the weekend I'd married Michelle. Since we didn't have money for a honeymoon, I figured I'd at least take a day off from school, to hang out with her and Valkyrie. The only class I had that day, was Theater. I never skipped classes and felt a bit odd about it, but figured I had as good an excuse as any. Ned dropped by that Sunday night and I got talking about my skipping my Theater class the next day, saying I hoped my excuse was good enough for my teacher, as I really liked and respected him. Ned said "I'll be your excuse!" We worked up this routine where I'd go in the following day, on Tuesday. From my seat on the front row, I'd announce I was sorry I'd missed class the day before, and that I had an excuse. Ned would listen for this cue outside the door, and then march in and be 'The Excuse.' He said he'd go into a litany of general excuses, like "The sun was in my eyes!" "I had a flat tire!" "I got snowed in!" And on and on. As he reached a crescendo, I'd pull out a little BB gun (as I said, I'd never owned an actual gun, but got the BB gun at a yard sale to plink targets in my back yard). I'd then yell "Enough!" and "Bang!" and pretend to shoot 'The Excuse.' At that point Ned would slap his chest where he'd have a couple of packets of ketchup taped under his white t-shirt. He'd then drop to the floor, as though 'The Excuse' had gone too far, and had to be stopped.

It went off without a hitch and Ned was 'crazy' dramatic, yelling one excuse after another at the top of his lungs, and when I yelled "Bang!" he splattered ketchup inside his shirt and fell to the floor. Right after hitting the floor, he got up, took a bow, and disappeared. Everyone was taken aback, though we got rousing applause when we'd concluded. The teacher however, was not amused. He told the class you NEVER do anything that resembles violence outside the context of a well-established plot line, as it had the potential to cause bedlam in the audience. I apologized for my actions, and on behalf of 'The Excuse,' and the teacher let it go. I think in some ways he was somewhat impressed at the lengths to which we'd gone. Not long after that, my teacher was working on a ladder when he fell onto his driveway and was seriously injured. He was to be out for the rest of the semester, and a junior instructor, Percival, took his place. Percival was in class fretting that he'd been named as Director for the upcoming production of *Fiddler on the Roof*, saying he'd no idea how to build a realistic and safe roof over the orchestra pit. I asked if he was serious, and he asked me "Why?" I said, "Because, that'd be pretty easy to do." He got a huge smile and said, "If I get you the materials, could you build it?" I said, "Absolutely! Especially if it counts for my Theater lab hours." He said that would be fine. I measured the area and gave him a lumber list. I built the structure and shingled it, and it looked amazing; and several people safely danced on it for rehearsals and several shows.

Percival was impressed and offered me a 20-hour/week work-study job. I'd be the Theater Lab Coordinator and Technical Director for productions in the regular season. I was glad to have steady work where I could schedule my hours around my classes, and thus more easily get Val to and from school. I'd never been in the 'arts' before, other than playing rock music. I got to use my construction skills in a highly creative way, which was gratifying. Directors of dances and plays described what kind of sets they wanted, and I'd figure out how to build them. In addition, I provided the lab tasks for students in the Intro Theater courses. The idea of the lab work was for students to get a taste of what it was like to work behind the scenes. Each student provided several hours of labor, which constituted most of the workforce for this theater, since they only had a tiny budget for production costs. I'd have the students do whatever needed doing, including sorting screws, nuts, and bolts, from disassembled sets. The theater's budget was so small, they kept everything they could keep, and use it over and over. I had to train many students how to use tools such as screw-guns, ratchets, and wrenches, and supervise them to make sure they worked safely. I also learned how to arrange and hang lights and run the lighting board, as well as the soundboard (where the latter was already an interest of mine). I was never a top-level technician, but was good enough for their purposes.

After I transferred to UNCC, I was able to keep the CPCC job, which gave me a small but steady income, with a very flexible schedule. During 'summer stock' theater, they hired me as support for an expert Technical Director, who was a true artist in every sense, and a genuine professional. That gave me a continuous job for a couple years. Yet I continued to work small construction jobs, on the side, for extra income. Michelle never worked steadily, and once she became pregnant, she hardly worked again with rare and brief exceptions. So, we needed all the money I could make.

Like I've noted many times, we had my Dad's support for the rent and bills, and occasional 'emergency' issues like my adoption of Val, but I was adamant that I'd do all in my power not to abuse his generosity. I didn't want anything from him beyond what I felt was absolutely necessary for the well-being of the family. So with a baby on the way, I had to seek out welfare, particularly to get WIC, food stamps, and medical benefits, so we'd be able to get formula and baby food, and proper prenatal care for Michelle during her pregnancy. It turned out we only needed the benefits a few times, to buy food once and for a couple of doctor's visits. While we didn't actually need it as much as

I'd feared, it was nice to know it was there, if we did. I've always paid taxes whenever I had a job that deducted them from my check, though most of my side work was paid in cash, and thus 'under the table.' I've no idea how much I made that way, as I was lousy at record-keeping. I know I didn't make much. Yet ever since I went to grad school and had steady professional work, and eventually a career, I've always paid my fair share. I think that's how it's supposed to work: pay all the taxes you should and can pay, and if you need welfare assistance, get it. I've been very Blessed in my life, and haven't had any major issues with my health. Since starting my career, I've had insurance as part of my benefits. So far I've been lucky enough not to need such assistance again, except once (which I'll get to). If all continues to go well, I'll need nothing else but my Social Security benefits, when I retire.

I occasionally worked on the side with a guy I knew, doing vinyl siding and installing drop ceilings, in remodeling projects. He'd call sporadically when he needed help with something, and I'd work in the evenings or on weekends. He had an older girlfriend who had an enormous and steep yard, so I started mowing it regularly for a bit of additional income. She had an amazing artist of a son, about my age. I was able to get her son a job at the theater for one play, painting the back wall and flats to resemble a forest. He did a stunningly good job. I've met all kinds of people with fascinating talents and/or personalities. At one point, the faculty chair of my honors thesis in Philosophy at UNCC, wanted a gazeebo built to hide the well pump at his house on the outskirts of Charlotte. Knowing of my construction background, he asked if I'd do it. I said "For $10/hour and materials, I'd be glad to." Thus, I continued to pick up all kinds of side projects, including hanging sheetrock, installing floors, and so on. But having an infant, in addition to an almost-teenager, would require more steady money than I was able to get with my hit-and-miss side projects, and my relatively low-paying theater job. So, I went on welfare for the first and, as it turns out, second to last time (about which, more below). My Dad eventually got us health insurance, after Hunter was born and I was in graduate school, so the kids and Michelle could have regular access to doctors, as needed. But at this point, I was loathe to ask for more financial assistance from him, and did what I felt I needed to do. I mention this, because a lot of people who've been fortunate enough not to need welfare assistance, seem to have disdain for those who need it. Some smaller but vocal portion of them, seem to think welfare fraud and abuse is rampant. There surely is some, but there's no evidence for that view, and the people I met who were on it, all really needed it. Often there were kids involved. Regardless of the parents' situations, kids certainly deserve to have the best shot possible at getting life's basic necessities. I used assistance in a way I felt was appropriate.

Chapter 10

Phase V Continued, The Light Grows Brighter

Michelle's pregnancy was during my last undergraduate year and I had to figure out what I was going to do for a 'real' job. At one point she asked what I was going to do with a Philosophy degree. She'd never been to college, and neither had I, so I had to say "I have no idea." I really didn't know what one could do with a Philosophy degree. As it turns out, with additional schooling, one can do quite a lot: teaching, law, business, government, etc. Being hit with the realization that I was finishing college with no idea as to what I'd do for work, I scrambled to find a practical solution. Nobody at UNCC offered me the slightest bit of advice as to how I would transition from college to a career, at least at first. It occurred to me Psychology was a lot like Philosophy, with the Scientific Method added, which I liked. I thought maybe I could do Psychology as a major, and become a Therapist; and perhaps work with teens to help them avoid the mistakes I'd made in my teenage years. Nobody told me then that I couldn't be a Therapist without having at least a master's degree and a license. So, I picked up Psychology as a major. I had an 'Advisor,' who was terrible at that job. It was obvious he didn't care about me as a student, and he wasn't well-versed in the course catalog or degree requirements. So I read the catalog and advised myself. I discovered I could actually get 2 bachelor's degrees, if I added a few more classes, where I'd have a Bachelor of Arts in Philosophy, and a Bachelor of Science in Psychology. Having almost completed the Philosophy major and having 24 additional semester hours I'd need to get the Psychology major done, I figured I might as well finish my Philosophy degree, and get another in Psychology.

And, that's what I did. It made for an unbelievably hectic schedule. I could've just double majored without the extra courses to get a second degree, and nothing about my life since would've been any different. But I wanted the 2 degrees, and set about to earn them both. I was able to do it all within 4 years, having started CPCC in the summer of 1992, and graduating from UNCC in the autumn of 1996. I'd always taken full course loads, and often overloads, in every semester, including summers. In my last year, I took 20 semester hours in the fall, 24 semester hours in the spring, followed by a full summer load, all while working the Theater job and side projects when I could pick them up. Again, at that point I'd not heard anything about the need to go to graduate school, and becoming licensed as a Therapist. I just didn't know any of this going into the Psychology major. I had some good instructors in my Psych classes for the most part, but few did more than to teach their material. They didn't offer guidance without being asked; and, I didn't know what I didn't know, so I didn't know what to ask about.

I'd got a tutoring gig in that last fall semester, under an older Psychology Professor, Dr. Hagar, as my Supervisor. I tutored a young woman on the tennis team, in Introductory Psychology. She was a sweet kid, always showed up for her appointments, and seemed to really appreciate that I helped her understand topics with which she was struggling. That was my first inkling that helping people could be fulfilling, but it was just a couple of hours a week, to get a couple of credit hours. It was another thing to put in my schedule, which was already overly packed. But, Dr. Hagar helped me the next semester in a way I didn't then know I'd need. I knocked out my classes and ultimately graduated with a 3.925 GPA overall, with a 4.0 in the Psych major. I'd work all night anytime I needed to, which was frequently. I'd juggle my work hours with my course schedule, and drop off and pick up Val from school whenever I could, where Michelle would do that if I couldn't. When I'd get home, I'd make time for Val (and ultimately Hunter, too), to go over homework, hear about the day's activities, make dinner, and just hang out as a father.

Arguments with Michelle were also very frequent and time-consuming, as well as emotionally exhausting. The only time to do my homework and study was when they'd all gone to bed, and I could be alone and concentrate. It'd eventually get more hectic when I went to graduate school. Because of Dad's financial help with the bills and rent, and my own variety of employment, and as I'd qualified for the Pell grant, I'd graduate with no school debt. Again, I was very Blessed and benefitted from privileges I'd still not yet understood. People who heard about everything I did, what with working 20 to 30 hours a week, going to school with a full load or overload every fall/spring/summer, being married and being totally invested as a father of 2 kids, would later ask, "How on Earth did you pull all that off?" And really, I don't know. I was just a man on a mission at that point, having realized my purpose in life was to better provide for my children by going to college and then maybe helping other people for a living. I'd become laser-focused on doing everything that needed to be done to get to a career.

That spring semester rolled around, and I had 24 semester hours on my schedule. Two were technically already done, because they were for the tutoring I'd done that fall, but Dr. Hagar still had to give me the credit. Three more were in an Anatomy & Physiology course I needed to get my 2 degrees, instead of just a double-major. I figured out from reading the catalogue I could take it pass/fail, to make it a little easier to get through, as I'd not need to study much for that course to maintain my GPA. Turns out I loved it and made a 99/100 in the course. It was taught by a brilliant woman, and I learned a ton. Back then I had no idea I could become a doctor of any kind, much less a medical doctor, especially given my fear of mathematics, and my miserable experience in Chemistry for non-majors. Later I realized I could've been anything I wanted to become, if only I'd had the belief in my ability, because I certainly was willing and able to do the work. But at this point, I figured I'd get my bachelor's degrees and a decent job I could stand to do day-in and day-out, which would support my family and maybe come with benefits (which none of my construction jobs provided). I also took a senior seminar course in Community Psychology and a Practicum course that put me in a clinical setting to help people in a supervised training program.

With those 24 semester hours on my schedule for spring, I got called into the Dean's office. I thought perhaps someone was concerned I'd either lost my mind, or would lose it trying to accomplish all of this (especially if they knew or found out I had a family and a job). So, I went in with a ready explanation of how I'd had everything planned out, and could pull it off, and do it well. The Dean stared at me as I launched into my assurances, and stopped me. He said, "You know we don't get paid beyond 15 semester hours." I didn't know what he was talking about, and he explained, "Beyond 15 credit hours, each additional hour is given to students at no charge, so the university doesn't make any extra money." I was astonished. He didn't care about me, my mental health, or my ultimate career. He cared about money, which I found to be a crass concern given all I'd put into getting my education. I assured him it was necessary to get my degrees, that I'd be finishing up in the summer, and that thus, I wouldn't do it again. He approved my overload and I looked forward to finishing up and getting out into the 'real' world.

It always takes me aback a bit when people refer to students as not living in the 'real' world. Everything they go through is all too 'real,' from my view. It's not easy to get a degree of any kind, be it an associate or bachelor degree, not to mention masters or doctoral degrees. And many students work to pay for school and/or living expenses, and/or accrue serious debt in the process. Sure, it's not the same thing as having a long-term career under a boss, but if you get a bachelor's degree, you completed at least 120 semester hours, meaning you did 40 classes with up to 40 different 'bosses' (instructors), each of whom provides a syllabus full of readings, papers, projects, tests, etc. And you have to get at least an average of 75% of all of it done well (a C average), to graduate. That's 'real' enough, though it gets more 'real' in the working world.

In the Community Psych class, I headed up a project with 2 younger students, in which we went to the men's Homeless Shelter in Charlotte, to establish a self-advocacy group. I'd had my own experiences of near-homelessness and had met lots of people who were homeless. I also knew from them and first-hand of hanging out downtown, they could be treated pretty harshly. I had to do a lot of reading up on the topic in the course, and found Asheville had a pretty effective self-advocacy group. Thus, somebody had headed it up, gathered homeless people on a regular basis, helped them figure out some needs and priorities, and helped them work toward changing city legislation to be more favorable to those living under otherwise terrible circumstances. So, I thought we might have a shot at helping the Charlotte homeless population to improve their situations, at least somewhat. That was a little over-optimistic, to say the least. Being it was just me and 2 other students (who were frankly much less invested, though nice enough and willing to help out enough to earn their project grade), it wasn't going to be easy. And it wasn't. I went to the shelter on a weekly basis and met lots of people. There was some interest, but being that homeless people are transient by definition and many were jaded and skeptical of 'lobbying' for change, the project ended when the semester ended. However, it was a great learning experience, and I've since always tried to do charity work aimed at benefitting homeless people.

Where I work, you can have money taken out of your monthly check to give to a variety of charity organizations, so I do that. I always give to the Salvation Army and the Families First program, where the latter works to help entire families experiencing homelessness. I give to a few other groups, in rotation. I don't accept as a reason not to give, criticisms of charities not being run as well as they could be. One should certainly check out such groups before giving, and those to which I give have excellent ratings from independent watchdog agencies (e.g., CharityNavigator.com). All charities have overhead and all organizations are imperfect. But doing something is better than doing nothing. I don't give an enormous amount, but I give as much as I feel I'm able to, averaging about $1,000 a year. As I've been doing this since 2004, I've thus far given over $12,000 total in this manner, in addition to chipping in on other charitable campaigns, in an effort to tangibly and regularly help others. And, I plan to do this until I retire. Since one can deduct charity donations from their taxable income, I figure this has squared me up with not having paid all of my taxes a few years when I didn't keep financial records and/or got paid cash, even though my income didn't amount to much.

The Practicum class placed me at a Runaway/Homeless Youth Shelter where I became a 'Part-time Relief Counselor.' We could never call ourselves 'real' 'Counselors' or 'Therapists,' as I found out later those titles require having a license. That was when I first realized I'd need more than just a bachelor's degree. I was getting some experience, but apparently without at least a master's degree, I'd never be an actual 'Counselor' or 'Therapist.' Our instructor met with us regularly, and we wrote up weekly reflection papers on our experiences. The woman who was the Director of the shelter was all about empowering volunteers to make a difference. I still had my long-hair, but made sure to wear more 'professional attire' than what I wore on a day-to-day basis. I still have long-hair, but whenever I'm representing my profession, university, or college/department, I wear a button-down shirt and tie. I started wearing that 'uniform' as soon as I got my first 'professional' job, just prior to going into graduate school.

I found I was good at connecting with teens and pre-teens who were in some bad life situations. Many were somewhat wary of opening up to any 'authority' figure, but I rarely came off as such, though I did everything by the book. At the invitation of the Director, I got a summer job at the shelter at the end of the school year, working part-time, and on a flexible schedule. I remember one kid saying "You don't care about us, you're only here for the money!" Getting jaded starts early when you don't have the kind of privileges I'd had. I'd had everything I needed and a 'stable' home, and still became jaded. It was all the worse for kids who couldn't 'take for granted' having life's basic necessities. I understood this kid's reluctance to see me as sincere. I said "I make $6/hour here, and there's a restaurant hiring and paying $7/hour. And, I could make $15 to $20 an hour working construction. If I was all about money, you don't you think I'd be here, do you?" He seemed convinced of my genuineness. I told kids, when it seemed relevant and necessary to establish that I cared about what they were going through, about my having made major mistakes in my own past and truly wanting to be of service to people their age who were otherwise at risk for some pretty bad life outcomes. I got the sense that helping others was a route I could enjoy as a career. Even if I didn't make a ton, I'd feel good about what I did every day, which was something I'd never felt in construction.

I met people there who were giving their all for these kids in need. And yet I met a couple of full-time staffers, who made me wonder why they were in that line of work at all. There was one older guy in particular who seemed pretty jaded himself about these kids, and who had some pretty serious issues of his own. He had a real power-tripping problem, and I was offended that he would exert arbitrary control over children in desperate situations, apparently just for his own amusement. But they needed permanent staff. He'd been there for years and acted like he owned the place, and they weren't going to fire him over a few kids complaining about his behavior. Nonetheless I was getting some experience.

While I was still in the Practicum course, the instructor said, "You have the grades and maturity to do graduate school." I said "What's graduate school and why would I do it?" He said something to the effect of "you'd get more money, more job security, and more control over what you do." That sounded good to me. He told me to join some honors societies, which I'd been invited to do before, but totally rejected up to that point. I thought to myself, why would anyone pay to join a group to tell them they're smart; that doesn't sound very smart to me. He was the first faculty member to actually offer me professional guidance. People who don't understand something usually don't work to learn all the facts. Rather, most just dismiss such things as unworthy of their consideration. When I was still working at CPCC's theater, I did the lights/sound for a community college honors society induction. As those students were getting their credentials, the place was packed with supportive families. I just sat in the sound/light booth, thinking why are they wasting their time and money? Later, my Practicum instructor said, "That stuff goes on your vita." I'd be in grad school before I learned 'vita' was a fancy word for extended academic resume. I got his point: this was important for some future I didn't yet know about. So, I immediately joined 4 honors organizations. Just like that, my resume (vita) got bigger. I'd been wrong and I began to proactively challenge my assumptions as I continued my education.

He also said that to get into graduate school, it'd be good to have research experience. I didn't know what that would entail, nor why exactly I needed it, but it seemed pretty important to him. Up to then, my only research 'experience' was in a Research Methods class. All Psych majors took it, and I'd made an A. I designed and conducted my own study, again with the help of a few less enthusiastic and younger classmates. They were happy to have me do the organizational work, so they'd get a solid grade. We got an 'A' on our project. Later, I saw a flyer on a bulletin board encouraging students to publish their research papers in a journal. In my ignorance, I thought it was some silly departmental newsletter. But I'd written up my project (I designed it and did all the analyses and writing. The others just helped me collect data), and it earned an A, so I thought, "Why not?" I submitted it, and they asked me to revise it. I did, and it got published. I didn't realize the significance of this, because it turned out not to be a newsletter at all, but rather a national undergraduate journal. The Editor just happened to work in the department. I did put it on my resume, but I didn't know how to 'sell' it as an accomplishment when trying to get into graduate school.

Now knowing I needed additional research experience, I knocked on the doors of some Professors with whom I'd had classes. They all essentially told me the same thing: "I've already got a grad student and 2 undergraduates working for me, and I really can't use anyone else." When I got around to Dr. Hagar, who'd supervised my tutoring, she told me basically the same thing. I said "I get that you don't really need me, but apparently I really need this experience…can't you help me out?" And to her credit, she did. Knowing I was an older student, working with a family, trying to get into grad school, and having seen me take tutoring seriously, she let me join her small research team as the fourth member, evaluating a pre-school academic enrichment program. I only collected data one day, but it was interesting, and she said I did well. Her other team members showed me how to manually enter data on a mainframe computer. But, I only got to do that a couple of times. She talked to me about going to grad school and agreed to write me a letter of recommendation. My Community Psych and Practicum instructors also agreed to write me letters for grad school applications.

Thus, I only lacked the Graduate Record Exam (GRE), which is like an SAT or ACT for people getting bachelor's degrees. It was intimidating as it had 2 main sections: Verbal (which didn't bother me) and Quantitative. Quant worried me, as all I'd done were basic community college algebra classes and a probability/statistics course (in which I'd worked mightily, only to come up with a 'B'). And, I didn't study for those 2 sections. I found out there was a Psychology subject test you could pay extra to take, and I naively thought Psych grad programs would care a lot about that type of thing. Thus, I focused all my study time on it. I checked out a stack of Psych textbooks from the library and used my 'down' time at the theater to study, and it paid off…or as was often the case, so I thought. I hit the 80th percentile on the Psych subject test, so I was happy. I'd find out later that few, if any, Psych grad programs even take that score into consideration. So in my naiveté, I'd spent all my time studying something that didn't even matter in the end. I did grab a basic Geometry text book and reviewed some elementary formulae, like finding the volume of a cylinder. Sure enough, that one was on the test. With a pretty strong Verbal score and an 'okay' Quantitative score, I had about a 50th percentile total score, which as implied, was mediocre. But, this was balanced by a 3.925 overall GPA and 4.0 in-major GPA.

Thus with all my ducks now in a row, I was ready to apply to grad programs. I applied to the master's program in Community/Clinical Psych in my own department, and to 2 Clinical Psych doctoral programs. I got no response. I was peeved about not getting an interview for my own school's program, because my department had just named me co-recipient of the senior undergraduate award. As that award essentially said I was the best undergrad they had in the department, I was at a loss to understand why they didn't want me as a grad student. I went to talk to my Community Psych and Practicum instructors. Separately, both told me because I'd mentioned in my statement of purpose essay having been aggressive as a kid, that some Professors worried I might be a problem. Apparently, one graduate student "8 years ago" had gotten upset with one of his Professors, became incensed, and made some threatening remarks. They said some of the faculty were afraid I might be like that. I said, "The whole point of my mentioning that, was that I've become a pacifist; that I'm NOT aggressive anymore. Researchers talk about aggression as a personality trait, and if it's a trait, how could I *choose* to change it so thoroughly? That's why I want to do research on the topic." Both were sympathetic, and each told me they'd argued on my behalf to get me an interview, knowing me to be responsible and heartfelt in my desire to help others. But they were overruled by the committee, and there was nothing else they could do. One also told me that many graduate programs won't accept undergrad applicants from within their own departments. So, that was that, and I had to focus on finishing my classes that summer, graduate, and find a job…and, a new place to live.

The house on Euclid wouldn't have been a great place for an infant and a pre-teen daughter. It had only 2 bedrooms and I didn't want Val to have to share her room with an infant. And, there was no extra space in our bedroom. So, we moved to a house on Valley Stream Rd., in a blue collar neighborhood packed with good people and great neighbors. It had a very small third 'bedroom,' that was just big enough for a nursery. Just after we moved, Hunter was born, in June of 1996. It turned out that he was a 'difficult' baby, in that he rarely slept more than a couple of hours in a row and he got upset very easily. He was difficult to calm, even though there was no 'reason' for him to be upset, as he was always well-fed, clean, warm, and cared for deeply. I'd no idea at the outset, of the degree of 'stepping up' I'd have to do to make sure all his needs were met, and how hard it would be while going to school (and ultimately grad school) full-time, and working as much as I could, while also parenting a teen, and having a deeply troubled wife.

I graduated with both my bachelor's degrees August of 1996. Val was 12 at this point. She was amazing and loved her brother, and was willing and able to help out. But, she was in school and had her own social life to lead. So, I was reluctant to rely heavily on her to babysit, though she did that duty willingly and with some regularity. With their mom's sporadic mental, physical, and alcohol issues, the bulk of the childcare responsibility fell on me. As I finished up my classes that summer, getting ready to graduate, I began looking for a job, but that wasn't going well. I'd no idea that UNCC had a 'career services' office, that would've helped me with preparing a resume, networking, finding job opportunities, etc. Thus, I felt I was on my own. I did what I'd always done before when looking for work; checking the classified ad section of the newspaper. 'Helping' jobs were far and few between, and I found they paid very little at my level of education. I did get a few interviews, but no offers until I got an interview with Sunlight Behavioral Health Services. Sunlight had a new facility opening up a couple miles from our new house. The job for which I'd applied, didn't actually require anything but a high school diploma or a GED, as it was a mental health 'tech' position. It paid only $8/hour. I could make twice that in construction, but construction was the last thing I wanted to do. The job was 40 hours/week, with health insurance benefits. I desperately wanted my family to have insurance, which I figured to be worth something substantial. The 'tech' job was working with severely and persistently mentally ill people, who'd be coming to what Sunlight called a 'partial-hospitalization program' 5 hours/day, 5 days/week. It sounded interesting and I'd be helping people who really needed help. The Regional Manager was the only one who'd been hired at the facility at that point, and was based out of the office in which I'd be working. He was nice and enthusiastic, and offered me the job on the spot; so, I took it. I figured I'd take a second shot at grad school applications that next fall, and if I didn't get in again, I'd just look for better paying jobs. The timing was also perfect, as I could start the job right after I graduated that August.

I didn't go to my CPCC graduation ceremony. But, it seemed important to Mom and Dad that I go to my UNCC commencement.

Since they'd been so instrumental in me getting into college to begin with, and in helping all along the way, I thought I at least owed them this. And, my grandparents came. My maternal grandmother had passed away, which was terrible, as I loved her deeply. My maternal grandfather took that loss very hard, and his health wasn't good either. I'd tried to step up and be there for him, calling him every week. But with 2 kids, a job, and living 3 hours away, I couldn't see him much. He was coming to my graduation with Mom and Patrick, and to see his new great grandson. My paternal grandparents were coming, too. Realizing this was a really big deal for all of them, I didn't complain about having to buy a cap and gown, and sitting through a long, boring ceremony. I started to feel a bit proud of what I'd accomplished, after all the ridiculous and negative things I'd done in my teens and very early adulthood. I was moving into my late 20s, and actually making the people I respected most, proud of me. It was awesome to see them all at the ceremony. I also felt I was now a positive role model for Valkyrie, as she'd seen me go through so much to achieve this goal, while also showing her my total dedication. I was fulfilling the purpose Val had given me, which Hunter had extended, and for that I was grateful to GOD and everyone who believed in me. GOD knows that many people thought, and understandably so, that I'd amount to little or nothing, or worse.

My maternal grandfather died not long after my graduation, and I went to help Mom clean out his house. She'd lived with Patrick the previous year in the other half of the duplex my grandparents owned, so they could take care of him in his decline. He was a master carpenter as I've mentioned, and he'd built a workshop in his backyard, and she wanted me to have all his tools. So, I rented a truck and along with Luke and W.B., and got his equipment moved into the basement of our new house. I also got all of his ties and he had quite a collection. When he moved off the farm on which he grew up, and went into business as a salesman, he wore a tie every day. My paternal grandfather did the same thing, also being in sales. So, now that I was in a 'professional' job, wearing ties seemed the right thing to do. I felt I should take my new job as seriously as my grandfathers had taken their jobs. I got a few button down shirts, some slacks, and a pair of dress shoes, and that became my 'uniform.' I only owned one suit, which my Dad bought me so I could present myself respectably at my maternal grandmother's funeral. I'd also worn it to my interview for the Sunlight job, as that was the most 'professional' attire I had. Thus I started my 'career,' with my recently expanded family. It turned out the corporation for whom I now worked, was corrupt as could be, at the top. But, I'd only find that out much later.

I was soon ready to apply again for graduate programs, and yet still didn't know what I was doing. I knew that I needed to revise my essay to take out the part about my having been previously aggressive, and focus only upon wanting to research the topic, generally. The people who also got hired at Sunlight were really supportive. There were 2 licensed therapists, as well as a receptionist and a Clinic Manager, in addition to the Regional Manager who hired me. They also hired a Psychiatrist, but he only came in once a week. I became friends with all of them, though I'd later find out some problematic things about corporate cultures, or at least Sunlight's culture. I'd only had the one experience in a corporate-like environment, at the sheetrock company; and that didn't go well. The therapists had both left another regional mental health facility because it was so unethical. They didn't like having to lower their standards to work there, so they jumped at the chance to move to Sunlight, where it initially sounded like patient welfare would always be at the forefront. But, that would change.

My job was keeping charts organized and up-to-date following a strict protocol, and arranging transportation for patients for those who needed it, using a taxi service, which turned out to be all but one of them. Many were 'wards of the state' who lived in nursing homes, though most were not 'elderly' per se. I also arranged their daily snacks and lunches, generally kept the place cleaned up, helped orient new patients to the facility, and facilitated their moving between therapy groups, individual sessions, and breaks. The work wasn't difficult, and I took pride in my professionalism and my relationships with the staff and the patients, with whom I typically became friends. Most of the patients had very serious disorders, having either been diagnosed with Schizophrenia, Bipolar I, profound Depression, and/or Dementia. Previously, I'd met a few homeless people in states of psychosis, and they didn't frighten or bother me. In the same sense, I wasn't repelled by any of our patients. However, many in the public and often within their own families, rejected them. These patients couldn't hold jobs, as their symptoms would sooner or later flair up to the point they'd be fired. That's why most were on disability or in state-custody.

I particularly bonded with the male Therapist, Joe, because like me, he was also into music. Eventually, he let me co-lead a music therapy group, where he was listed as the official Therapist, for billing purposes. But, he also gave me lots of leadership opportunities. The patients liked our music therapy group best. We'd come up with a clinical topic, and go around the room and have each make a statement about the issue. I'd write what they said on the board, and Joe and I would throw in a line here and there, so we'd have a running rhyme scheme. I'd write it all down at the end of the session, and type it up. I'd then take my guitar and come up with a song structure and vocal melody for the lyrics we'd collectively written. We'd hand out updated lyric sheets at each session and I'd teach them the new songs we'd written. We also had them make rhythmic instruments, like putting dried beans inside plastic bottles for maracas, which they could play. We'd all jam our songs and write a new one almost every session. They loved it, and so did Joe and I. We'd used art to help them meaningfully work through struggles they faced, and everyone had lots of fun doing so.

As Joe and I got to know each other, he offered me a lot of advice on the graduate school application process. When I told him I'd only applied to 3 schools the first time, he said "Three?!? You don't apply to 3, you apply to 23!" I said, "Applications are like $50 each; that'd be pricey!" He said, "Do you want to keep making $8/hour doing menial tasks, or do you want to be a licensed Therapist?" His point was well-taken, and he told me how to find more programs, how to figure out which faculty had which research interests, how to customize a paragraph of my essay that was specific to each program, and how to detail my interests to match those of particular faculty. It was an onerous process, especially with a new baby, a teen daughter, difficulties with my spouse, and a full-time job. But I applied to around 20 programs, some master's level, and some doctoral level. I didn't really understand the difference, but at the time you could be licensed at the master's level to be a Therapist/Counselor. The doctoral level meant you could do a range of jobs you couldn't do with a master's degree. I got 6 interviews.

Chapter 11

Phase VI, Moving Onward & Upward

My first interview was at Appalachian State, where both Fred and Luke had graduated. Luke was still living there with his wife, Mary. It was in the mountains and they loved the outdoors and had an active lifestyle. For my interview, I wore my only suit again. When I crossed the campus, I encountered people waving and saying "Hey!" I'd look over my shoulder, thinking they must be talking to someone behind me. Strangers in Charlotte never said "Hey!" to each other. But at Appalachian, strangers acknowledged one another while walking across campus. It was a nice experience, though completely unexpected and new to me. I had a series of one-on-one interviews with the faculty. I'd done my homework, so I knew who researched what, or had particular clinical interests. Joe had given me some interview pointers, and I thought it went well. At the end of the day, the Program Director offered me a slot on the spot, and I immediately accepted. I contacted the other schools where I had interviews, thanked them for considering me, and cancelled because I'd accepted a position at Appalachian. I found out later that was a bad move. Apparently, I should've gone to all the interviews and if I received other offers, compared them all and picked the best. But, Luke lived there, the place was friendly, and I liked the faculty and graduate students I met, so what more could I have wanted? The interview was in spring, and I had the summer to go before I'd move.

In late summer, my co-workers and I found out about the shady dealings of the CEO of Sunlight, and what he'd done to our company. Basically, the guy had been barred from doing business in Georgia, having engaged in massive Medicaid fraud. He wasn't sent to prison and was free to go set up a new company in another state; so he picked Florida and did just that. Sunlight had set up clinics all along the East Coast. Lots of people were employed with them, and lots of seriously ill patients were being served by well-meaning people. The first hint I had there was a problem, was when our vendors started calling about not being paid. That included our transportation company, on whom almost all our patients relied. The head of the taxi company was as understanding as he could be, and continued to provide services as long as he could, as charity for the patients. Then we got wind some Sunlight clinics were being shut down without warning. At those sites, everyone was losing their jobs without notice and not being paid their final checks. Patients were summarily discharged, regardless of their mental health status.

Our Clinic Manager seemed friendly enough at first, and appeared to be invested in what we were doing. When my first evaluation had come that past spring, she'd given me a rating of 3/5, across all criteria. I was perplexed. When we met, I said, "I'm the only one in my position, I do everything I'm supposed to do, and I do it exceedingly well; so, why wouldn't you give me at least 4's, if not 5's?" She agreed with me, and told me that's "just how it goes" in a corporation. She said if she were to give me the ratings I deserved, she might have to give me a raise. She added, "And, everyone has room for improvement, right?" I told her I couldn't see how I could possibly improve beyond doing everything perfectly well, but that if that's how these things went, I could live with it. Around that same time, she called me into her office to talk about my interactions with the patients. Her office was right beside the break area I'd take the patients so they could smoke. She told me she'd heard me talking and that I was "too friendly" to them. She said I needed to maintain a "professional distance." I just couldn't understand. In at least a couple of cases, I seemed to be the only friend they had, and the Therapists were strictly clinical with them. I just had conversations with them on topics they thought were interesting or important, and they seemed to value this kind of contact. So, while I understood that clinicians needed boundaries, my job there wasn't really that of a clinician. I was more of a friendly facilitator, getting them what they needed and making sure they got where they needed to go. My conversations put me on a personal level with people who were either experiencing, or had experienced, some very serious psychosis. It was a privilege to get to know them. Anyway, it felt like it'd be a slap in the face if I had to tell them I couldn't be "friendly" anymore.

As the systematic Sunlight shut-down began (spurred on by a new Federal investigation into the same types of practices the CEO had engaged in before), it became apparent we'd soon close. The Clinic Manager's response to this, was to tell our Psychiatrist all our patients were much better now, and should all be discharged. Even though that was preposterous, he complied and started discharging them one after the other. That happened on one single day, where the patients were coming out of meetings with them, totally confused and telling me they were being "thrown out" of the program. I couldn't believe it. While they were able to maintain okay within the program, without it many, if not all, would rapidly deteriorate and be quickly as bad off as when they'd arrived. I felt compelled to do something, so I talked to the Regional Manager, who happened to be in his office. He said, "They're doing what?!?" I said, "They appear to be discharging every patient, without warning and without regard for how they're actually doing." He went and confirmed what was happening, and fired the Clinic Manager on the spot. She was livid and held an impromptu staff meeting on her way out. She told us she didn't care about Sunlight's situation, because her husband was finishing up his doctorate at a school out West. She said she was moving to be with him, so basically, we could all go to hell as far as she was concerned. She didn't care about our patients, after all. She was trying to unload them and get 'let go,' so she could get unemployment and move as soon as possible. Being stopped in the middle of the mass discharge, about half the patients still had the benefit of the program for as long as we remained open, though that wouldn't be long. I could've quit and moved my family to Boone. But, I just couldn't do that to our patients and staff. So, I worked a 2-week notice, knowing I'd never see my last paycheck. Not only was it the right thing to do from my view, but I figured it would make for a great reference from the Regional Manager and the Therapists, where they could say: "He knew he wouldn't get paid, but he stayed anyway." Which was true.

As Sunlight collapsed, I also found out they'd been robbing me, too, as well as every other employee in their health insurance plan. I'd really wanted health insurance, not only for my kids, but also because Michelle had major physical health issues. She had degenerative disc disease and was often in tremendous pain from that, in addition to the endometriosis. Having what I thought was health insurance, I'd encouraged her to go to the doctor as often as necessary. It was a 'self-insurance' plan, where employees paid a chunk of their monthly pay into a pool, managed by the company. Michelle had several medical procedures in the previous 6 to 8 months. I'd gone through proper channels to get them all 'pre-approved' by our insurance plan and each was 'approved.' But it turned out, they never actually paid any of the claims we'd made. In fact, they'd never paid any employee claims. They'd taken everyone's money. So, I was now stuck with $10,000 in medical bills, without a job other than the low-pay Graduate Assistant position I'd get at Appalachian. Thus, I was without any way to pay the bills. I had to go back on welfare again, for the second and last time. They actually got all the bills negotiated down tremendously, and paid off. As soon as they were paid, I came off welfare. It made the papers when Sunlight finally shut down, and that's when we staff learned the notorious back story of our CEO. Once again, my corporate experience was disheartening.

We got ready to move. Dad was characteristically willing to help out, and bought a house in Boone for us to live in, rent-free! That was stupefying to me, but as I've also mentioned, he'd done really well for himself, and could afford it. He figured he could sell the house after we moved out, and at least get back what he'd put in, and potentially make some money. At that point he also gave me a monthly check to put toward health insurance for my family; another mind-blowing Blessing! My privilege was starting to hit me, and I'd learn more about what that meant as I continued my education. A benefit of that graduate program was getting my classes tuition-free, so I only needed to pay for books and some fees. And, they gave me a 20-hour/week Graduate Assistantship (GA), where I'd work for a faculty member and get a small stipend.

I also learned that having held myself to the highest academic standards in my undergraduate career, would later pay me back in ways I'd never anticipated. Appalachian had a box to check on the application, to be considered for grants and fellowships. I didn't even know what a fellowship was, but I knew a grant was where they'd give me money I didn't have to pay back. So, I checked the box. Apparently because of my undergrad GPA, I was awarded an Alumni Fellowship, which paid for my books and fees. So, I always tell students to take great care of their GPA. It's really hard for young people in college to see how all their time, effort, and costs, will eventually pay them back. But if they stay diligent and keep up their grades, it can open doors later in life that they don't even know they'll need access to while they're just trying to get through their undergraduate years.

Still, the GA position wasn't going to cut the monthly bills, even not having rent. Thus, I immediately applied for and got, a food-service job in one of the campus dining halls. I bussed tables, washed dishes, and prepped calzones to be cooked on a later shift. I was able to work at 7:30am, right after I'd drop Val off at her new high school. And, I was done with my short shift before my first classes and my GA work, where my GA was flexible with my class schedule. Michelle was home with Hunter, and she was relatively stable at that point, so he was taken care of, for the most part. Either she or I would get Val after school ended. Val got involved in extracurricular activities and adjusted quickly and well to the move and new school. My master's program was a real eye-opener and quite the challenge, especially with all my other work and family responsibilities. I noticed my peers often complained of the workload, and not having any time to spare, which vexed me. Only one guy in my class, which was just a handful of people, even had a 'significant other.' None of them had children, nor jobs outside their 20-hour/week GAs. It showed me that no matter how good people have it, they'll often see the difficulties as more prominent than the benefits. I mean, who'd tell their families/friends: "I spend all my time learning fascinating things, getting relevant skills to help others, and talking to great people about important topics?" That just doesn't sound right; so it makes sense that people tend to focus on "how hard things are" rather than "how good things are." I'm sure they had other challenges, of which I was unaware. But as much work as it was, I compared it to my previous life in construction, and would tell myself on my harder days: "At least I'm not carrying a 36-foot ladder through the mud in 36-degree weather."

I got another job not too far into my program, and was able to quit the food service gig. I got a 10-hour/week GA position in the Graduate School office; the very office enforcing rules for grad students, including the one that said grad students couldn't have more than 20 GA hours/week. Here I had a total of 30 GA hours/week, with 20 in my department and 10 in the Grad School. Thus, I found most school rules can be bent, in the right circumstances. I was the assistant to the Office Manager, Peg, who was very knowledgeable and quite maternal towards me. I was grateful for her thoughtful support. She ran all the major operations, on behalf of the Graduate Dean, who was a nice and scholarly woman. I was a secretary. Having had filing experience with Sunlight, I was able to quickly handle the main tasks. Aside from Peg, all the other older workers in the office had a real aversion to computers, which were relatively new on the scene in 1998. They were all happy to let me do anything that involved computers and the Graduate School website. I'd taken a computer course at CPCC. I started at CPCC with an electric typewriter. Around the time I went to UNCC, I got a DOS computer. By the time I got to Appalachian, I had a Windows-PC. Everyone but Peg wanted things to be the way they'd always been before computers, but that wasn't how it was going to be. Thus, I saw how well-meaning and otherwise competent people often resist even the most basic (and potentially beneficial) changes to the point of serious counter-productivity. I became a top-notch secretary and learned all kinds of things that benefitted me as I went through grad school and into my career.

In my Department GA, I worked for Dr. Wolf, an older Professor, running his Educational Psychology laboratory. He did a lot of testing of computer programs, on very basic and old machines, so I had to figure out a lot of obscure software. I also supervised students doing make-up tests for a variety of professors. One of those professors, Dr. Skippe, was 'way out there,' and had a student in there taking a make-up test one afternoon. She was looking through the textbook while she took the test. She actually had the audacity to ask me for an answer to one of the questions, saying "Do you know anything about the Super Ego?" I said, "Only that you don't appear to have one." She didn't get my joke, of course. So, I did my duty as a Proctor and went to ask Dr. Skippe if he let students use the book on his tests. He said, "Egads,

No!" He went and set her straight and let her finish the test, unaided by the book or me.

Luke had an anecdote he related about Skippe, when he found out I'd met him. Luke was at a crowded bar when Skippe, whom he'd never met, came up to him and said, "That guy over here just hit me in the face!" Luke asked, "Did you deserve it?" to which he replied, "I don't think I did!" But a young woman standing beside him said, "He absolutely deserved it!" Once coming out of the grocery store the night of a full-moon, I saw him in the parking lot, literally howling like a wolf, into the sky. He'd been suspended the year before I'd arrived, apparently for showing pornography to one of his classes, for what he said were "educational purposes." Dr. Skippe thus had quite the reputation for oddity. And, he was a 'long-hair' like me, so I thought if he could be a Psychologist, perhaps I could make it, as well.

I ran the Educational Psych lab well, and Dr. Wolf let me put together a research project based on his data and present it at a professional conference. That was my first real research project, outside of the one I'd done in the Methods class in undergrad. I was pretty intimidated by research in general, as I never felt I had the hang of statistics. I'd made a 'B' in undergrad stats, and it was one of the hardest grades I'd ever earned, other than my 'A' in General Chemistry for non-majors.

I was now in Dr. Zarb's graduate statistics and methods class, and this guy was brilliant beyond understanding, but not much for niceties. Zarb kept telling us all we understood what we were doing, though all but one of us disagreed. The one who disagreed was brilliant with statistics, and she'd tutor the rest of us. He said we'd be taking a test his entire class had failed the previous year, which was more than a little daunting. She asked him bluntly, if he'd make it a take-home test. I was impressed she had the guts to ask that, and figured he'd shoot her down. Instead, he thought for a moment and said "Okay." I worked on it at home, with the benefit of all my notes and the book, which were permitted. I logged my hours on the task, which totaled just under 24 across 3 days. When I got it back, I made something in the low 90s. It was no wonder everyone failed the previous year, as they had to do the same test in class, in just 3 hours.

While most students didn't like Dr. Zarb because he was difficult to grasp and not pleasant in his dealings with us, I looked for a sign he was an okay guy, and found it one day when he said: "I have an undergraduate class taking a test on Saturday, and I have a daughter turning 4. She's having a party and I'd like to be there…would one of you proctor the test for me?" I said to myself, "Yep, I knew it, he's totally human…he has a daughter and he loves her." So, I did that for him. And, when it came time to do the stats for the presentation I was creating from Dr. Wolf's data, and Dr. Wolf had no time to go over it with me, I asked Dr. Zarb for help. He spent 3 hours going over stats with me. He talked at a level I couldn't understand, and yet he'd really tried to help. When I took the results to Dr. Wolf, he didn't understand them either, and told me to do something much simpler, which did make sense to me, so that was good.

I found out from talking to students in Dr. Zarb's research lab, they often failed to understand him. But I discovered he cared deeply for his students, and virtually all went on to doctoral programs. Once I was sitting just across from Peg in her office, and Zarb came in to discuss something he needed from her. I'd been in his classes for a year, had talked with him directly many times, and did him the favor of proctoring that test Saturday of his (I've no idea why he scheduled a test for a Saturday). While I was literally 5 feet away, looking at him and Peg, he never once acknowledged my presence. He walked away after he was done, and Peg was offended he'd not spoken to me. I told her it was okay, that he just operated in a very different way from most people, socially, and that he cared about his students. As I was speaking to her, he popped back in, continued right where he'd left off, with me now sitting 2 feet from her. Yet he still never looked at, nor spoke to, me. He left just as abruptly, and she said "Wow, you're right; I guess he's just put together different." It was another lesson for me that one can't judge a book by its cover and that there's good in virtually everyone, if you look hard enough.

Dr. Wolf taught a class on teaching Psychology the first year I was there. I took it thinking it wouldn't be hard, without much thought to teaching as a possible professional route for me. And, I loved it. We got to design lectures, syllabi, and even 'guest teach' a class. Having been a 'front man' for several bands, I found this a natural role, being in front of people and commanding attention, for the sake of imparting knowledge that'd been imparted to me by others. The department gave me an Introductory Psychology class to teach the following year, and I've been teaching ever since. It seemed I'd found another calling.

I'd gained so much practical knowledge from my undergraduate and graduate courses in Psychology, it helped me transform myself into a better person, as a better father, and a more positive and engaged citizen, in general. I'd also learned a lot about how people suffer in this world, what contributed to their problems, and how to help them. As a teacher, I could help others obtain the same knowledge, and hopefully get similar benefits. And, I could do it in addition to helping people with mental health struggles. It became clearer to me, I'd need yet another degree, to become a doctor, to get the broadest array of career options, better pay, more control over what I did, and superior job security.

But first I'd need to finish my master's degree, and I also had to do a master's thesis, which was also a source of concern for me. While I felt I'd not mastered statistics, I was comfortable with research design and basic analyses. And, I couldn't graduate without a thesis. I finally came up with a topic, driver aggression. I found little had been published on the topic, so I thought this might work. I needed to form a faculty thesis committee. Dr. Stallard had been my Developmental Psychology instructor, and she'd been doing a lot of work on videogame aggression. Being a related topic, I thought she might be willing to Chair my thesis committee. She was a fascinating person. She was quite small in stature, but she held a black belt in martial arts. I remember she once posted a notice in the department's main office. It said she often worked in the building at night and that if she encountered anyone unannounced in a dark hallway, she'd kick their ass first, and then figure out who they were. Thus, she recommended people turn on the lights when they came in at night, and not skulk around.

She said she'd be my Thesis Chair, but also that she didn't know much about driving as a research topic, and that I should add Tim to my committee. So, I went and talked to Tim about joining my committee. After about 5 minutes of explaining my topic, he said "I think you have the wrong Tim." So, I went to the other Tim, and he agreed to serve on my committee. This Tim had been a former doctoral student of Dr. Pressley, a long-time professor at Virginia Tech (VT). When I realized I needed to get a Ph.D., Tim suggested I call Dr. Pressley, with whom he'd worked on driving research, and who was seeking a big grant from a national agency to study dangerous driving. I wasn't much for cold-calling people I didn't know, and had ignorantly thought 'networking' meant 'ass-kissing,' which is something

I'd absolutely not do. But, I took Tim's advice and called Dr. Pressley. We hit it off immediately, and talked not only about research ideas, but also about music, because it turned out he was a drummer. I then realized that in 'networking,' you generally have a lot of latent things in common when meeting people in your field. There was nothing insincere about engaging in genuine conversation. Dr. Draper, another wonderful instructor at Appalachian, was also a graduate of VT. She suggested when I went to an upcoming conference that I talk to Dr. Drummond, her former doctoral mentor. Again, it was weird opening a conversation with someone I'd never met, especially since this guy was an internationally-recognized expert on Anxiety Disorders. But, I found him at a poster with some of his students, and just like that, we found we had lots of things in common and had a delightful conversation. Like Dr. Pressley, he suggested I should come up and visit the department before they reviewed applicants.

I went up to visit VT, and Dr. Pressley. I arrived on a Saturday, and was walking around the department when I ran into a hard-nosed Professor who immediately asked me what my GRE score was. I told her, and she said "You'll have to take that again!" That was a bit shocking, as I hated taking it the first time, and didn't know if I'd be able to do any better. That was before I realized it was just a test, like any other test, and that dedicated studying on the right subjects could help anyone raise their score substantially. She asked, "Who are you going to work with?" I told her Dr. Pressley, and she said "Oh, he can get you in." I wondered what she meant by that, but she moved on and I then met with him. He said he had his own line of GA funding, since he had some major research grants. Thus, if he wanted me working with him, and as long as the clinical Professors wanted me in the program, he could write a letter to make my GRE scores a non-issue. That sounded good to me.

When it came time to apply to doctoral programs, I knew better than to apply only to Virginia Tech, but it seemed VT would be the best fit for me. And, I got an interview for their doctoral program in Clinical Psychology! When I went for the interview, I wasn't nervous at all. Typically, I'm never nervous. But, I'd taken the 'roll with the punches' attitude of the *Tao of Pooh* to heart, and figured if they didn't want me, I must be meant to do something else. I enjoyed talking to the faculty and other grad students, and they fed us interviewees a nice lunch. I felt I'd represented myself genuinely, with no sycophantic BS, and left without concern. As it happened, I got in, and so I didn't have to re-take the GRE. All seemed to be going well.

Moving again was going to be a hardship on Valkyrie, which I regretted. She'd gotten well-adjusted to her high school in Boone, and made lots of friends. But, here I was about to make her move again, and in the middle of high school. I explained it was for the good of the family for me to get a doctorate. She was sorry to leave her friends, but seemed to understand. Frequent moving had been a way of life for her, so this was nothing new. Hunter was still a preschooler, so he had no opinion on the subject.

But, I'll finish with my Appalachian experience. I'd continued to work side jobs when I could get them, and had installed windows for my sister-in-law's parents in a cabin they had in the mountains, amongst other things. I also installed windows for a faculty member in the department. Hunter was wild, and rarely slept, and went from being fine to highly agitated, back to fine, without seeming cause. I'd pulled lots of all-nighters for grad school, and was frequently in his room in the middle of the night, trying to soothe him and get him to sleep. He wound up in a day care at a local church, where Valkyrie had taken to going to services, and where she'd made friends. I always explored churches with her, serving as a kind of guide, but letting her make her own decisions, and she really liked this particular church. The day care program was a real bonus, because it was on the edge of campus. So I could take Hunter there in the morning after dropping Val off at school, and get him later in the day on my way to get her from school. He was wild there as well. One great caregiver there knew just how to handle him. One day he said he was going to "Escape!" and walked into the hallway. She said she'd followed him and convinced him she needed his help with something, and he came back in the room.

She and her husband needed some flooring installed in their bathroom, and I said I'd only charge them for the materials and $10/hour to do the work. The subfloor had rotted, so it turned into a bigger job than expected, but I explained what needed to be done, and they were willing to get extra lumber and plywood. When I finished, her husband asked if he could pay me in weed, since apparently, he was also a dealer. That worked for me, as I'd felt I shouldn't be buying weed, given the tightness of our financial situation; and yet, I couldn't seem to give it up either. I'd taken to buying a single quarter ounce bag a month, from an in-law relative, whom I could trust. I'd divvy it up into 30 of those large capsules you can get at a local herbal shop. Then I'd smoke from a bong. That way I could hit it a few times, a couple of times a day, which seemed to take the edge off my stress. But again, it never impaired me in any way. Nobody ever seemed to have anything but the highest (no pun intended) regard for me and the work I did in school or my various jobs. Still, it was a burden to 'need' weed.

At the end of the year I graduated Appalachian, I ran out of on-campus funding sources. My GA ended, as did the class I'd been teaching, as well as the internship I'd been doing in the school's counseling center. I'd picked up a lot of temporary academic and clinical jobs here and there, but none were available at that time. The previous summer I'd worked for the campus Archives office cataloging an accession of a previous President's office materials, and also as a student-therapist at a Cardiac Rehabilitation program, teaching stress-reduction techniques to people who'd had heart surgeries. But this summer nothing seemed available, and it'd be a couple of months before we moved, so I needed extra work. I was working nights part-time at the gas station around the corner from my house, which was convenient, but that was a low-paying, part-time job. I'd occasionally have a student in the store say "Hey! You're my Psych teacher!" And, I'd reply, "Yep, and I'm also your friendly neighborhood gas station attendant."

By this time, Hunter was in the on-campus pre-school, where he'd adjusted well, and was as convenient as the church. It had the added bonus that it was a training facility for education majors, who were attuned to the individual learning needs of all the children. There was a kid there whose dad, Dave, was the manager of the Ring Clean Carwash in Boone. That was a franchise location of the same company I'd worked for as a teenager. Knowing that workforce was high in turnover, I asked him if I could work a few months in the summer and quit when I was ready to move. He said that would be fine. So there I was again, working as a buffer of vehicles. The crew was mostly younger college students, and I was an older long-haired guy always wearing mirrored shades. Having a family and lots of responsibilities to attend to when not at work, I didn't hang out with the kids after work, as they hung out with each other. And they didn't seem inclined to talk to me, so I didn't get to know them. They thought I was an undercover cop or

DEA agent, scoping the place out and looking to bust them, as most smoked weed. Dave thought that was hilarious and didn't do anything to set the record straight with them, so we had some laughs over their talking to him about who they thought I was.

One day the Preacher from Val's church came to get his Cadillac detailed at Ring Clean. He and I'd had a couple of interesting theological discussions when the kids had become part of his church. He held a doctorate in Theology, so talked deeply on a lot of topics. I'd gone to one of his services where he did an entire sermon using Freud's Psychoanalytic Theory as the basis. I thought it was fascinating to see the kind of reach Freud had, showing up as a central theme in a Baptist church sermon. He did a great job with it, and made it completely relevant to Christianity, though Freud himself was not a fan of religion. In one of our discussions, he'd offered me a parking pass so I could park on the edge of campus for free. I took him up on that, because I often had to park off-campus and walk over. I think he thought I'd join the church with this incentive, which I didn't do. I'm not much for joining any group, even if I totally support their mission, which I did in this case. It was a great church, and filled with good people. Anyway, I wound up detailing his car that day, and he had no idea how to interact with me in this new setting. I was very friendly, but he was awkward. He tipped me a dollar and drove away. People can sometimes be very odd when they encounter one another outside of traditional roles.

The house we lived in had a lot of flood damage, being located next to a creek in a 100-year flood zone. They'd done lots of commercial development upstream the previous decade, adding parking lots that created far more runoff. The water problems were so frequent that all the sheetrock in the basement had become molded. The first thing I did after we moved in, was to strip it all off the studs and get it out. As noted, Val had asthma, so half a house of mold was the last thing she needed. Dad had a sump-pump system installed to prevent further water damage. My intention was to get around to putting up new sheetrock and finishing the whole basement, to improve the re-sale value. But with all my other jobs and duties, I never had the time. I did replace the floors in the kitchen and dining room, with some close-out ceramic tile, to keep the costs down for Dad. I also did several other upstairs improvements. Having put a lot of work into it when I could, I was hoping he'd be able to make a profit when he sold it. As it turned out,

FEMA declared half the neighborhood a disaster area of sorts because of the dramatic increase in regular and severe flooding. They bought the homes on our side of the street and bulldozed them. They paid market value, so Dad did make a little cash, though not much. He was able to roll that money over and buy another house in Christiansburg, VA, about 10 miles from Virginia Tech. Again, I was Blessed in how things worked out. It was only about a 15-minute drive from VT, and we were a couple of blocks away from Val's new high school.

Chapter 12

Phase VII, Moving On, Again

Thus, we moved again. Luke had helped me move a couple of times in Charlotte, and in moving to Boone. He helped me again in moving to Virginia. He's as awesome as a person can be, and I don't know what I'd have done without his help. I always rented a truck and moved us myself, as I couldn't afford a moving service. I still had all my grandfather's tools, and a house full of junk I'd picked up along the way from yard sales. Luke told me, jokingly, if I didn't get rid of at least half of it, he wouldn't help me move anymore. We got settled in at our new Christiansburg home, and I started up the program to become a doctor.

Michelle decided she wanted to be a Realtor. I was game for her doing anything that might make some money, and learned the hard way that Realty isn't easy, nor cheap. Being smart, she got her license in short order, and started working for a national franchise. Realtors have all kinds of fees to pay to just be in the business, which amounted to hundreds of dollars a month in her case. The only way I had to handle that was by credit card. Within several months it ran to a few thousand dollars' worth of debt. She only sold one house before she quit, and the commission didn't come anywhere near to paying down the debt. So there I was with new money owed, and no additional money coming in. She never worked steady, so that was just the way it was, and she did no additional work of note while in Christiansburg.

Val adjusted quickly to her new high school, and started making friends. She joined several clubs and the marching band, where she soon became the lead snare player, leading the band onto the football field during games. She'd become a drummer in junior high. I was all for her being a musician, and she needed a snare to join the school band. I bought her a really nice one, 'on time,' making $15 payments each month, for a couple of years. It was worth it. I remember complaining about the cost to Spook one day, who'd amassed a really nice kit with Creature Sack. He gave me $5 and told me to put it in the 'drum fund.' I said "What about contributing to her college fund?" Spook said, "No way man! I don't support Education!"

While in Boone, I'd not only received the Alumni Fellowship, but also another scholarship, which one semester left me with $400 after all my books and fees had been paid for; so, I went to a pawn shop and bought a used drum kit. I'd always wanted one and thought when would I ever have an 'extra' $400? Spook later gave me some of his old, cracked (but functional) cymbals, so I didn't have to buy any more. I still have the kit, and the cymbals (I sentimentally kept them, as we lost Spook from this world). Hunter, who's become a great rock guitarist and drummer, keeps the kit at his house.

I'd always told Val she was a 'drama queen,' and that she should get into acting. Having been in the theater gig at CPCC, I met lots of very dramatic actors. I said it mostly to aggravate her when she was in a tizzy over something, and she'd always get more dramatic when I did. But she took me up on it at her new school, and got the lead in a couple of plays. She was an outstanding actor, as I predicted. She could also sing and dance, which made her a triple threat. She also met a really nice kid there, Alan, and they started dating. His parents had been born in Puerto Rico, and his father was a physician and a US Army veteran, and his mom stayed at home to raise him and his brothers. They were wonderful people, and I was grateful for the way they took to Val, and were supportive of them both. Of course, I had no problem with his ethnicity whatsoever. Not so for Val's grandfather, Michelle's father, Doyle, who'd give her a hard time for dating a "Hispanic," though he used racial epithets instead. Doyle had gotten used to me, a long-hair for whom he'd had initial disdain when I'd married his daughter. I was never a 'holier than thou' type, having been prejudiced before myself. But, I wasn't just going to sit around while he spouted his racist views at my daughter.

One day Doyle was visiting which happened only very rarely, and Alan came by to respectfully meet his girlfriend's grandfather. Doyle was totally dismissive of him. We were watching football on TV, and one of the guys ran in a touchdown, and did a triumphant bobbing up and down of his head. Doyle said "Why to those 'n-words' always do that?" I said, "You mean why do African-American football players celebrate when they score a touchdown?" He said, "Yeah!" I said, "Probably because it's difficult to do, and your team benefits when you pull it off, and you feel pretty excited about your accomplishment…I don't play, but I imagine I'd do something similar, if I did that." Doyle then let it go. About 5 minutes later, Alan said, "Well, I have to get going." I knew he was feeling uncomfortable, so I went out with him, and said "I'm sorry about Doyle. He doesn't know better." Alan said, "I know; it's okay. I've dealt with a lot of racism growing up, being in the only Hispanic family in town. Nobody ever 'means' anything 'bad' by it, but it gets old."

Doyle was pretty abusive, physically and verbally, to Michelle growing up, and he was very opinionated on most matters. So it was always somewhat edgy when we visited him or when he came to our house, though again, he rarely came. I recall he visited us in Charlotte right after Hunter was born, and was staying with Michelle's sister, Tammy. When he came to our house, I had Val on a grounding for the day, for something she'd done. He got angry because I only let her come out of her room for a few minutes to visit him. He said "You should just whip her, if she acts up!" I told him that wasn't how I operated, and it was fine if he didn't like it, but I had to stick to the punishment. I said he was welcome to hang out with her in her room as long as he liked. Of course he wouldn't do that, and he left shortly thereafter. Later that night, he called me. He said he was sorry he'd gotten upset with me, and that he respected the way I was trying to raise his granddaughter "right." I said I appreciated the gesture, that she'd be off grounding the next day, and that I hoped he'd come visit with her. He didn't. Doyle was an ornery fellow, and a product of his own rough childhood. He'd grown up working hard on a tobacco farm with his brothers and no mother (she died when he was very young). Getting beaten was pretty common for them. And racism was just 'the way it was' in his experience, so he'd come by it 'naturally.' Eventually, we got along well. He even made me the Executor of his will, because he trusted me. However when he died, complications with his daughter prevented me from serving in that role.

Things were getting really bad again with Michelle's drinking in Christiansburg, and it was frequently a 'Jekyll and Hyde' scenario. At times, she'd act absolutely 'demonic.' She was terrible about tearing into Val verbally, over nothing at all usually. She'd accuse Val of doing drugs (which she didn't), having unprotected sex (which she didn't), being a terrible daughter (which she wasn't), and so on. They'd argue, where Val only tried to hold her ground, which never worked. Val would always try to disengage, but her mom would follow her wherever she went and continue her verbal assaults. She was never physically abusive to Val that I saw, but she physically intimidated Val a lot. I tried to intervene when I saw this happen, and that would just make me the target, and I'd get the same treatment. But I'd always rather have it been me than Val, as I was an adult and had learned how to manage my own anger fairly well, though not completely. Her accusations of my 'cheating,' being a 'pot-head,' amongst many other vile things I'd never done, were relentless. She'd occasionally physically attack me, and I'd just take it, or try to get out of arm's reach. At this point, I'd had my non-violent commitment tested many times, and never retaliated physically. However, I'd argue back and scream back, at times.

This made life very difficult on me and my kids. After weeks or months of this 'craziness,' she'd sober up a while. During those brief breaks, she'd admit to having been out of control, apologize profusely, and promise it'd never happen again. But, it always happened again. During our 15 years together, she did some form of rehab 6 times, and it always seemed promising at first. But, sooner or later, and usually sooner, she'd be back to drinking, justifying it because she was depressed, anxiety-ridden, and/or in physical pain. Nonetheless, the kids and I stuck it out the best we could.

She'd had a hysterectomy while we lived in Boone, and they also took out a lot of the fibroid growths (where they'd also removed some when we lived in Charlotte, contributing to the bills Sunlight never paid). So while that issue had gotten better, the degenerative disc problem had only worsened. People in chronic pain often self-medicate and/or get addicted to opioids, and/or alcohol, and/or other drugs, and from a clinical point-of-view, it's hard to blame them. But, living with the disastrous results of massive addictions and 'crazy' behavior makes it impossible to maintain a wholly clinical and objective stance. Her "but you're a pot head" accusation became null and void, soon after we'd arrived in Christiansburg.

Dr. Pressley had a very active research laboratory, with a postdoctoral fellow in charge of major projects, several graduate students besides me, and a few dozen undergraduate research assistants. The postdoc was Kenny, and he was a happy-go-lucky guy who'd graduated, but never left as he was able to make a pretty good living off grant money, as they'd stayed perpetually funded. He was also a partier, and smoked a lot of pot. He was very friendly with many of the undergrads, as he supervised a lot of their research. And, he had connections with a few of them to get his weed. The first semester I was there, I had no weed, and I wouldn't ask undergraduates to sell me marijuana. I had no supply, but I'd still not 'quit' per se. One day Kenny asked if I wanted to get high, and I said "Absolutely!" I thought we'd go to his place or something, so I went with him to his truck. But instead of leaving, he fired up a bowl right there. It hit me that we were the only vehicle left in the lot. Thus, the VT police could roll up on us, and if they did, I'd be arrested, my name would be in the paper, and everything I'd worked for up to that point, would be gone. That was it for me. It wasn't a moral thing, and I certainly never feel superior to others who use. I'm happy for others to make life choices as they see fit (assuming they don't hurt others). I decided right then and there: I was done with weed.

I told Michelle, and of course she never believed me, needing to have something to 'hold over' me. I also told Val, and she was proud of me, which made me feel good. I was generally becoming a better person, and while I'd quit for practical reasons, I soon found another, more personal reason to stay committed to my new sober lifestyle. I always figured myself to be a pretty 'hard core' person, and never backed down from challenges. Krull once said, in a brief attempt at quitting drinking, "Sobriety Sucks!" I had to agree. I'd not been able to quit drinking or weed back when I hung out with Krull. Life can be beautiful, certainly, but it's also full of pain, both physical and emotional. And here I was without having any sort of 'buzz' with which to escape bad times, anymore. I thought there's nothing more 'hard core' than living a sober life, taking everything, good and bad, as it comes, and not retreating into a 'buzz' for solace. Thus, living 'clean and sober' became one of my life's enduring missions.

Working with Dr. Pressley at VT, I'd taken the lead on revising the dangerous driving grant they'd submitted to a major government agency, and we were awarded just over $99,000. Dr. Pressley made me the Grant Manager, which was helpful because I was able to make a little money on the side. I also was successful in authoring another grant to get a driving simulator, in collaboration with other faculty in our department and another department. I wasn't what they call the Principal Investigator, but I'd initiated the process and did all of the writing, though Dr. Pressley did some editing. I was becoming a fairly successful researcher, in addition to becoming a more skilled Therapist. My clinical training was pretty intense, as was my course load, and I was putting together a substantial dissertation made up of 4 separate studies. Having come with a master's degree in hand, and a thesis that the VT department approved, I was moving through the program at what I found out was a record pace. And, I was making great grades as well.

The stress of my home life only increased, as my academic and work life remained very busy, though very productive and successful. Michelle began to threaten me to the point I worried something serious might happen, likely while I was asleep. I had to reveal this to someone I could trust. Dr. Pressley wasn't actually a Clinical Psychologist, and thus wasn't as directly involved with my overall doctoral program. So I talked with Dr. Drummond, who I knew would keep what I revealed confidential, unless something happened which suddenly took me out of the program, in which case I knew he'd speak up on my behalf. I thought I could potentially wind up in the hospital, and miss classes or important meetings without warning, which would be unacceptable. It was a relief to be able to tell someone, and he was totally understanding and supportive. Much later, after we divorced, Dr. Pressley said "I never knew anything was wrong!" I said, "I know, because it was nobody's business but mine, and I had to take care of my own business without putting it on anyone else." I told him I'd let Dr. Drummond know what was happening, just in case I needed a hasty advocate. Dr. Pressley had known Michelle from coming to our house every month or so, to play music in our basement, which we enjoyed a lot. She was fairly put-together when he'd come over, and sometimes even sang with us. She sang at his wedding, and did great. She was quite talented, and when 'put-together,' was kind and charming, and a 'hit' with everyone. So, nobody outside of our house really knew what was going on, except

Tammy, who was long-aware of her sister's issues. A few years later, I informed Dad when it got so bad that I needed some external assistance.

As noted, Val was in high school, and was involved in lots of extracurricular activities, and taking a ton of shit from her mom. I'd come home to hear 2 very different sides of what 'had happened.' I tried to be diplomatic, and not completely believe either was completely 'right' or 'wrong.' I'd try to calm tensions and get them to move past whatever conflict had occurred. Val had continued to date Alan, and they were quite the couple. He knew what she was going through, and was always sympathetic. With his support, she was able to cope remarkably well with the situation. Hunter was very young, and none of his mother's vitriol of was directed at him at that point. Thus, while he frequently heard and saw lots of loud arguments, and heard a lot of horrid accusations hurled at me and separately at Val, he seemed to be okay.

As I neared finishing my classes, I had to apply for a pre-doctoral, year-long, full-time internship. That's required in order to get a doctorate in an APA-accredited program, and ultimately to get licensed as a Clinical Psychologist. I only applied to 2 local sites, one at the VT Counseling Center, and the other about 45 minutes away at a Veterans Administration Hospital. I knew this was a bad strategy for getting placed at an internship. The process is highly competitive, and as with grad schools, one should apply to well over a dozen sites, to best ensure 'matching' with one. But, I wouldn't apply to any that would require me to move Val again, as she'd be entering her senior year of high school that upcoming year. Having moved her twice before for my continued education, from her Charlotte friends and then from her Boone friends, I couldn't bear to pull her out of high school in her senior year. I got interviews at both sites, and I thought they went well. But, I didn't get 'matched' to either one. This wasn't a big deal from my view, as I was still working as Project Manager on the grant, and could still work as Dr. Pressley's GA. In this latter role, I was in charge of all tests and recitation sections of his Intro Psych course. The course had 1,200 students, and was the biggest in the department. It had 30 or so recitation sections, where other GAs covered material in additional depth. I was in charge of training and supervising 14 GAs, and keeping everything running smoothly. They always had a GA dedicated to the course, and the department Chair thought I did a good job. So, I'd still be able to make money if I didn't get an internship that next year, and I'd be able to complete my dissertation, while Val finished high school. I'd just apply to more sites the next year, and be free to move wherever we needed to go. But in that spring, I got a call from the VT Counseling Center, which usually had 3 pre-doctoral interns each year. They'd lost a staff member and their budget was tight. So, instead of hiring a new staff member, they decided to add a fourth intern. They knew I was local, and asked if I'd be interested in the position. Of course, I said "YES!" That way, I'd be able to keep running the grant, stay involved with Dr. Pressley's lab, do my dissertation, and polish off the internship hurdle (which was slated to be 40-hours per week, but actually took up about 50 hours a week on average), all at the same time. With all of that, and the pressures at home, I was pretty stressed, but never seemed to identify that way.

One day during my internship year, I had an 'episode' in the grocery store parking lot. Both of my legs went weak, and trembled a bit. It persisted for about 20 minutes, and only subsided after I'd gotten home and put up the groceries. My paternal grandfather had major bypass surgery about 10 years earlier, and my Dad's brother also had some cardiovascular event that put him in the hospital briefly, a few years prior. Plus, I'd worked in a cardiovascular rehab facility that one summer, and knew the symptoms of a heart attack, but this didn't seem to fit that description. However, I also knew the cardiovascular system was complex and that I might be experiencing atypical symptoms. I began to wonder if I had a heart issue. Having struggled with my weight off and on, when I could afford to eat more than just in a subsistent fashion, and not having any alcohol or weed to help me deal with stress, I'd taken to stress-related overeating. I never liked exercise of any kind, and was pretty much a sloth. Being a glutton and a sloth, I was overweight again, and knew eating the junk I tended to consume put me at heightened risk for cardiovascular disease. With the negative heart history on Dad's side of the family, I decided I should consult a cardiologist. Again, Dad set me up to be able to get health insurance for the family. Though I'd never used it myself, at this point I thought I'd be foolish not to do so, and made an appointment with a heart specialist.

After the physician reviewed my medical history, which was negligible (I'd had the tonsillectomy and broken ankle, but that was it), I gave him the run down on what had happened. He actually laughed at me. That seemed a totally inappropriate response. Eventually, I'd go on to train medical students (as well as nursing and doctoral pharmacy students) in communication skills. As this guy demonstrated, not everyone provides healthcare equally well. He concluded I'd had some kind of anxiety attack. I said that was ridiculous, as that was my area of clinical expertise, and that I'd treated dozens of anxiety-suffering patients myself. He asked if I was under any stress, and I said I wasn't stressed, just busy. He delved in a little further and asked about my daily routine. I told him I was a research laboratory Coordinator, doing a dissertation, running a major grant, working 40 to 50 hours/week as a Psychology intern with about 25 regular clients and lots of training activities, and that I had a teenage daughter and young son I looked after. He said, "But, you're not stressed?" And it hit me: I was. He sent me out with a new perspective. I then made a commitment to myself to eat less and get in better shape.

Val and Alan graduated from high school, and both got accepted to Radford University, where they'd be attending the following fall. When she started college, Val had no job. She didn't really need one because she lived at home. Alan had a part-time job and paid for all their dates. They often did things with his parents, who were well off financially, like going to movies, out to eat, and taking skiing trips. With Dad's help, Val had lived a life of considerable privilege, going to good schools, having a room of her own, having a computer and the Internet, plenty to eat, etc. My Dad always gave Gwen $400 at the beginning of each school year, from the time Val started junior high, to take Val shopping for fashionable clothing. He didn't want her to have to rely only on clothes I'd get from thrift stores. Gwen was also much invested in my kids, and showed them lots of love. So, other than the ever-escalating conflict with her mom, Val did well materially, and got lots of support from me as well as from Alan and his family. Doyle and Tammy got together and bought Val an old Toyota, when she graduated high school. So, Doyle had his brighter moments as a grandfather.

The escalation between Val and her mom continued as she started college. Hunter was in kindergarten near VT, and continued with 'after school' care at the pre-K facility he'd been in previously. So I dropped him off and picked him up each day. It seemed every time I got home, Michelle was ranting that Val had started arguments with her. Val would say the exact opposite. It was exasperating, and at that point, I wasn't really sure who was at fault, not having actually seen the conflicts. Val was strong-willed, and I'd taught her not to take flak from people, if she didn't deserve it, or if it was inappropriate criticism. So it was theoretically possible, though highly unlikely, as she was a peaceable child, that on rare occasion, Val was firing on Michelle. I finally told Val her one obligation for continuing to live at home, was to avoid conflict with her mom, at all costs and by whatever means were necessary. She agreed. Alan's family being aware of the problem, had offered for Val to come live with them, in their guest bedroom. But the peace just wouldn't last. One day I came home, later than usual, and the two had been into it heavy. Michelle again claimed Val started it, and said that she had to go.

So, I told Val she had to move out. It was the hardest thing I'd ever done and I felt absolutely horrible. I just thought it was the only course of action, and would ultimately make everyone's life more tolerable. So she took Alan's family up on their offer to move in with them. They got a truck and I helped them pack up all her stuff. I followed them over to help unload. I never cried much as a kid, and almost never as an adult; but the entire way over to their house, following the truck, I cried. I composed myself before getting out of my car. I figured Val had enough to deal with, without seeing her dad in tears. I thanked Alan and his parents profusely. They were gracious and said they were happy to help.

Val then got a job, and she and Alan made plans to get married. His parents agreed to co-sign for an apartment they could live in, where Val could live there on her own until they married. My contribution was to install a new vinyl floor in their kitchen, as the place was old and in need of updates. After they married, they moved into the place together, and Val continued working. She soon dropped out of college, being unable to focus on her studies with all the major changes coming her way fast and furious. She'd withdrawn from her classes, instead of taking F's, which made me feel good, as I'd always told her that withdrawing was better than flunking. Withdrawing preserved her GPA, and that helped in picking up the pieces and going back when she was really ready. She did go back, and did very well.

Much later, after a decade of marriage, Val and Alan split up for reasons I'll not go into, other than to say it wasn't her fault, and I think they did their best. They're still friends, but she'd not found a career of her own, living in a college town up north, where he'd been going to graduate school for several years. But she was fluent in Spanish and had been working as a secretary in an elementary school. She'd worked with a lot of Hispanic families and their children, often serving as an interpreter for the parents, and helping the kids adjust as they entered the school system. She found her calling. She later started a job as an entry-level, bachelor's degree-level, Social Worker, with a heavy caseload and not a great salary, but it was fulfilling. As of the moment I'm writing this, she was recently accepted into a graduate program to earn her master's degree in Social Work, and is thus preparing for a full career. I couldn't be more proud of my daughter.

I finished up at VT, and did well. I'd won the Outstanding Graduate Student Award in 2002, served in the graduate student governing body (as I'd done at Appalachian), as well as an award for my dissertation. As I was preparing to graduate in May of 2003, I was on the job market. I thought I'd have a great shot at an Assistant Professor's job in a university Psychology Department. However, while I had a great academic record and excellent clinical training experiences, I only got one phone interview, and didn't get that gig. I was now used to 'rolling with the punches,' and started looking into Postdoctoral Fellowships. I really didn't know what was wrong with my CV that I didn't get more interviews, given I'd applied to around 30 positions. It was disheartening, but I had to get a job, as staying on at VT in the Psych department wasn't really an option. Dr. Pressley didn't have enough grant money to keep me on as a second postdoc, already having Kenny there. Since I wasn't a student anymore, I couldn't continue as a GA, nor would teaching a class or so a semester as an Adjunct Faculty Member really cut it for us, financially speaking. And, I just couldn't keep relying on Dad's generosity, having finished up my graduate school years.

Chapter 13

Phase VIII, Sorting Out Some Things

I was going over Postdoc options with Dr. Pressley, one of which was at the University of Memphis. He said he knew a Professor in the Psych department there, whom he'd gone to college with, and told me to give him a call. That was Dr. Dreyfus, and he was quite the character. He'd been there a few decades and said he'd never had a Postdoc before, and that therefore the department "owed him one." I got an interview, and they hired me. So, I was now a Clinical Psychologist, working in the Industrial/Organizational (I/O) wing of the Psych department. Dr. Pressley was really an I/O Psychologist, and Dr. Dreyfus was an I/O Psychologist as well. Dreyfus had hundreds of thousands of dollars in grants with the state, to help reduce DUIs and enhance police computer systems. As most of my own work had been in driving safety, the gig was a good fit. Hunter got into the elementary school on campus, so I could take him in the morning and pick him up in the afternoon.

I got my own office with a window, which was very cool. I still had a mini-fridge I'd found in the church parking lot in Boone, where some college kid abandoned it with a sign that said "Take Me!" taped to the front. I still have it. Thus, I could take food to work, to keep from having to buy lunch. Dreyfus was very controversial in the department, being big, loud, and the antithesis of politically correct. I found him very amusing. In my first meeting with his research students, he announced, "This is Dr. Sage, only he's not really a doctor, because he's Clinical." I said, "That's funny Dreyfus, because I was thinking you weren't really a doctor, because you're not Clinical." He just smiled, and we had a jovial relationship the entire time I was there. Dreyfus took me to the top floor one day, which was exclusively for animal research. One of the professors saw him and said, "What are you doing up here, Dreyfus?" He said, "I have the most grant money in the department, so I'm going to take over the top floor and throw you doofuses out; I'm looking to see which office I want." At one point I was working on something for him, but headed to a conference to present my dissertation findings. I said, "Dreyfus, I'll be out of town a few days, and won't be able to work on your stuff until I get back, because I don't have a laptop." The next morning, he came into my office and plopped a new laptop at my feet, and said "Here! I hate whiners!" I laughed and said I'd only been telling him the situation, and wasn't complaining. He smiled and said, "I know." He hooked me up with the lead authorship on a research paper he'd had in mind, and set me up as Principal Investigator on a small grant with the U.S. Navy, both of which were big deals professionally. Dreyfus took good care of me.

When I moved to Memphis, I bought my first house, where Dad loaned me the down payment. Blessed and privileged, again! It was small, old, and relatively cheap, but it was mine, which was a great feeling. I was getting about $35,000/year, with an option of staying for 2 years. I could make my house payments, cover my bills, and get plenty of food. Thus, all the education I'd amassed allowed me to live a very good life! It was 8 miles from the U of M, but it took me a half hour to drive there, due to the traffic. And that was if no train stopped traffic completely. There were metal bars on all the windows, and metal security doors on the front and back. The first week a police helicopter came over the house every night and spotlighted the back yard, moving up a few doors before leaving. I wondered what kind of neighborhood I'd moved to, if there was a cop chopper checking it out every night. As it happened, it was a great neighborhood, and the guy who lived next door was the officer who flew the police helicopter. He worked the night shift and spotlighted the area as a way of saying 'Hello' to his wife. They were both huge NASCAR fans, and so was Hunter, so we had lots of great conversations, where they'd talk driver stats with Hunter. They also invited us to watch races on their big screen TV. We had other great neighbors, and I loved living there.

Before the trip I was going to take to the conference mentioned above, Michelle got really paranoid about her and Hunter's safety in my absence. She wasn't drinking much right after the move, so I didn't worry about leaving her with Hunter for a few days, but she was still extremely anxious. The fact we had a cop living next door didn't soothe her fears. She said she needed a gun for protection. So, exercising my second amendment rights, I got an inexpensive shotgun, which was the first and only gun (other than a BB gun) I've ever owned. I took her and Hunter to the local range, to show her how to load and fire it, and to make sure he knew as much as possible about gun safety. I locked the gun case, and stored the ammo separately, other than a single shell in a compartment of the gun case in case of an emergency. As it happened, nothing happened. When I got back, I took the shell out of the case and locked it back up. That gun later became a problem I should've anticipated, but didn't.

Memphis was a lot like living in Charlotte, and I'd loved Charlotte. It was very diverse, which was fine by me, but not for Doyle. When we were getting ready to move he said "Memphis!?! There's a lot of ni... uh...um...black people there!" He'd learned not to use certain language around me, because that meant we would have a 'conversation' he didn't want to have. I said, "Yes...and?" He said, "What are you gonna do?!?" I said, "Live as a minority for the first time in my life, and be fine." He said, "I don't know..." We were fine, of course. Hunter joined a t-ball team there, and I did some assistant coaching, and it was a great bunch of kids. I sent Doyle a picture of the team, where Hunter was only one of two White kids. Everyone was smiling, and I wrote him a note: "Just wanted to let you know all is well, and we're very happy." Things were going fine, and Michelle did fairly well, other than her anxiety and occasional binges on alcohol.

One day I was coming in to the Psych building and a professor was headed in at the same time. He asked me how it was going, working with Dreyfus. I told him it was going very well, and I enjoyed it. He said, "The way I see it, your only job is keeping Dreyfus happy." I said, "Well, I hate you think that's my job, but keeping him happy is easy." He looked surprised and said, "Easy?!? How on Earth do you do it?" I said, "I argue with him. I disagree with him on virtually all his opinions. I just say what I'm thinking, and we debate. He loves that!" The desktop computer I had was old and not able to run the stats program without lots of delays. I told Dreyfus, "I need a new computer to do our analyses. How does one go about getting one?" He said, "One goes about that by kissing my ass." I said, "I guess I'm not getting a new computer." He smiled and left. Within a week, a new computer was delivered to my office, without further comment from him.

Another Professor asked if I'd come talk to his graduate class, as they were in a course on preparing for careers, and he wanted someone to tell them what a Postdoc was like. I went and gave a short history of my background, and said, "Honestly, I didn't want a Postdoc. Before getting this job, I didn't really know what they were. I applied to tons of Assistant Professor Positions, but didn't get any interest." I said that had surprised me because I'd done so well in graduate school, and had tons of research presentations on my CV. The instructor said "Did you have any publications?" I said "Only one from my thesis." He then looked up the opening of one of their textbook chapters, and read: "Beware creating a CV of all presentations and no publications." I was dumbfounded and said, "They actually have a book on how to get Professor jobs?" He said, "Yes, that's what this class is all about." Neither Appalachian nor VT had such a class, and I'd no idea I needed publications to get into an academic job. In fact, it's a cliché that academic jobs are 'publish or perish' situations, but I'd never been told that up to this point.

I didn't know what I didn't know, so I never asked Dr. Pressley how to go about getting a Professor's position. Had I asked, I'm sure he'd have told me. Thus, getting lead authorship on Dreyfus' article was a really good thing. It was 'in press' by the end of the year, which meant I could put it on my CV as being 'virtually' published. I did a literature search of my own name, to see if my thesis article made it into the database, and it had. And apparently I had 2 other publications to my credit, as a third-author, of which I wasn't aware. I'd helped a peer with an article at Appalachian. The other was one I'd done substantial editing on, for the Director of the clinical program at Appalachian. He was second author on both, and never told me they'd been published. So just like that, with 4 peer-reviewed articles, I was more qualified for the type of job I'd hoped to obtain. I saw an Assistant Professor's job posted for the Psych department at ETSU in Johnson City, TN, near where Michelle had grown up. She had a laundry list of reasons she wasn't happy, and always said if she lived 'back home,' she'd be happy. I always found that with the right attitude, one can be happy virtually anywhere. I'd never planned to move away from Charlotte, but felt compelled to do so, and was now in my third different city in a span of 7 years. And other than the issues with Michelle, I was pretty satisfied, especially having been able to spend as much time as possible with my kids. I figured I had to give applying to that job a shot. I still had another year on my Postdoc, if it didn't work out. I got an interview, and went down to give a 'job talk' and meet the faculty and students. Apparently, I wasn't their first choice, but their first choice turned them down. So I got the gig, and have been there ever since.

Rather predictably, moving to Johnson City didn't make Michelle happier. She'd cut back on drinking in Memphis, a bit, but within months of moving, that changed. I was able to sell the house in Memphis quickly, and bought a house near ETSU. I was making more than at my Postdoc, around $43,000/year. So while it was still going to be tight, as mine was the only money coming in, I could pull off my house payments. And, it was close to a good school for Hunter and a 5-minute drive to work. Within the year, Michelle got really bad again. I was reluctant to do anything drastic, other than to leave with Hunter whenever it got threatening, where I'd take off as necessary to stay at Dad's house, about 3 hours away. At this point, Dad was aware of what was happening. Then came the incident with the shotgun, where Michelle was really intoxicated, and had been up for days, and had been relentlessly accusing me of imagined infidelities and of being a horrible person. One night she pulled the shotgun case out, and was trying to get it open (I kept the key hidden), saying she was going to kill me. While I could handle this, it was in full view of Hunter. I got the case away from her, and hid it.

A couple of years went by, and she started accusing me of abusing her, physically. As I've said, I'd become completely non-violent. So when she physically attacked me on occasion (pulling my hair was a common move, along with scratching and slapping), I'd just carefully extricate myself and go to another room and lock the door. After her most recent threat on my life, I took to sleeping in the third bedroom when she got 'crazy.' I'd take Hunter with me, set out a sleeping bag and pillows, lock the door, and press the futon against the door, with the weight of my body holding the door closed as she pounded her body against it. She cracked that door trying to break it open, as well as those of the bathrooms when I hid out in those places.

But at no point had she ever threatened Hunter, until I got a call at work from him one day. He said she'd tried to start a physical fight with him, telling him to "put up his dukes" and disconnecting the phone from the wall so he couldn't call anyone. Without Val to belittle, and without me home to accost, she'd finally turned on Hunter. He'd gotten the phone plugged back in and called me and I went and got him. He was now old enough to realize she truly had a major and unresolvable problem, and that while he'd seen me and Val go through a lot, he was going to be a target for her rage from then on. So, I talked with him about the possibility of his mom and I getting a divorce, and he was very understanding. He'd always opposed me divorcing her before this incident, and I'd read that the best predictor of kids coping well with divorce, was *perceived control*. Wanting him to be okay, I'd never taken it upon myself to try and divorce or separate from her, without him being ready for me to do so. So, I told Michelle she should move out, and that I'd help her to pay for an apartment, and that we'd be getting a divorce. She refused to go, and I had no way to 'make' her leave.

I'd never laid a hand on her, though the provocations she constantly sent my way did push me into verbal tirades on occasion, of which I'm not proud. But I had my limits in taking nearly constant unchecked verbal, and sometimes physical, abuse. But she falsely told her mother, Betty, that I'd been physically abusing her, which further complicated things. Betty had recently been so overwhelmed by her own drinking that she developed sepsis (infected flesh) all along her backside from her thighs to her upper back. This came from her being unconscious on her couch for many days, laying in her own waste. She was discovered by her landlord, perhaps hours and certainly not more than a day away from death. She was taken to the hospital, and had to spend weeks in physical therapy to regain her ability to walk, where after an extensive period of immobility her muscles had atrophied. When Betty got out, I tried to get her situated in an apartment in Johnson City (she'd previously lived a town over), so we could help her out. She apologized for all she'd done and pledged to live sober the rest of her life. That lasted only one week after she got settled in her new place. The mother of my kids and her mother, took to drinking together and commiserating, and conspiring about how to 'get' me. Once a city police car came by my house to check on my wife, because they'd received a call from Betty. That happened to be a moment of sobriety for Michelle, and she denied I'd ever done anything to hurt her, which was fortunate for me.

Once, not long after Val first moved in with us back in Charlotte, Betty called Child Protective Services (CPS) to say I'd been abusing Val. CPS came to Val's school and took her out of her fifth grade class, to interview her, and Val said she had no idea what they were talking about, and that I always treated her very well. CPS came by the house to interview me, and investigate the conditions of our home. I was offended, but realized they were just doing their job. They'd had a report of child abuse, and had to follow up. It was just so insulting that Betty had the audacity to accuse me of abusing my daughter, after I'd gone in the middle of the night to get Val away from her drunken irresponsibility. Anyway, CPS checked the home, saw the 'strike chart' I had on the refrigerator for progressive and reasonable discipline for Val. At that time, Val was understandably quite rambunctious coming into my home where I had rules, where she'd not had any living with Betty only a few months before, and being only 10-years-old. The CPS worker was impressed, and said, "That's exemplary." I said, "I learned that from a Psychology class." Between talking to Val, her teacher, Michelle, and me, they declared Betty's accusation against me to be "unfounded," and said they'd ignore any future accusations from her, and prosecute her for filing a false report, if she did it again. She never did it again. Eventually, Betty apologized for doing that to me, saying she'd been drunk when she'd called CPS, and offering me her appreciation for my deeply committed caring of Val. That's just how she rolled, alternatively sweet and 'crazy.' And, that's how it was with Michelle.

Michelle had lots of extended relatives in the area, including an aunt and uncle, and cousins, who owned a local greenhouse. One day they found her on their lawn, passed out. When they finally roused her, she'd claimed I'd been abusing her and she'd run away to them. They were part of a local church, and immediately consulted the Pastor, who was coincidentally serving on a local coalition of community members and law enforcement personnel, trying to combat drug abuse in the area. I also served on that coalition, having been recruited for my Psychology background. As it turned out, I'd not only long ago left behind my own illegal activities, but starting with Dreyfus in Memphis I'd been working along with police at state and local levels, to help deter DUI and help people get treatment for drug abuse. Again that wasn't out of some sense of moral superiority, having had my own prior addiction issues, but rather out of a sense of wanting to help others. I found there were lots of compassionate police who wanted to help people suffering from addictions, and to prevent them from putting others at risk. Anyway, the Pastor was a former law enforcement officer himself, and on hearing her accusations about my abusing her, he cordially offered to counsel us. He met with me alone first (having heard her side of the story) and I gave him the run-down on all that had happened, including her bouts of semi-psychosis, her prolonged states of intoxication, and her false accusations of me abusing her. He then sat down with her, and when confronted with the information I gave him, she relented and said my version was true. She said she didn't know why she'd accused me, and moreover, that I'd tried to help her get sober for many years and to thus help her to be the mother she really wanted to be.

This was now getting precarious for me, professionally. If she ever made such an accusation to the wrong person, and they seemed fairly random to me, it was possible it could get back to people with whom I worked, or in the press, without my being able to provide the factual narrative prior to people making negative judgments about me. So with all that'd happened with her accusations and her having accosted Hunter (and him understanding and approving of my plan to divorce her), I was resolved to do something. I called Val and asked her to come help me convince her mother to try rehab once more, hoping once more might finally do the trick. When Val came, Michelle released a torrent of abuse on her, and me, and ultimately it was Hunter who convinced her to go to rehab. Both kids went with her, and were beside her when the Counselor inquired about her bruises. The Counselor immediately assumed spousal abuse. Michelle actually denied it, somehow seeing through the fog she'd been living in. Both my kids witnessed her confession, and spoke up on my behalf, saying this had been happening for years. The Counselor asked how she got the bruises, and Michelle, again truthfully, said she had a serious problem with alcohol and blacked out a lot, fell down a lot, was prone to easy bruising, and that the bruises had been unintentionally self-inflicted.

Michelle completed their short residential treatment program, and was supposed to follow up with weekly counseling sessions and 12-step meetings. She was once again repentant, and declared her intention to stay sober, and to make up for all she'd put us through. This phase was short-lived, and she never did the follow-up she'd said she'd do. She stayed sober about 3 weeks, and was back to drinking heavily, which she always tried to hide, but where it was impossible to conceal. It got terribly bad, but still she wouldn't agree to a divorce, nor would she leave the house and separate, despite my offer to help her financially. I was at a loss for what to do.

Val had previously planned to come visit and help Hunter paint his room, which he wanted in the colors of his favorite NFL team. Michelle declared she'd "take all that paint and dump it" all over Val's car, when she arrived. I told Val this via phone before she arrived, and she said "She'll calm down when I get there." She didn't. When Hunter was at school, and I was mowing the lawn, and Val was preparing the walls for painting, Michelle confronted her, and got physical. Val came running outside, with marks on her neck where Michelle had grabbed her by the throat. I called the police. They came and Michelle said Val had attacked her, unprovoked. They saw her state of drunkenness, and the marks on Val's neck, and arrested Michelle for assault. While she was in jail, we gathered her clothes and anything we thought she might need or want, and took them all, along with our second car, to Doyle's house. We told him everything that happened, and he agreed to let her live there when she got out of jail. That happened immediately, because he bailed her out, which was fine. I gave her our second car, so she'd have transportation. She'd actually totaled another one we had previously, in a DUI episode, for which she'd also been arrested about 6 months prior to this incident. None of us wanted her to be in jail, much less go to prison, no matter all that had occurred all the years prior. So, Val ultimately dropped the charges. I changed all the locks on the house, and she never came back again. Within a week of living at her dad's place, she took up with a guy working at the convenience store on the corner and they were soon engaged.

In the process of our divorce, I had only one condition: that I would get full custody of Hunter. She got half my retirement account, and I had to buy out her half of our house. That required me to get yet another loan from Dad, and refinance the house with an increase in my loan amount, to pay him back. In the mediation process, I also offered her an additional $5,000 in cash (also borrowed from Dad) and said I wouldn't expect any child support, so long as I got full custody. She agreed. The court set up supervised visitations at first, where I'd be in the restaurant in which she'd meet Hunter, but where I'd hang back so as not to be seen by her as interfering. She moved in with her new fiancée and the visits moved to their places, which were in two different towns within a 6-month period. I'd drop Hunter off, and then go to a local restaurant or library to hang out, because within 30 minutes to an hour he'd always call me, saying she was drinking and going off about me and Val, and that he just couldn't take it. So, I'd swing by, he'd jump in the car, and we'd leave. This went on for a couple of years. Within a few more years, nearing his 16th birthday, he decided he didn't want to do visits anymore with her. I supported this, and she was furious, assuming I'd tried to turn him against her (which I didn't; he was old enough to have his own impressions of her behavior). Yet she didn't press the issue, so he was free of that experience.

On an aside, it seems stereotypes continued to plague me outside of work, where I always wore professional attire. I was at a library in a town Michelle and her husband were living, in case Hunter needed me to come get him from one of his visits (he did). It was a nice facility, with a gas fireplace. I was wearing a t-shirt, jeans, a leather jacket, and a baseball cap. I moved one of the chairs over to sit by the fireplace, while I worked on my laptop. An off-duty officer was working security, and he said "Hey hotshot! How 'bout you move that chair back?!?" I said "I'm perfectly fine to put it back when I leave, if you don't mind." He said "Put it back!" So, I complied and then went over to where he'd stationed himself. I said, "I don't know what you think, but I assure you I'm a responsible citizen. I'm actually a doctor who works at the university." He seemed quite surprised and started apologizing, saying "I thought you were homeless, and the homeless around here cause a lot of problems in the library." I don't pull out the 'doctor' title much, and try to avoid mentioning it generally. I only need the title to demonstrate my qualifications for working with patients, teaching classes or seminars, and to use on letters of recommendation I write for students seeking jobs or applying to graduate school. I don't see myself as being more important than anyone, and I just keep that information to myself where it's not relevant. But, being challenged over my moving a chair, set me off a bit, and I tossed in the 'doctor' comment. He even walked over to me later while I was sitting by the fire, and apologized more. I said it wasn't a problem and that I appreciated his changing his mind about me and the chair. About then, I got a call from Hunter, put the chair back where it belonged, and left to go pick him up from yet another ruined visitation.

Years later, Michelle wound up in a legal situation involving the deaths of Doyle and her sister Tammy, which occurred within a week of each other, having to do with their estates. She wound up in a very weird conflict with the kids. I won't go into it other than to say it laid bare the fact that money was more important to her than sharing with the kids what was rightfully and legally theirs. Both decided not to have any more to do with their mom. She'd later call relatives and friends of ours, always intoxicated from what I was told, and rant about the kids and me. When a couple of her remaining friends questioned me about my kids' loyalty to their mom, and why they wouldn't have anything more to do with her, I said it was far more complicated than they could possibly know, and they'd received only a one-sided and false story from their mom. I asked them to please leave my kids be, and said I supported their decision. I never talked shit about Michelle, and I'm not trying to do so here. It's just how it was.

Michelle actually died recently, from a combination of health issues, including liver disease induced by chronic, heavy alcohol consumption. Addiction is one of the worst things anyone can experience, and it destroys lives and families. There's a line from a KXM song that I think sums it up: "Words can be as powerful as drugs, and drugs are more powerful than love." After all I've been through, and all I've seen both personally and clinically of people consumed by addictions, and knowing alcohol is a drug (I've never understood how some seem to classify it otherwise, saying at times 'alcohol and drugs,' as if it wasn't also a drug), I believe that statement to be all too true. I'm truly compassionate about substance abuse/dependence with everyone I encounter who struggles with it, or who have family members in the throes of addictions. But it's nearly impossible to stay completely compassionate when you're living with the effects of a family member's addiction, and I wasn't always as supportive as I'd wished. I still have respect for Michelle, who was the mother of my children, and now just see it all as a terrible tragedy. She was a wonderful person when she was sober, being beautiful, smart, loving, and talented, amongst much else good. But when drunk, she wasn't herself, and eventually she lost herself completely, and ultimately her life.

After the divorce and my attempts to protect Hunter from negative situations during visitations, I was actually pretty depressed. Nobody would've been able to tell that, as I'd always been good at hiding sadness. But I spent a lot of time browsing 'Myspace,' and playing mindless computer games like solitaire, in a kind of daze, when not at work or actively spending time with Hunter, where in both cases I gave my all, at all times. And, work was going really well. But in my 'down' time, I was pretty down. And pretty lonely, though again, I wouldn't let that show. And, I was well past having 'one-night stands.' So, while I wasn't 'on the prowl,' I was interested in the possibility for a relationship. While in the netherworld of Myspace, I happened across Lynne, the goddess from high school. She was single, with Addison now a teenager, where Lynne had continued to raise her on her own. We got into online conversations, and I revealed my previous reverence for her. And, she was receptive to getting together for dinner. She lived in Charlotte which was 3 hours away, but this was an opportunity I couldn't pass up. Even if nothing came of it romantically, I really wanted to see her in person, if only to reminisce about the Creature Sack days and catch up.

So I went to Charlotte, where I took Hunter to hang out with W.B. and Jan, who were very much his uncle and aunt. Lynne and I hit it off and embarked on a long-distance dating relationship. Addison, who was about 15, of course knew who I was, as I was an old and good friend of her dad, Obie, and she was very kind to me, as well. She seemed to approve of her mom going out with me. Things became pretty intense, quickly. In many ways, our getting together long-term seemed 'preordained' in a way. Of course I thought she was gorgeous, but I'd always had tremendous respect for her independence and willingness to do whatever it took to raise her daughter well. And, she was a bright and caring person, qualities to which I'm also attracted. Within months, we'd decided to get married. She'd never been married, though she'd been in long-term relationships. I was very honest about my past, and about my need to focus on raising Hunter to the best of my ability.

We worked it out for her and Addison to move in with me and Hunter, while we prepared for our wedding. The move went well with the assistance of her brother and his wife, who were likewise very supportive of our relationship. Addison had a room of her own in the house, and got enrolled in the local high school, and seemed to adjust well. I was as committed to helping her as my step-child, as I was to my own kids. I take parenting of any type, very seriously. Though our relationship was in the 'honeymoon' phase, cracks began to appear even prior to our marriage. Lynne and I were both extremely strong-willed people, and though not necessarily disagreeing on anything major in life, we started to argue, though it wasn't anything particularly serious at the time. We had some pretty stark differences in parenting styles, and she was not a fan of the way I raised Hunter, where she thought he should have substantially more responsibilities, and be substantially more deferential to me and her as authority figures.

However, I raised Val and him to own their own personalities, and question authority. Hunter and I had a sarcastic and witty repartee where if one didn't know us, it might seem on the surface as disrespectful toward me. But, I very much enjoyed our banter, as did he, and we still do. To cut to the chase, it wasn't a very good step-parent/ step-child pairing for those two. That wasn't the only issue, by far, and after we were married, Lynne and I continued to have conflict. Conflict seemed par for the course to me for intense romantic relationships, and I was committed to being a good husband and step-father. We thought we'd work our way through our difficulties. Not to cut things too short, but also not to belabor this phase of my life, within a year it was clear that living together wasn't going to work out for the rest of our lives. I still have nothing but admiration and respect for her, but we separated and eventually divorced. In the process, we thought we might try couples therapy. As a Psychologist, it seemed only reasonable to me that if I was having struggles beyond my own ability to cope, I should seek therapy. As I always tell people who wonder about Therapists, we all have our own issues. Our jobs are not to be 'issue-free,' but to be trained well-enough to ensure our own problems never enter into our therapy with others, and to always strive to be open-minded, respectful, and supportive of our clients, regardless of their issues. And, I've always been able to do that well. An analogy I find helpful is the notion that Physicians know a lot about viruses, bacteria, and diseases, but they aren't immune to them. Therapists know a lot about all kinds of issues that commonly afflict people in life, but they aren't immune to them.

Anyway, Lynne didn't really feel the therapy was a good fit for her, which I respected, but I continued to go to individual therapy for about 5 sessions total. After all, if someone has been through multiple committed relationships, there's only one common denominator…in my case, me. People in love always think the other person is an 'angel' at first, and by the time they break up often figure their former partner to have become a 'demon.' Some relatively few unfortunate people may be deceived multiple times by partners who are actually bad people, but who put up a 'good front' at first. But, I'd wager it's most often the case that one who seems to be the victim of multiple 'demons-in-disguise,' is potentially an 'angel-killer.' It's certainly worth considering how one contributes to causing situations that lead to multiple bad relationship outcomes, if one really wants to become a better person and avoid continuing the pattern.

Being willing to be honest about myself and to work on my issues, I quickly got a lot out of the therapy. I'd been working on my various issues for some time by this point, but the process led to the Therapist giving me feedback on my patterns, which had honestly not previously occurred to me. I took stock of my tendencies, and made a commitment to make better relationship choices in the future, and to make sure I didn't contribute to their demise. If I wanted a healthy relationship, I couldn't do anything other than change myself further. So, I took responsibility for my own issues, and never faulted Lynne for being the person she was. And, we finalized our divorce on relatively good terms.

When teaching on the topic, I make an analogy between therapy and athletes/coaches. Therapists don't 'make' people better, any more than coaches 'make' athletes better. When they're doing their jobs well, coaches establish respectful/trusting relationships with athletes, observe their performances, and give them analytical and supportive feedback. If the relationship is one of mutual respect, and the athlete accepts and uses the feedback, then any improvements which result are due to the athlete's work on him/herself. The coach facilitates, but does not 'cause' the improvement. It's the same way with therapists. They also give analytical/supportive feedback, but any resulting improvements are solely due to the client's own efforts.

Chapter 14

Phase IX, Recognizing and Stabilizing

I believe even adverse things tend to happen for important reasons that we may not be able to understand at the time. Not necessarily because it's GOD's plan, but perhaps it is; I certainly wouldn't rule that out. But in 'rolling with the punches,' we can learn a lot about ourselves and life from the mistakes we make, and/or suffering we endure, if we so choose. We can become more appreciative of good times, and bad times can make us stronger. We can use life's hard lessons to become better people, and I've made this an enduring goal in my own life.

My first marriage led me very directly to change myself to become non-violent, if not perfectly peaceful at first. I'm sure she got something out of our difficulties, if only to more fully appreciate better relationships later. My second marriage directly led me to quit drinking. It also helped me figure out ways to better manage my own anger issues. Most importantly, it gave me my two children, and I'd not change anything if for that outcome alone. My third marriage led me to better understand my own relationship issues, and become better on that point. And, by Addison moving from Charlotte to my town, she wound up meeting the love of her life, an absolutely wonderful young man in every respect, whom she married. And they now have two amazing children. Thus, Lynne got a great son-in-law, and two grandchildren, whom she loves dearly. And, that wouldn't have happened if not for the relationship she and I had, regardless of its unfortunate outcome for ourselves.

My rejection of my privileged childhood, and 'discovery' of
how good I actually had it, made me realize how bad some have it.
Ultimately, I rejected racism, homophobia, xenophobia and sexism.
I'd never really had negative feelings toward people outside my own
country, nor toward women, though the music I loved growing up and
still love, contains an awful lot of sexual objectification. I can't even
hate people who hate others unlike themselves, because to me hatred
is hatred, and I reject hate. I feel I've grown a lot and worked my way
out of much ignorance, and I believe everyone has the potential to do
the same. I think everybody should be given a chance to do just that,
though I won't sit idly by when somebody inflicts their ignorant hatred
on others. Again, that's not out of some sense of moral superiority,
because I realize if things had not progressed for me as they did, I might
well have the same ignorant views I had early in life. But, I now feel I
have a responsibility to try and help make positive changes in society,
when presented with opportunities to do so.

And, if not for the path I took, I'd never have met the woman who
became the truest love of my life, Renea. It's an interesting and beautiful
story. Having ended yet another marriage, exiting with as much grace
as I could muster and accepting my own responsibility for the mistake,
I started dating this lovely woman. I'd started using Facebook (instead
of Myspace) after Addison showed me how it worked. I found I was
friends with Renea. I've got lots of Facebook friends of all stripes. I
often don't know how I got connected to them, as many are current or
former students, whom I always accept as 'friends' without personally
knowing them. I use Facebook as a means to reach out to others with
announcements of events, promotions of charity events, etc. Renea's
daughter was a student at ETSU, so perhaps that's how we connected.
In any event, being suddenly single and wandering around the 'virtual'
world, I read Renea's profile info, and found we had a lot in common.
And, she was stunningly gorgeous. I took a chance and reached out with
a message, introducing myself and wondering if she'd like to converse,
without expectations of any kind. She was thoughtful and positive in
her response, and got in touch by phone and we talked for 8 hours! We
arranged to go out for dinner, and became inseparable after our first
date.

Renea and I soon felt we were meant for one another. Of course, I
was completely honest with her about my own past, and my recently

'discovered' issues with my own patterns in my relationship history. She never judged me negatively. She'd been married once before and wasn't 'looking' for a relationship. She was completely reciprocal of my love and we got married 5 months later after a whirlwind courtship, which was blissful. She moved in with me and Hunter and we began our life together, in earnest. We've been married for almost 6 years at the time of this writing, and I've never been more in love, nor more grateful for my life's Blessings.

She shared the lyrics of a Rascal Flatts song with me, which says in part, "God blessed the broken road that led me straight to you." Yet again, with my 'roll with the punches' philosophy, I feel that's a true statement. Without all I'd been through, including my previous 3 marriages, alcohol and pot addictions, a lot of drama, as well as my dedication to self-improvement (slow as it was in coming, and as it still continues), I'd never have crossed paths with this truly amazing woman. Having made a better commitment to discovering and working on my own issues, I was finally prepared to have a relationship that didn't consist of constant arguing, nor eventual bitter dissolution. We've had a few differences, as any partners will, but they've indeed been few and far between, and always resolved with mutual esteem and peaceful discourse.

Renea's an angel on Earth, to me. She's most certainly physically beautiful, and goddess-like in that sense, but she's just as beautiful on the inside. She's kind to everyone, cares deeply for her family and friends, and compassionate. She's also absolutely brilliant. And yet for all these qualities, she doesn't see herself as anything 'special,' and doesn't recognize herself as 'beautiful.' Her humility is truly astonishing and I'm utterly humbled by the fact that she's chosen to spend her life with me. Though in many ways I'm undeserving, I'm deeply thankful for her love. I wouldn't say Renea is my 'reward' for turning my life around, but other than raising my children, my time with her has been the most rewarding phase of my life.

I had a wise supervisor, Dr. Waters, with whom I worked while accumulating my 2,000 post-doctoral clinical hours for licensure as a Clinical Psychologist. He said "Marriage should be easy." He explained while nothing between two people could ever be 'perfect,' that when two people are truly right for one another they'll resolve difficulties without drama, will always be appreciative of all they have together, and will unconditionally support one another. I now know what he meant. Renea also didn't agree with my parenting philosophy, having raised her own daughter largely with the support of her extended family, but she was respectful of my need to raise my child according to my own views. That's true graciousness.

My step-daughter is an incredible woman in her own right: caring, intelligent, and talented (she teaches fiddle and guitar for a living and is a violinist in a symphony orchestra). It's a delight to be involved in her and her husband's lives, as well as with Renea's whole family. In fact, I count as two of my best friends, my 95-year-old grandfather-in-law and 5-year-old niece-in-law. It's a joy to spend time with them. With our niece, I get to hang out with an energetic kid who loves to do all sorts of things. I often get to see life again through the eyes of an innocent and engaged child, helping me to remain appreciative of all this world has to offer. With our grandfather, the only grandparent I have left in my life, I learn from a person who lived as a child with no electricity or indoor plumbing, lived the hard life of a farmer, became a multiple award-winning fiddle-player, and who raised a huge family, all of whom revere him. He and I love to play music together, where he taught me to play bluegrass and happily tolerates what he calls my 'unique' guitar playing style. And, we write music together, on occasion.

I'll back track a bit, to speak to my career development at ETSU, which is a joy and a Blessing. As I noted, I joined the Department of Psychology in 2004. When I arrived, I had completed the 1-year postdoctoral fellowship at the University of Memphis, but it was a research and teaching position, so I'd not obtained any of the required 2,000 post-doctoral hours of clinical practice needed to get licensed. During my second year there, I partnered up with the Family Medicine Clinic to provide therapy under a provisional license, under the supervision of Dr. Waters. The deal was that he'd provide my required supervision free of charge, and I'd give a half day a week of service to the clinic, without additional pay. This also gave my department a training connection for our graduate students to shadow and work in the clinic, as we were starting up a doctoral program in Primary Care Psychology.

As it turns out, when people suffer from mental health issues, they usually don't go to a 'mental health clinic' or a Therapist in their area, but rather, they go to their Physician. That's not a bad thing per se, but Physicians are primarily trained to take care of physical health issues.

They get some basic training in frequent mental health diagnoses, like depression and anxiety, but are not trained in complex diagnostics (e.g., multiple mental health concerns, or prolonged/severe mental illnesses), and are not trained to act as Therapists. And, that's as is should be. Nobody can be an expert in everything, and being an expert in physical healthcare is daunting enough. But, those with expertise in mental healthcare are not always accessible by people in need. And, enough myths and stigma still surround mental health issues that many are far more comfortable, at least at first, going to their Physician. That's fine if it's a relatively straightforward diagnosis, and if medication were the only option for treatment, because that's the 'tool' that Physicians' have in their 'kits.' But for most diagnoses, talk therapy is just as effective as medication, has no side effects, and has less relapse associated with it. In some diagnoses, such as depression, both routes are virtually equally effective, but there's a bit of an efficacy boost (on average) when both medications and talk therapy are used. So, one needs to have information about talk therapy as an option, and needs to have access to it, in order to make use of it. However in most situations, around 2/3 of people referred to therapists by their Physicians, don't actually go. This is likely because of stigma and access issues, and perhaps with many wanting the benefit of what's seen to be an easier route to alleviation of suffering (i.e., medication), and hoping it's enough to help. Surely it is, at times. But if we really want people to have access to therapy, it makes sense to put Psychologists, Licensed Clinical Social Workers, and Licensed Counselors, where people are most likely to go: medical settings.

I remember once being asked by a Physician to see a woman he said was crying, where he thought she'd benefit from psychotherapy. I readily agreed and I'm sure being introduced by her doctor helped alleviate some concerns she would've had going to see a Therapist without having met them first. She related a history of trauma, relationship problems including abuse, and said her husband had thrown her and her kids out as he'd 'decided' he wasn't the father. There was no paternity test, and she was adamant he was the biological father, but he no longer recognized the children as his. She was unemployed and overwhelmed with anxiety and worry, both of which were long-standing issues. She said people had told her for years that she should go to the local mental health center, but she wouldn't go because as she related to me, "I'm not crazy!" I said "I don't think you are crazy. It sounds like you've led a hard life, and that you're working hard to be a good mother under difficult circumstances. What I do is help people get a good understanding of what's going on in their lives, in terms of the ways they think and feel about things and themselves. Then I help them find strategies and techniques they can try out to reduce their stress and suffering, and build up their support and coping abilities. I'd be glad to meet with you regularly, if that sounds like something you'd want to do." She accepted immediately. Thus, putting Psychologists or other mental healthcare providers into medical settings has a synergistic effect enhancing patient care.

After 5 or so years at a half day a week, I was able to go from a provisional license, to being a fully Licensed Clinical Psychologist, Health Service Provider, which I've been ever since. As noted, this also helped provide training for our students as we launched our doctoral program. I helped build that program, which was also quite fulfilling, and my hire was the first in a series designed to support its development. We've since gone from 7 faculty to 17. And while the graduate program brings me great opportunities to help students achieve their career goals, I'm just as invested in our undergraduates. In fact, I started a research laboratory with the main aim of providing experience to undergrads, as it was so hard for me to find such an opportunity when I was in their place, once I realized I needed it. I based my lab on Dr. Pressley's at VT, though I've never had the grant support he had, despite having a few grants of my own and with colleagues. Based on Dr. Pressley's model of having graduate students and highly qualified undergrads in mentoring roles, we've been able to produce around 250 professional presentations, all first-authored and co-authored by students. This gives them accomplishments for their vitae, which were unavailable to me. And, I've witnessed some remarkable transformations of others, two of whom I'll describe.

I mentored students through the McNair program, which is named after Ronald Erwin McNair, who held a doctorate in Physics, and who was the second African-American to fly in space. Unfortunately, he died in the Space Shuttle Challenger disaster. To commemorate his accomplishments, this national program seeks underrepresented undergraduates, including ethnic/racial minorities, first-generation college students, and low income students, and provides training and support for them to get into graduate programs and build careers. It's recognized that people in such groups may not have thought themselves capable of such accomplishments. The program tries to lift them into believing in themselves academically and to further their education to the highest levels. It's a competitive program, and if selected after a rigorous summer program, they're paired with a faculty mentor who's supposed to guide them. I've served as a McNair mentor to 15 such students.

Landon was one of my first McNair students. He was older than the average undergrad, and had a wife and young child. He'd worked industrial jobs up until he got his hand caught in a machine at work, which tore off two fingers. He was remarkable in many ways, but certainly he is highly adaptive. After his accident, he wasn't able to return to work, and had no idea how he'd support his family. He came across a program called Vocational Rehabilitation, which provided him funds to go to college. Like me, he started in community college. On transferring to ETSU, he heard about the McNair program and found his way into my lab as my mentee. And he took off. Landon and I worked very closely together, and he presented at several conferences, including getting a paper published in a refereed proceeding. Undergraduates with publications are exceedingly rare, and with that and his other accomplishments, he got into our doctoral program. Again, it's often not the case that graduate programs take students from their own undergraduate programs. But, our doctoral program does just that, hoping to train Psychologists and place them in jobs in our semi-rural area, to help fill the gap in mental healthcare providers. Landon is now a Licensed Clinical Psychologist, and works in a Primary Care Clinic in a very rural county in Virginia. For many in the area, he's the only mental healthcare provider to whom they have access. He's helped, and continues to help, an unbelievable number of people. His life's transformation helps others transform their own lives.

While I could relate many stories of positive transformations as a result of people obtaining higher education, I'll give just the one more example. Walter came to ETSU fresh out of prison. He'd been a drug dealer and had gotten into some serious trouble, and was in prison long enough to actually earn a bachelor's degree in English. He wound up in my senior-level History & Systems of Psychology course, and I had a paper students had to write, due near the end of the semester. Walter turned in his paper the week after it was assigned. I told him it'd be better for me if he'd wait and turn it in when it was due, so I'd not lose it in the interim. He said, "No problem dude, I'll just write another. This one only took me a few hours and some change." With that kind of seemingly casual attitude toward writing papers, I figured it couldn't have been very good, and I told him he didn't need to write another paper, but rather, to just make sure this one was as good as it could be before he turned it in with the rest of the class. But, he insisted I keep it and that he'd write another. So, I decided to go ahead and grade it, and give him feedback so he could make the one he turned in later, better. To my astonishment, it was outstanding. I didn't know his criminal history at the time, or that he had an English degree. I ran it though software to make sure it wasn't plagiarized, as I couldn't imagine a first draft from any undergrad being that good. I wasn't stereotyping, because I knew better, but he was a fairly 'rough' looking guy, stocky, close-cropped hair, beard stubble, and arms covered in tattoos. Thus, he'd been treated as 'lesser than' by many, though I'm proud to say, I wasn't one of them. Nothing in the paper had been plagiarized.

But Walter brought in another paper on a different topic after a week, despite me asking it be turned in with the rest of the class. He just enjoyed writing research papers, which is an unusual attitude. I read it and it was just as good as the first. I told him I was opening a research lab, and that someone with his writing skills, should join it, because I saw in him graduate student potential. Thus, he joined the lab, and quickly distinguished himself as motivated beyond belief. He took to research like a duck to water, and I got to know him in the process. Walter had a young daughter with his ex-wife, and still had one foot in the underworld to make extra money to provide for his child the best he could. We talked a good bit about my prior history, and how going to school had opened a whole new world of opportunity to me. He saw the light. After a year in the lab, he told me he knew he'd left his old life behind him, when he'd gone to a dealer he knew, to be 'fronted' a pound of weed. He'd planned to sell it and pay his tuition that semester. Walter said when he got in his car with the weed, he realized it was wrong, and not in his best interest nor that of his child. He said he went right back into the house, and 'returned' the weed. He said in that moment he knew he'd never do anything illegal again. As he didn't have the money for tuition, he dropped out of school that semester. I hated that for him, because he was on a roll. But, he'd been working a part-time job as well, and he went to full-time status at work and saved money to pay tuition the next semester, which he did.

Walter continued to work in the lab, and eventually became a McNair student, where he met Maude. Maude joined our lab, too, and both of them became key project members on a major grant, to which I'd been added as an Evaluator. The project had more data than they could handle. When I came on, I told the PI we needed to hire part-time data personnel. Thus, the two started working as a team, with my fullest confidence, and their help made all the difference. They not only learned how to manage databases, but also mentored a host of undergrads helping with the project. Walter became completely invested in helping others learn what he'd learned, and he and they got lots of conference presentations as a result. And, those two became an item, and are still together to this day. Walter also became an excellent role-model for his daughter. He got into school, much like me, without knowing what it could really do for him, but with a vague sense that he could make a better life for himself and his kid. Moreover, he got into a master's program, and obtained his MA. He now works for a major city, doing safety training.

Chapter 15

Phase X, My Final Frontier

I know that I'm truly Blessed, and I recognize that fact and give all my thanks to GOD. I'll spend the rest of my life trying to live up to the forgiveness, privileges, and potential given to me. I very much resonate with these words attributed to John Wesley, to "Do all the good you can. By all the means you can. In all the ways you can. In all the places you can. At all the times you can. To all the people you can. As long as ever you can." Some claim he never said that, which may be the case, but I love that credo all the same. While I'm far from perfect, and always will be, I think to improve upon ourselves, as relentlessly as possible, is a very laudable goal, and to really help ourselves, we must endeavor to help others.

While I love being able to help patients/clients clinically, I rarely do that these days, having so much going on in other realms. Instead, I focus on training our next cadre of clinicians each year. And, I love doing research and teaching students to do quality research. I've also been able to teach 8 high school classes this past year on topics requested by teachers. I've also done talks in the last year for groups such as the Kiwanis Club, the Junior Monday Club, a local regional Career Development Center, and the Johnson City Seniors Center. Further, I gave 35 seminars on campus last year, which were always open to the public, on the topics of Anxiety/Stress Management, the Science and Practice of Mindfulness, Career Planning, Developing Study Skills, and Why People Should Go to College. I also gave over a dozen guest lectures for various faculty and groups on campus last year. This is a fairly typical load of extra projects for me, annually. And, I take absolutely no money to do any of it, feeling Blessed to be able to provide such services to others for free, so they can benefit from the knowledge I've acquired, as I've benefitted. I don't do what I do for the money. If I was all about money, I'd be working in I/O or at a bigger and better-funded university, or run a private practice, or all of the above, which I could do. Where I am, we get paid in the lowest quartile, compared to others doing the same thing all over the country. However at this time, I'm making a base salary of $63,000. And where I live, that's a lot of money. The cost of living is low, and many people have to work two jobs to make ends meet. And, I've got great benefits, like health insurance (subsidized partly by the university) and a retirement account (with a small match of my contributions by the university). I know how good I have it. Johnson City is great and in a beautiful area, and the people in my community are wonderful. In terms of quality of life, I'm rich beyond my wildest dreams. I can definitely see doing what I'm doing until I'm absolutely unable to do it anymore, physically and/or mentally. We all get older and I'm okay with that, but I envision doing this job until it's no longer possible. I'm a man on a mission, and that mission is two-fold: 1) strive to be a better person every day, and 2) strive to have a positive impact in my little corner of the world.

I'll say again that learning Psychology helped me change my life for the better in many ways. Thus, part of my mission is imparting this information to others, at undergraduate and graduate levels. While it may be obvious that working with graduate students leads pretty directly to those students going on to make a positive impact in the world, it may be less obvious how I translate my mission to undergraduates. I do it by having the largest classes I can have. Loving what I do, and emulating the best of those from whom I've learned, I'm a popular teacher. I was told I was the first person to ask to teach Introductory Psychology (naturally enough, many prefer to teach higher level courses that reflect their own areas of expertise), and the first to ask to increase my enrollment cap. For many years now, I've been fortunate to have a class of 320 Intro Psych students in the fall and spring semesters. Some ask how I handle such a large class, but having been a GA in charge of a class of 1,200 students at VT, 320 is not a big deal to me. And, I have a GA of my own to help with various tasks. While many undergrads might love Psychology and become majors, as happened to me, many more will never take another Psychology course in their lives. Therefore, I've got to get as much practical information to them as possible, in one semester. I've found that for everything except the discipline's early history, I can easily show the real-life relevance of virtually everything else I teach. They can use that information to better understand themselves, better understand others, and improve their own lives and those of others.

Another way in which I strive to have a positive impact, in a persistent and consistent manner, is through the music I play. I have a band, of sorts. We play under the name 'Steven Sage & Friends,' where my Friends consist of about 25 outstanding musicians. The lineup for any given event depends on who's available. As a rule, we never take money to play events, as I've got a great day job and can perform without compensation. We frequently play charity events to help support a variety of causes. We're capable of playing virtually any event, with set ups ranging from acoustic to full band formats. We can play Rock, Celtic, Bluegrass, and Folk genres. I can also provide PA (a sound system) for small to medium sized venues for organizations who can't afford to rent gear. At this point, we've even opened for the national acts Train and James Durbin. As an example of the level of our activity, we played around 30 events last year for about a dozen charity causes and/or organizations. We also played for student organizations and festivals. We have two other rules, besides not taking money, and they are that we never practice (because technically, we're not a band, as the only thing consistent about this enterprise is me), and that we must have fun. And, we always have fun, and by extension, most everyone for whom we play, also has fun. This is a way for me to indulge one of my most long-standing passions while also doing something positive for others.

My final frontier, as I see it, is to continue on the positive path I finally set myself upon. And hopefully, I can inspire others to do the same, and where possible, assist them in doing so. Valued reader, if you've stuck with me this far (or even if you skipped to here), all I can say is Thank You for taking the time to read my story (or whatever parts you read). And, if you bought this book, I really appreciate that as well. Again (repeating from the introduction), if this book makes me back what it cost me to self-publish it, which was substantial, I'd be very happy. If it doesn't, I'll still be very happy to have simply shared it. But, if it makes more than it cost me, then I pledge to donate at least half the revenue to charity causes.

Likewise, I have to thank my parents, the rest of my family, and my friends, without whom I'd likely not be here at all, and certainly wouldn't be writing this book. Who am I, to deserve all the good things which have come my way in my later life? Nobody special, for sure. We're all deserving of having good things happen in our lives. I now think our biggest responsibility is to recognize when we make mistakes, apologize, correct them (or at least not repeat them too much), and do our best to be better people every day. With that, I'll leave you with an excerpt from the speech about *Success and Teachers in Our Lives*, lightly edited for reading vs. speaking, which it was my honor to deliver at the 2016 Spring Commencement Ceremony at ETSU. Having won the University Distinguished Achievement in Teaching Award, I was invited by our President to address the graduates. Here is that speech, in part:

"I know there are many [teachers in life] for you all as well. Thank them, whenever you have the chance. In fact, do that today. Also, thank your parents, siblings, friends, and personal mentors. And, thank the enemies who put stumbling blocks in your way. Their purpose was to force you out of your comfort zone and challenge you; and should you accept such challenges, to improve yourself. I'm not talking about the enemies who would do you physical harm, for there is no excuse for evil. But, even those who have engaged in the worst behavior, have the potential to change for the better. For if we're lucky, life lasts long enough for us to be confronted "by the better angels of our nature," as Lincoln put it. To selectively quote from Lincoln's first inaugural address, from whence that phrase came: "We are not enemies, but friends. We must not be enemies. Though passion may have strained, it must not break our bonds of affection. The mystic chords of memory... will yet swell... when again touched, as surely they will be, by the better angels of our nature." And, this is a difficult calling. To accept different others, not just tolerate them, but really accept them, is a goal toward which it is well worth striving.

My teachers also included my grandparents Tommy and Ina, and Clyde and Helen, to whom I owe a great deal with regards to the depth of my Faith. They loved me unconditionally, and thought highly of me when I was at my lowliest. They seemed to accept everyone. And, they instilled in me a love for GOD. And yet my own Faith doesn't separate me from others who don't believe what I believe. Others' views are not a threat to my own. I have meaningful and important relationships with people who identify as atheists, agnostics, Christian, Muslim, Buddhist, Hindu, and more. And, I'm not separated from people in different demographic categories. I have meaningful relationships with a wide variety of people different from me with regard to such things as socio-economic status, race, ethnicity, culture, and sexual identity. Nor am I separated by political ideology, as I have meaningful relationships with members of such political parties as Republican, Democrat, Green Party, and Libertarian, as well as within my own group, the Independents. None of us are better than any other, at least in my humble opinion. And I recognize the privileges I have as a member of historically dominant demographic groups in our society, and that others do not have the same privileges. I owe it to them to always speak about that, when it is relevant, as it often is, such as now.

One of my dearest friends these past few years has been Gwen, who is in her 70s, and I learn from her example of doing all she can to help everyone she can. We don't share the same politics. We don't share the same subdivision of religion. But we share love for one another, respect for one another, and support for one another, and a willingness to learn from one another. She will do whatever she can for anyone, regardless of whether she agrees with them in matters such as religion or politics. Though I did not always, I now very much agree with Thomas Jefferson, who said "I never considered a difference of opinion in politics, in religion, in philosophy, as cause for withdrawing from a friend." And, isn't that what America is about? Freedom to be yourself, to think what you want, to believe what you want, and to do what you want? Do we really want everyone to be just like those in our own in-groups? Would that be true freedom, if we were all exactly the same? And, I acknowledge those who make our Freedom possible, those in our military who protect our Constitution; and who along with our police, firefighters, and other emergency responders, often protect our lives. And to those who take such risks and who sacrifice so much, and to their families who support them, I say 'Thank you!' You helped me be here today.

And in politics we see challenges to respect and acceptance everywhere. I have long heard people lament that there should be higher quality candidates for elected offices. But, you know who runs the world? People who show up. They showed up in high school clubs, college organizations, local and regional elections, and the candidates we have for any election are the ones who showed up. Where are the people who complain about them and yet want others to choose from? They didn't show up. Resist apathy. Another way to increase success is to show up. Everyone in this room could potentially serve society by showing up locally, regionally, nationally, and internationally. Be the change you want to see in the world. But not only in politics. Show up to do charity work. Show up to fill in for a struggling co-worker. Show up to help when a family experiences a crisis.

And resist bigotry. Fred Rogers took to the airwaves with a Public Service Announcement after 9-11 to try and sooth children struggling to make sense of what was happening. He said "When I was a boy and I would see scary things in the news, my mother would say to me, 'Look for the helpers. You will always find people who are helping.' To this day, especially in times of disaster, I remember my mother's words and I am always comforted by realizing that there are still so many helpers –so many caring people in this world." He also said "I'm convinced that when we help our children find healthy ways of dealing with their feelings –ways that don't hurt them or anyone else– we're helping to make our world a safer, better place." And, he always said, "I like you just the way you are." To these ideas, I say "Yes! a thousand times, Yes!" We're at our strongest, our best, when we are at our most compassionate. And it shouldn't have to take tragedy to bring that out in us. Success includes bringing out that aspect of ourselves every day, showing up in every way. Doing new things, learning new things, and helping others when we can.

It can most certainly be a hard world out there, but it is most certainly also a beautiful world out there. And, you have the power to change it for the better. We have an obligation to try. Viktor Frankl, who survived the horrors of a Nazi concentration camp, and the loss of his family in that genocide, was a profound believer in the possibilities of people to triumph despite the tragedies they experience. But you have to be able to make true meaning out of your negative experiences. He thought you need to have meaning in your life to have happiness, and that constructing such meaning took effort. He said the Statue of Liberty on the East Coast should be balanced by a Statue of Responsibility on the West Coast. In other words, we have to take responsibility and make the most of whatever we have. And, while all the moments of our pasts explain how we got to any given negative places in our lives, explanation is not the same thing as excuses. To succeed, we can't make excuses. If we screw up, we need to be bold enough to admit it, do our best to do whatever we can to fix it, learn from it, and do our best not to repeat the same mistakes. And we must forgive ourselves for our human frailties while working to strengthen our characters. And importantly, we must learn to forgive others. To truly succeed at that, we must give up hate. There is evil in the world, and we sometimes need protection from it. But evil feeds on hate, and we must give it up.

Love thy neighbor as thyself. Those are very straightforward words; yet it is likely the hardest thing on earth to do. You first have to give up hate. MLK showed us that pacifism is the furthest thing from cowardice. To look in the eyes of someone who hates you and return that glare with love; that's one of the toughest things you could ever do. "Love thy neighbor as thyself" is an important imperative. It is also one of the hardest things for humans to learn to do consistently. And this is not just a Christian imperative. In addition to Jesus, this life-changing philosophy has been advocated by secular philosophers such as Immanuel Kant, Gandhi, Buckminster Fuller, Ram Dass, and Robert Anton Wilson, to name but a few of millions. But in a world of billions, we need more to adopt this perspective. And, to do it, you'd actually have to love yourself first, which means again, to forgive yourself and accept you errors and do what you can to make amends.

But doing this is going to take persistent and committed effort. So, let's put ourselves to it. Let go of hate. Let go of anger. Let go of jealousy. And to do this, you must also let go of fear. Fear and hatred are deeply intertwined, and ignorance promotes both. We know what must be done, we must open our hearts and our minds. And we all have the power to do this. Alice Walker once said, "The most common way people give up their power is by thinking they don't have any." You have power. Pain and suffering happen. And growing from those experiences make us deeper and more appreciative individuals. And, greater appreciation for what goes well for us, leads to satisfaction, which is a type of success. Ups and downs come and go, but we can be satisfied in the down times, knowing that if we did our best, we learned, and deepened our appreciation. Appreciation is an active thing. Love is an active thing. Continued success is an active thing."

Peace & Love to All,
Sage

CPSIA information can be obtained
at www.ICGtesting.com
Printed in the USA
LVOW11s0634060717

540419LV00002B/251/P